"Clear, engaging, and a welcome challenge to think beyond the familiar landmarks."
—**David Smith,** Director of Kuyers Institute for Christian Teaching and Learning at Calvin College

"Higher education can get caught up in a game of change, unaware of subtle compromises being made to achieve sustainability. *Echoes of Insight* provides compelling ideas for reimagining faith based education. By balancing "Glitz, Glue and Hope," institutions can consider how remaining anchored in their strengths can provide greater longevity."
—**Deana L. Porterfield,** President, Roberts Wesleyan College and Northeastern Seminary

"This eclectic account of eleven gifted thinkers about education resists the modern vogue for flashy academic innovation. Instead, *Echoes of Insight* looks toward the past—not with sentimental nostalgia—to uncover a rich heritage of wisdom."
—**Susan VanZanten,** professor of English, Seattle Pacific University

"Educators—including those involved in Christian higher education—are part of an ancient practice and craft. As such, there is much to learn from those who have insisted that education in liberal arts and the humanities matter. Patrick Allen and Ken Badley have engaged ancient and more contemporary sources and in dialogue with them provided contemporary teachers and administrators—those called into higher education—insight in the art of teaching, but more, guidance for the mission and curricula of universities and colleges that are resolved to form women and men in wisdom."
—**Gordon T. Smith,** President of Ambrose University

Echoes of Insight

Echoes of Insight

PAST PERSPECTIVES AND THE **FUTURE** OF **CHRISTIAN HIGHER EDUCATION**

PATRICK ALLEN
AND **KENNETH BADLEY**

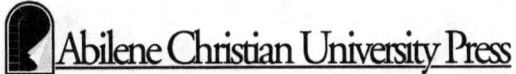
Abilene Christian University Press

ECHOES OF INSIGHT
Past Perspectives and the Future of Christian Higher Education

Copyright © 2017 by Patrick Allen and Kenneth Badley

978-0-89112-332-3

Printed in the United States of America

ALL RIGHTS RESERVED
No part of this publication may be reproduced, stored in a retrieval system, or transmitted in any form by any means—electronic, mechanical, photocopying, recording, or otherwise—without prior written consent.

All Scripture quotations, unless otherwise indicated, are taken from the Holy Bible, New International Version®, NIV®. Copyright ©1973, 1978, 1984, 2011 by Biblica, Inc.™ Used by permission of Zondervan. All rights reserved worldwide.

Library of Congress Cataloging-in-Publication Data is on file at the Library of Congress, Washington DC.

Cover design by Kent Jensen
Interior text design by Sandy Armstrong, Strong Design

For information contact:
Abilene Christian University Press
ACU Box 29138
Abilene, Texas 79699

1-877-816-4455
www.acupressbooks.com

17 18 19 20 21 22 / 7 6 5 4 3 2 1

We dedicate this book to our own professors who first introduced to us many of the writers we treat in this book. They taught us not only a love of learning but also pushed us to think clearly, write carefully, and read constantly. And we wish to thank our own students over the years, literally too many to mention by name, with whom we have shared our love of these thinkers and the ideas they express. With kindness, they have endured our stories; with creativity and some courage, they have enlarged our ideas; and with care, they have encouraged our hearts.

Acknowledgements

The authors wish to thank Jason Fikes, Mary Hardegree, and the editorial staff at Abilene Christian University Press for their support of this book, as well as Bina Ali, of Toronto, Ontario, for her administrative and editorial work on the project.

Contents

Preface.. 13
Introduction.. 17

Part 1:
The Classroom and the Student:
Instruction, Formation, and Vocation

Chapter 1
    Alfred North Whitehead—*The Aims of Education (1929)*.................. 27

Chapter 2
    Dorothy L. Sayers—*The Lost Tools of Learning (1947)*..................... 51

Chapter 3
    Hannah Arendt—*The Banality of Evil (1963)*............................. 71

Chapter 4
    Flannery O'Connor—*A Good Man Is Hard to Find (1955)*................ 97

Chapter 5
    Maria Montessori—*The Montessori Method (1912)*..................... 117

Part 2:
The Faculty and the Administration:
Mission, Vision, and Values

Chapter 6
    John Henry Newman—*The Rise and Progress of Universities (1872)*....... 141

Chapter 7
    Abraham Flexner—*The American College (1908)*........................ 167

Chapter 8
    Thorstein Veblen—*The Higher Learning in America (1918)*.............. 191

Chapter 9
    José Ortega y Gasset—*The Mission of the University (1930)*.............. 215

Chapter 10
    Robert Maynard Hutchins—*The Higher Learning in America (1936)*...... 237

Chapter 11
    Karl Jaspers—*The Idea of the University (1946)*.......................... 265

Conclusion... 291

Preface

WE ARE BOTH THANKFUL FOR RICH AND REWARDING CAREERS IN HIGHER education and for the opportunity to serve in faith-based institutions. We believe that teaching at the college level can be one of the most rewarding occupations on the face of the earth, and particularly so at an institution that sincerely claims Christ as the foundational and organizing commitment and pursues its educational mission with passion and intentionality. At such an institution, rather than thinking of the professorial task as simply teaching and scholarship, we can reframe our work with a faithful commitment to teach, to shape, and to send. It is indeed honest work with eternal implications.

And we are philosophers of sorts, too. We know that the rare air of higher education for faculty and students alike is a rich, shaping discourse about things that matter, and sadly, we confess that such discourse is often a rare and sometimes unwelcome commodity at faith-based institutions. This concern has led us to write this book. The dominant discourse we see in Christian higher education today swirls around three concerns: (1) how to embrace a business model for higher education with an emphasis on money and margins, (2) how to market effectively and brand our institutions, and (3) how to focus faculty and curricular efforts on getting jobs for graduates. Now, we are the first to say that there is nothing wrong with margins, marketing, or job preparation. Losing money and enrollments is no way to bring energy to an institution, and having an alumni base that cannot find meaningful work or repay student loans is a disaster of a different sort. But as John Henry Newman would tell us, these efforts are sufficient for *being* a university, but not for its *well-being*. This book is dedicated to a conversation about the well-being of the Christian university, particularly as we look to the future.

A culture of fear now hangs over higher education's landscape like a dark cloud. We believe this to be an unintended consequence of the emphasis on business tactics and margins, and it is debilitating to the well-being of our institutions, too. According to Parker Palmer, ignorance is not the biggest impediment to learning; rather, it is fear.[1] We agree. Fear drives discourse underground, stops innovation in its tracks, pits colleague against colleague, diminishes personal and professional commitments, and ultimately kills the spirit of a place. Fear may be a motivator, but it is ultimately a toxic one.

Certainly, there are many pressing issues and concerns facing faith-based institutions: the loss of denominational and theological identity, declining financial support and alumni loyalty, increasing political interest in free community college education for all, competition from other educational providers, cheaper models for the delivery of instruction, the heavy demand and expectation for job training, the public's willingness to accept less in exchange for a credential, and a general malaise regarding the mission and priorities of Christian colleges and universities. Many wonder if Christian higher education is a relic of an age now past, or at best an example of a broken business model. Of course, these concerns are real, and our institutions had best take them seriously. The denial of reality is no way to run an institution.

Nevertheless, we are hopeful about the future of Christian higher education. Higher education as we know it has been around since the twelfth century, and we have no reason to believe that it will soon go out of business. The concerns we now face are not new. In the late 1970s, for example, serious predictions were made that one-third to one-half of all private institutions in the United States would not see the 1990s. In fact, most did.

Why? Colleges and universities developed new programs and markets to supplement their traditional enrollments. In short, they were nimble and adaptive. We hear the same woeful predictions today, but we are optimistic that faith-based institutions can be nimble and adaptive again. We look for strong and vigorous leadership from trustees, administrators, and faculty members. With a sense of partnership and a commitment to shared governance, our institutions can enjoy a sustainable future.

However, our universities need something richer and better than mere sustainability, and this is what we are aiming at in this book. Sustainability is fine for *being*, but not for *well-being*. We are after something bigger here, something that is built on hope, a hope that will not disappoint. We offer in this book older, forgotten, and ignored voices that invite us to consider new perspectives and to do fresh thinking about our work, our rich heritage, and the amazing calling we who work in faith-based institutions possess. We trust that across our campuses such ideas will lead to renewed, vigorous discourse about the nature of our common work. Ultimately, we will argue that our future is based not on optimism, but on a hope based on the very character of God. It is this hope that will inform our efforts and shape our institutions as we look to the twenty-first century.

NOTE

[1] Fear is a major theme for Parker Palmer. He has addressed it in major speeches, in personal conversations with one of the authors (PA), and in publications. For example, see Russel Edgerton, "Community and Commitment in Higher Education: A Conversation with Parker Palmer," in *AAHE Bulletin* 45 no. 1 (September 1992): 4; and chapter 2 in Parker J. Palmer, *The Courage to Teach: Exploring the Inner Landscape of a Teacher's Life*, 1st ed. (San Francisco: Jossey-Bass, 1998).

Echoes of Insight

Past Perspectives and the Future of Christian Higher Education

ABOUT A YEAR BEFORE WE WROTE THIS BOOK, HIGHER EDUCATORS around the world whipped themselves into a fury over massive open online courses (MOOCs). By some accounts, these courses would become the financial salvation of every struggling college and university. All the college had to do was find a few all-star lecturers, record their lectures, make those lectures available on the Web, and hire adjunct workers to interact with the hundreds of thousands of students who were guaranteed to enroll. Boatloads of tuition revenue would then pour in. Within three months, the storm had passed and many academics could not remember if a MOOC was a music synthesizer, a character from a science fiction movie, or something else altogether. Many of our readers will remember this flurry of worry and activity. We start with this story to remind our readers that educators are particularly susceptible to falling for whatever is the flavor of the week. And our readers know that there's no shortage of new flavors in the world of higher education and Christian higher education. Whether we talk about curriculum, instruction, assessment, technology, or students, we're guaranteed to learn of some revolutionary new proposal every day if we keep our eyes and ears open.

This book is not about new ideas. We believe that Christian higher educators ought to consider and, in some cases, reconsider some old ideas, ideas that have been around for decades or possibly centuries. Educators have tried some of these ideas before. In those cases, we think a reminder might be in order. But some of the ideas we write about in this book have never been implemented in higher education or even considered as to what application they might have. In those cases, our task becomes one of introduction and application more than reminder. For example, a search in major educational databases using these two search strings—*Montessori* and *college teaching*—yielded two records. Intuitively, that may make sense; after all, did Montessori not focus on the education of young children? In fact, wasn't her original interest in developmentally delayed children who lived in poverty? The answer to both questions is yes. But her ideas about the psychology of engagement and the need for teachers to be aware of students' prior learning have as much application to contemporary teaching in higher education as they did a century ago in the slums of Rome where she began her work. And without the benefit of what we now know about the human brain, she argued that children are hungry to learn, hungry to make connections, hungry to organize and classify new knowledge, and hungry to make sense of the world around them. If she were writing today, she would likely be using phrases such as *the synaptic cleft* and children's hunger to make new *neural pathways*. Her ideas may be old, but we think we should reconsider them, or, in this case, consider them for the first time with reference to higher education. So relax; we will not propose that Christian higher educators use wooden blocks to help their students understand the concept of squaring a number. But we do believe that this educator, who died more than half a century ago, has something to tell us as higher educators.

She is not the only one whose ideas we believe warrant a first or second look for those of us who work in Christian higher education. In Part One, we will introduce five thinkers, wisdom keepers of sorts, and make connections between what they have to say and the challenges faced by Christian higher education in the twenty-first century. We believe you will be surprised by the relevance of their writings. These thinkers include Alfred North Whitehead, Dorothy L. Sayers, Hannah Arendt, Flannery O'Connor, and Maria Montessori. Whitehead and Montessori were educators and will be familiar to at least some educators (usually in name, if not in content), and of course, O'Connor will be familiar to most of us. However, few have thought about her work as it speaks to Christian higher education. She has much to say to us, especially about sin and grace. And as you will see, the works of Sayers and Arendt are fresh, powerful, and insightful.

In Part Two, we will reintroduce some thinkers and their classic works about higher education: John Henry Newman, Abraham Flexner, Thorstein Veblen, José Ortega y Gasset, Robert Maynard Hutchins, and Karl Jaspers. Some philosophers and historians will be familiar with their work and their contributions to higher education, and faculty members may be familiar with their names, but few have read these writers or connected ideas to the realities that face Christian higher education today. We intend to make some of those connections, and we hope to start a conversation that is honest, relevant, and helpful.

The names we listed above may surprise some readers because we have included some names not primarily associated with education or not well known to contemporary educators. As we have noted, our list includes writers of fiction, theologians, and philosophers. We include these names for good reason. Some who have focused their thinking and work on matters other than education have good ideas that we believe educators should consider.

Certainly, other names in this volume are more familiar to the higher education community—Newman, Flexner, Veblen, Whitehead, and Ortega—but we fear that while their names are familiar, their ideas and concerns have been largely shelved away or dismissed as goods with expired "use by" dates, irrelevant to the pressing concerns of faculty, administrators, and trustees serving in Christian colleges today. We believe that there is much to be learned from these gifted thinkers, and many of their concerns and observations about higher education transcend time and place. If we come with a thoughtful humility and a cool passion, they will have much to say to us as we strive to improve our work and be instruments of God's kingdom work here and now.

Of course, the people we have named had more than one idea each; most were prolific writers. In this single work, we lack the scope to treat these figures exhaustively. To streamline our project and your reading, we have focused on one or two main ideas or major works from each of the figures we review. We mention other aspects of their work, of course, but we want to suggest in each case that we should pay attention to one or two key ideas at this time in Christian higher education.

Before we conclude this introduction, we want to explain in more detail our intent, our approach or methodology, and our selection process for the thinkers we treat in this book. To be clear, our intent was not to add to the scholarship on any of the individual thinkers we discuss in this volume. While that is certainly a noble task, it was not ours. Those who read this book to find newly discovered or nuanced ideas or positions about these thinkers will be disappointed, although we did try to be faithful to the existing scholarship. We do not claim to be Newman, or O'Connor, or Veblen scholars, nor did we attempt to be. Rather, our intent was to create meaningful conversations about the future of Christian higher education at a time when it seems to us that it is particularly needed. The contemporary conversation, in our view, is much too dominated by margins, markets, and metrics, while faculty voice and issues of quality and spirit have been pushed to the rear, and in some cases out the back door altogether. We believe that discourse is the rare air of higher education, and we wanted to start or rekindle serious conversations on our campuses. We trust that this book will do just that.

In order to engender these important conversations, we looked for voices from the past (over the past 150 years) that we believed could help frame these conversations by highlighting important issues and questions that have been forgotten or ignored. Those in Part Two of this book (Newman, Flexner, Veblen, Ortega, Hutchins, and Jaspers), along with Whitehead from Part One, are considered classic thinkers about higher education. They would be covered in any serious graduate course or standard work on the idea or mission of the university. In many respects, the reasons for their inclusion in this book are self-evident. Yet we note that their ideas are rarely seriously embraced or thoroughly discussed by Christian college faculty and staff today, so we wanted to feature their voices. And in the case of Newman and Flexner, we wanted to highlight a lesser-known but important work about college life.

The reasons for selecting the other voices in Part One (Sayers, Arendt, O'Connor, Montessori) are less obvious. Why were they selected, and why not others? Of course, there could have been others, but these four thinkers (two writers, a philosopher, and an educator) were familiar to us. Their writings have been read and discussed in many of the philosophy of education courses we teach, and we note that students particularly gravitate to their ideas and their application for Christian higher education today. As you will see, these writers have concerns about the coherence of the liberal arts, the use of power, the impact of sin in our lives, and the place of theology in our work—all issues of great importance as we look to the future of our institutions. Certainly, the inclusion of voices from both genders was important to us, too. Beyond this, however, there is no secret method to their selection. They are familiar to us, and in our own professional experience and judgment, they contribute to the conversation we wish to kindle. But are there other voices worthy of inclusion in such a volume? Certainly. In fact, we are already in discussion about an *Echoes of Insight, Volume II* for that very reason.

One final note about method. According to Gerald Gutek, emeritus professor at Loyola University, existentialists practice "an epistemology of appropriation, in which the person comes to an area of knowledge and chooses what she or he wants to take from it and make her or his own."[1] We appreciate this approach to knowing very much. Far too often, ideas are rejected because we do not accept a person's entire philosophical or theological framework. We think this is sad; so much can be learned from those with whom we disagree. So we have appropriated ideas from serious thinkers, some who do not even believe in our work or share our faith. That is fine with us. Their ideas and concerns do speak to those of us who care deeply about the future of Christian higher education.

In the conclusion, we try to connect some dots. That is to say, we will identify the conversational threads, common themes, major disagreements, and common concerns. We will point out that most of the challenges we face today in Christian higher education are not new, although they are real and troubling nonetheless. We will also point out that both glitz and glue are needed to maintain institutional vitality in today's turbulent times, and we try to make a helpful distinction between the two. The glitz has to do with such things as effective branding, marketing, technology, and image. We find no fault with these efforts. Contemporary students and their parents are influenced deeply by these factors, so having some glitz is essential. However, efforts in marketing will ultimately dry up like an old leaf if an institution cannot live up to its own recruiting brochures. To do so, it must be clear and firm in its mission (what it is to be primarily, and what it is to be in addition, to use Ortega's terms), it must have a clear understanding of students and how they learn, and it must know how best to teach them. This is not glitz; this is the glue that holds things together.

Finally, we will end by suggesting that there is good reason for both optimism and hope, using Moltmann's distinction of the two from *Theology of Hope*. Ultimately, we trust in the character of God as our ultimate reason to have hope in our efforts to teach, shape, and send.

One final note—while this book can be read and studied solo, we suggest that it be read and discussed in a small (or large) group setting. To that end, we have included some questions for reflection and discussion at the end of each chapter. Crafting a compelling future for Christian higher education is truly a team sport, not a marathon.

NOTES

[1] Gerald Gutek, *Philosophical and Ideological Voices in Education* (Boston: Allyn and Bacon, 2004), 91.

The Classroom and the Student

Instruction, Formation, and Vocation

PART 1

Alfred North Whitehead

The Aims of Education (1929)

WE BEGIN WITH WHITEHEAD (1861–1947) AND WITH A SMALL COLLECtion of papers, lectures, and public speeches he gave from 1912 to 1927, which were finally gathered in 1929 under the title *The Aims of Education.*[1] Despite working primarily in mathematics, Whitehead frequently voiced his interest in the liberal arts and the necessity of the humanities in education. An urgent call to avoid teaching inert ideas runs through several of his works, the main one being the title on which we focus here. Another theme running through his work is that we should teach for depth rather than breadth. He complained that the secondary curriculum and the undergraduate curriculum had both sacrificed in-depth knowledge about a few things for a survey of too many things. Another theme—almost a lament—running through Whitehead's work is that the standardized examination cannot possibly reveal all that students know. He also wanted to see teachers have control of curriculum because he believed that they knew their students and their students' needs better than others higher up the educational food chain.

Already, we see that despite the book's being called *The Aims of Education*, Whitehead was also interested in curriculum, instruction, and assessment, the three core things that professors and teachers do. As is true with every other author we treat in this book, Alfred North Whitehead offers far more ideas than we would ever attempt to treat in one chapter. However, by concentrating on just this one collection of essays, we can narrow our focus to a few ideas that have the most relevance to our project in this volume. Some educators speak of *covering* material. We will attempt simply to uncover a slice of the range of wisdom that Whitehead offered nearly a century ago. And within that range, we will give most of our effort to his concern that students see or make the connections between their various subjects of study and, furthermore, that they make the links between their education and life itself.

Whitehead lived and taught in London and at Oxford from the day he graduated until age 64. While at Oxford, he became a friend and colleague of Bertrand Russell, and Whitehead published with Russell in both philosophy and mathematics. Their best-known title remains *Principia Mathematica*, which appeared in four volumes between 1910 and 1913.[2] Despite his obvious brilliance in logic, mathematics, and philosophy, Whitehead did not simply take refuge in his ivory tower. He served in professional organizations and was also a member of a national committee appointed to recommend educational reforms to the British government.

When Whitehead faced retirement from Oxford, Harvard offered him a position, which he filled from 1924 to 1937. He viewed this offer as an opportunity to write up and present a systematic explanation of his philosophy, a philosophy famously difficult to understand. Besides earning a reputation for offering complex ideas, he also became known for being either contrarian or simply a persistent member of every possible philosophical and theological minority. He refused to bow to the empiricism that dominated Anglo-American philosophy during his time and instead worked on metaphysics. There, he proposed an organismic view in which we should think of matter more as interconnected processes than as individual objects (thus *process philosophy*). In his theory of perception, he also parted company from the majority by arguing that nonliving entities also have a kind of perception. His views of God put him at odds with most theologians, and his views in epistemology ensured his marginal status among scientists.

For reasons that are perhaps already obvious, interest in Whitehead in the West remains only a fraction of what it once was, with two noteworthy exceptions. A center for the study of process theology at Claremont University in California continues to work with Whitehead's ideas, as does the center for the study of Whiteheadian educational thought at the University of Saskatchewan. Whitehead's legacy in the East may turn out quite differently, because the government of China has established a couple dozen research centers focused on his philosophy.

Levels of contemporary interest in his philosophy and theology are not so much our concern here as are some of the ideas he presented in *The Aims of Education*. We have organized our treatment of Whitehead's thinking about education under several headings. These headings are completely fair to and reflective of Whitehead, but they have the potential to mislead our readers. Therefore, we need to make clear here that in the final section of the chapter—on curriculum integration—we argue that the discrete headings may mask the single vision that Whitehead advocated throughout all his writing on education. Obviously, different readers will read and interpret Whitehead (and every other author) in different ways. That being said, we humbly propose that a single driving vision energizes Whitehead's work: all the parts of a student's education should fit together epistemologically and should connect to the student's day-to-day life. We will provide road signs along the way, but please be aware that that is our destination in this chapter.

The Liberal Arts and Vocational/Technical Education

Whitehead recognized the importance of technical education along with academic education. The conversation about the relation between those two kinds of education has come back to life in recent years, largely due to one book: *Shop Class as Soulcraft*.[3] Its author, Matthew Crawford, a philosopher working as a Washington consultant, abandoned his office and his office job to open a motorcycle repair shop. In his bestselling account, he laments the closing of shop classes in schools, and he argues quite compellingly that we lose something when we abandon interest in the trades. Crawford notes that the person in China who assembled your computer cannot come and fix it for you. But for Crawford, it's much more than that. His lament is that we lose something essential to human being when we lose our knowledge of craft and of how to fix things. In his writings, Crawford makes no mention of Whitehead's *Aims,* but his title's having achieved bestseller status interests us because Whitehead said some of the same things nearly one hundred years earlier. Whitehead saw technical skill as part of "the educated strength of the nation,"[4] and in "Technical Education and Science and Literature," Whitehead develops his defense of technical education at some length.[5] In short, he honors technical education. He does so not just because society needs people with technical skills, but he sees an inherent value in technical skill, as did Crawford who followed him by almost a century.

Higher education or even Christian higher education does not need to be reduced to job preparation, whether that job might be in a motorcycle repair shop or in the financial district. The authors whose ideas we explore in this volume have repeatedly reminded us to keep the big questions at the core of our educational undertaking. So we will not try to use Whitehead or Crawford to reduce education to employment preparation. But we do call on educators to remember that many people have the dispositions and skills needed for technical work. In fact, technical work may well be their vocation, their God-given means of serving in this world. And as Whitehead reminds us, society needs people with technical skills. For those who name Christ, the high value Scripture places on work should clinch the argument.

Interestingly, Whitehead sees liberal education as essential for the person who will go into nonacademic or technical work.[6] In fact, for him, "The antithesis between a technical and a liberal education is fallacious. There can be no adequate technical education which is not liberal, and no liberal education which is not technical: that is, no education which does not impart both technique and intellectual vision. In simpler language, education should turn out the pupil with something he knows well and something he can do well. This intimate union of practice and theory aids both."[7] Later in the same paragraph, Whitehead puts it this way: "Geometry and mechanics, followed by workshop practice, gain that reality without which mathematics is verbiage." We will avoid baptizing Whitehead here with an out-of-context citation such as "faith without works is dead," but we agree with him that education must put to rest the fallacious distinction between theory and practice, between the liberal arts and technical skill. Clearly, individuals and societies need both.[8]

We include this rather extended treatment of Whitehead's view of technical education because of its consistency with his overall concern for integration in students' experience of their education. Whitehead believed that "every form of education should give the people a technique, a science, an assortment of general ideas, and aesthetic appreciation, and that each of these sides of his training should be illuminated by the others."[9] On our reading, for Whitehead, the curriculum is all of a piece. The theory/practice dichotomy is resolved. Crawford's *Shop Class as Soulcraft*, albeit a bestseller worthy of a careful reading, turns out to be something of a repeat of what Whitehead already said (but we must note, a repeat in clearer language).

Whitehead seamlessly incorporates scriptural allusions and language in all his writing, sometimes explicitly and sometimes implicitly, often in such a nuanced way that one wonders if he was in fact attempting to be mischievous. Nowhere in his writing, however, have we found reference to Paul's words to the Colossians regarding Christ's role in holding the whole creation together (Col. 1:17). Paul claimed that Christ was before all things and that in him all things were held together. Readers of Scripture have historically read Paul at this point to mean the created world. Without doing too much violence to Scripture, we believe Paul's words might apply as well to the curriculum; that is, the whole world of learning is held together and makes sense in Christ. If we're right in this reading, then we all need to recognize with Whitehead that both technical and academic learning have value, and that they in fact may be the building blocks of any education worthy of that honorific name.

The Tension between Depth and Breadth

Whitehead famously issued two commandments for education: "Do not teach too many subjects. What you teach, teach thoroughly."[10] When first encountering these two commandments, contemporary readers may want to object that Whitehead is simply wrongheaded in calling for more specialization. But there's more to his argument than this. His commandments are embedded in a larger concern for what we now call integrated education. In his own words, "the devil in the scholastic world has assumed the form of a general education consisting of scraps of a large number of disconnected subjects."[11] He lays the blame for that disconnection on the universities of London, Oxford, and Cambridge and then continues in this way: "Culture is activity of thought, and receptiveness to beauty, and humane feeling. Scraps of information have nothing to do with it. A merely well-informed man is the most useless bore on God's earth. What we should aim at producing is men who possess both culture and expert knowledge in some special direction. Their expert knowledge will give them the ground to start from, and their culture will lead them as deep as philosophy and as high as art."[12]

His exclusive language notwithstanding, Whitehead makes clear that he concerns himself not about specialization per se but rather with the lack of connections between the different components of the curriculum. Again, we will return to this question of connections when we discuss the experience of the student—integrated or not—at the end of the chapter.

At one point, Whitehead asks about the breadth/depth tension by talking about the amateur and the expert. The amateur in this picture is broadly educated and has mastered a routine. Whitehead asks how we are "to produce the expert without loss of the essential virtues of the amateur."[13] In this, he sounds a bit like educational philosopher R. S. Peters, who expressed his concern that specialization without connection produced a lack of "cognitive perspective."[14] Peters wrote long after Whitehead, but on this point, they share the same concern. Certainly, it remains a challenge for all of us who teach in the Christian college classroom. If we do not intentionally teach for depth and explicitly point our students toward potential connections, it is unlikely that they will make such connections on their own. In fact, it is sheer folly to think that they will. In this regard, and of course in others, students need a Sherpa, a wise guide who knows the way up the mountain and safely back to base camp.

Imagination and the Adventure of Education

At several points in *Aims*, Whitehead insists that education should be an adventure. In his view, "the adventure of life cannot be disjointed from intellectual adventure."[15] He expands on this idea in detail in "Universities and Their Function," a speech he first gave at the opening of the Harvard Business School campus in 1924. In his view, "education is discipline for the adventure of life; research is intellectual adventure; and the university should be the home of adventure shared in common by young and old."[16] He highlighted the importance of imagination in the educational adventure, writing this way: "The justification for a university is that it preserves the connection between knowledge and the zest for life, by uniting the young and the old in the imaginative consideration of learning. The university imparts information, but it imparts it imaginatively. At least this is the function which it should perform in society. The university that fails in this respect has no reason for existence."[17] On his account, even schools of business should be imaginative. The "proper function of the university is the imaginative acquisition of knowledge," and for Whitehead, "A university is imaginative or it is nothing—at least nothing useful."[18] Strong words indeed, but words with which we agree.

He elaborates on what he means by education as adventure, although more in Whiteheadian fashion than orderly fashion. Nevertheless, the conception of education he lays out in that speech contains some elements that we believe higher educators—and Christian higher educators—need to take seriously today. To begin with a massive generalization, the contemporary cliché *lifelong learner* points in the direction Whitehead seems to go with his use of *adventure,* but as we will see, that is only the threshold; he implies much more.

For Whitehead, education as adventure implies a fresh view of curriculum. He writes:

> For successful education there must always be a certain freshness in the knowledge that it is dealt with. It must either be new in itself or it must be invested with some novelty of application to the new world of new times. Knowledge does not keep any better than fish. You may be dealing with knowledge of the old species, with some old truth; but somehow or other it must come to the students, as it were, just drawn out of the sea and with the freshness of its immediate importance.[19]

We see at least two curricular implications in that citation. First, every academic field has cutting edges. To meet Whitehead's criterion of freshness of knowledge, professors need to keep reading. In the summer of 2006, one of us witnessed a senior professor present the survey of his field in a lecture. His last overhead slide (yes) took the field up to 1986 (yes), and when a student asked for a summary of the field in the intervening two decades, the lecturer replied that the field had not really developed since. Everyone—including the presenter—knew that they had just witnessed a fraud. If it was not fraud, the field had conveniently stopped developing the year that professor stopped teaching and entered the dean's office. Why tell this story? Whitehead calls us to stay fresh in our disciplinary specialty. If we ignore his advice, students will know. The evidence is there in the reading lists in our course syllabi. It is there in how we shape the central themes and driving questions of our courses. It is there in our answers to classroom questions. There are other good, principled reasons to keep reading in our fields, but we offer this simple tactical one: avoid looking like an idiot.

We said we saw at least two curricular implications in Whitehead's remarks about freshness. The first related to staying fresh in our fields and the impact that freshness might have on our curriculum and courses. The second relates to instruction and to how we present that which is not fresh in our fields, a challenge for anyone teaching introductory material and for many who are teaching historical material. How do we keep the old material from rotting like fish or drying up like an old leaf? How do we lead our students into it so they perceive it as fresh, "just drawn out of the sea," as it were? In this passage, Whitehead indicates at least one direction for our attempt to answer this question: we must invest it with some "novelty of application," some links to the world in which our students study and live.

Two quick examples come to mind. Both students and professors know and sometimes joke about the digital divide between generations. We sometimes frame that divide in a comment about the effects of technology. In the *Phaedrus,* Plato addressed the effects of introducing a new technology to a society. This would be a novel (and dare we say interesting) way to begin a discussion on this very important issue for students intending to go into the professions. Our second example comes from the nineteenth century and the habit of intermarriage among European royal families, a habit formed in part out of the misbelief that such intermarriage would help prevent war. Such intermarriage may now be passé, but nations still form alliances, and in the new millennium we have learned (or should we say "some have learned") that those alliances do not always turn out for the best. We may face an accusation of cherry-picking with these two examples; after all, the university curriculum involves hundreds or thousands of courses with many different subjects and sections in each. Finding contemporary links to all those bits will be as hard as finding the elusive element unobtainium. Still, linking the past to the present is a solid step forward.

Whitehead offers another perspective on his criterion of "novelty of application." Instead of (or sometimes, in addition to) seeking parallels between the historical and the contemporary, we should help students identify links between our curriculum contents and their own lives. We have already referred to these kinds of connections as practical integration. Integration of this kind is a recurrent theme in Whitehead's book, and we will explore it in some detail later in the chapter. But we need to note here that connecting course contents to life is central to his conception of integration, and to his understanding of how learning can go beyond inert facts.

We have argued that Whitehead's call entails our understanding and approaching both curriculum and instruction in ways more likely to help education become an adventure, but he is also concerned about our own intellectual development as faculty members. This concern may hark back to what we said a couple paragraphs back about curriculum. On Whitehead's account, "the whole point of the university, on its educational side, is to bring the young under the intellectual influence of a band of imaginative scholars. There can be no escape from proper attention to the conditions which—as experience has shown—will produce such a band."[20] And what are those conditions? He offers an idea somewhat like that of Ernest Boyer,[21] that those who teach best should be freed to teach and those most suited to research should engage in research. Whitehead believes that the greatest mistake a university can make is to estimate the value of faculty members by the number of pages they produce. While recognizing that a whole faculty should produce some kind of quota of research, he makes it clear that his concern is that we not judge the quality of individual factory members by page count. "Efficient pedants and dullards"[22] can produce research and the corollary page counts; Whitehead wants to know what kind of faculty can run a university successfully. We note that efficient pedants and dullards can offer courses, too, but they cannot teach. The bank of teachers imagined by Whitehead must have a passion for instruction, a love of students, and a serious calling to the work of learning.

In Christian higher education, we need to take Whitehead's challenge seriously. We should stop acting like R1 (research) institutions and recognize our teaching responsibilities; we should free those who teach well to do so. We need to let our students come under the "influence of a band of imaginative [Christian] scholars," whether those scholars focus primarily on the scholarship of teaching, or the scholarship of discovery, or the scholarship of engagement, or the scholarship of integration, to use Boyer's categories. Faculty and administrators must all give proper attention to the conditions that will produce such a band. Like our readers, we do not take our ultimate instructions for living from Whitehead. Nevertheless, on this point, we think all of us who teach in universities should hear his call. And we should rise to the standard he describes. Students coming to Christian universities deserve an adventurous and imaginative education. And they deserve to have a transformative (T1) educational experience.

Rhythms and Readiness

In "The Rhythm of Education,"[23] Whitehead argues that there is a "fitting appropriate time" for students to encounter each of the various curriculum contents. He takes pains to point out that he knows his thesis to be perfectly obvious, but he takes a dig at those educators who apply the principle of readiness too slavishly. In his words, the "uncritical application of the principle of the necessary antecedents of some subjects to others has, in the hands of dull people with a turn for organization, produced in education the dryness of the Sahara."[24] He also digs past the readiness truism to suggest both that the student's year has a rhythm of its own that educators should recognize, as well as that students are more receptive to some contents at some points in life than at other points. In fact, in his last proposal, Whitehead reveals himself to be a full-fledged stage theorist, albeit one offering less detail than Piaget or Kohlberg.[25]

We note, however, that Whitehead used the word *rhythm* to mean more than readiness. In his discussion of the rhythms of education, Whitehead also argues that students should continuously cycle back through material they have already encountered, but at greater depth with each pass. A student first encounters new learning in a kind of romantic stage characterized by excitement.[26] In Whitehead's view, this romantic stage is part of the adventure of education. Most university professors know something about the power of attraction that new topics have. So we need not comment on Whitehead's point at length here, except to note that he does not propose that we simply set students free to explore what they want. According to him, we should structure our courses so that students can explore within whatever boundaries will induce them to use their time most effectively.[27] On Whitehead's account, the romance stage gives way to a desire to learn more of the detail of the area, what he calls *precision*. In his chapter on freedom and discipline, and in language that sounds lifted from a marriage manual, Whitehead argues that we need to keep the romance alive during this part of the learning cycle. That being said, while the romance stage may have its share of mystery and freedom, in the precision stage, the student learns that subjects have their own allotted tasks.[28] Inquiry into the details of an academic discipline implies disciplined inquiry. Finally, there's a stage of generalization and application; the new learning must make sense within the student's larger understanding; it must fit into the student's life, what we have called practical integration at several points already in this chapter.

But Whitehead identifies two problems related to these stages or moments, one at the front end and one at the back, so to speak. First, most educators do little to engage the romance stage of the learning cycle with its ad hoc character, starting instruction instead at the next stage, that of precision and details. In his view, we have the responsibility as educators to capture the imagination of our students with some mysterious or exciting property of the subject rather than simply launching into the topic with a mass of details. He does not call for catalyst metaphors of instruction in so many words, but he does say that we need to set "a ferment stirring in the mind[s]" of our students.[29] In calling on professors to engage students' imaginations with "some mysterious or exciting property of the subject," Whitehead provides a further answer to the question we asked in the previous section about the meaning of teaching with imagination, or teaching as adventure. He also moves rather obviously into the kind of teaching that many K–12 educators now call inquiry learning. On the student-driven end of the continuum, inquiry learning requires that students identify the questions they will answer. On the teacher-driven end, students conduct research to answer questions set by their teacher or professor. We will not debate the merits of the various models here but will simply note that those advocating inquiry learning point to student engagement as a major benefit. We think if Whitehead were alive today, he would affirm that inquiry learning has great potential to set a "ferment stirring" in students' minds.

The second problem Whitehead identifies related to this three-part cycle of learning has to do with generalization and application. He complains that university courses repeat too much of what students have already learned in their secondary education. As he puts it, they spent their secondary years bent over their desks but now need to be able to stand up and look around.[30] He complains that we fail to move beyond the precision and detail moment of the cycle to the application moment. By arguing this, he raises again the problem of inert knowledge. But he also points again to his ongoing concern for what we call practical integration. On Whitehead's account, if we fail to engage the romantic dimension as we begin a topic, and we fail to attend to generalization and application at the end of a topic, then our failure is twofold. We have succeeded only in contributing to students' accumulation of useless, inert knowledge.

No Inert Ideas

Whitehead begins *Aims* by raising an objection to any education built on inert ideas. By *begins,* we mean the second sentence on page 1. He starts his book in this way: "Culture is activity of thought, and receptiveness to beauty and humane feeling. Scraps of information have nothing to do with it. A merely well-informed man is the most useless bore on God's earth." Later on that first page, he defines inert ideas as "ideas that are merely received into the mind without being utilized, or tested, or thrown into fresh combinations."[31] In the first citation and the first part of the second, we see seeds of a theme that runs throughout Whitehead's work: theory and practice must connect; inert ideas are those that are not applied. In the second part of the latter citation, we see the seed of a second theme: the connection between the various fields of knowledge.

If unused ideas are useless, Whitehead raises the stakes just two pages later by claiming that they are not only useless but that "ideas which are not utilized are positively harmful."[32] He qualifies his use of the word *utilized*; ideas must connect to our own and our students' day-to-day lives (again, practical integration). This discussion leads a page later to the first definition of *education* Whitehead offers in *Aims:* "Education is the acquisition of the art of the utilization of knowledge."[33] In defining this key term this early, Whitehead has put his cards on the table in *The Aims of Education* before one might ordinarily expect him to have done so. Recall that this volume is a set of papers and lectures given over fifteen years; it was not written as a book with a beginning, middle, and end. Still, we find it interesting that Whitehead began his collection with such a bold claim.

Teaching inert ideas is the antithesis of adventurous education. A complicating factor for anyone wanting adventurous education is that the easiest knowledge to test—and Whitehead recognizes this as a problem—is inert knowledge. The most meaningful knowledge (by definition) is that which the student has connected to life. On Whitehead's account then, schools face a difficult choice between standardized assessments and meaningful or adventurous education. Whitehead's repeated criticisms of inert knowledge grew in part out of his concern with a view, popular in his time, that the mind could be sharpened by the discipline required to learn useless knowledge, the easiest kind of knowledge to assess.

Standardized Assessments Are a Disaster

We cite one more passage about inert ideas to make our transition to Whitehead's view of standardized, external examinations: "Theoretical ideas should always find important applications within the pupil's curriculum. This is not an easy doctrine to apply, but a very hard one. It contains within itself the problem of keeping knowledge alive, of preventing it from becoming inert, which is the central problem of all education."[34] How to address that problem, Whitehead claims, depends on "the genius of the teacher, the intellectual type of the pupils, their prospects in life, the opportunities afforded by the immediate surroundings of the school, and allied factors of this sort. It is for this reason that the uniform external examination is so deadly."[35] Whitehead takes the rest of that paragraph to cycle back to his claim that with so many variables at play, the classroom teacher—in our case, the professor—is best positioned to know how to assess what students have learned.

Slowly but inevitably, he moves his argument to what for him is a paradigm example of useless knowledge tested by a useless test: the quadratic equation. He asks what the point is in teaching it to students who will not become mathematicians. For Whitehead, the argument that learning the quadratic equation sharpens the mind simply does not wash. For the average student, according to Whitehead, a quadratic equation is inert because the student has no place to apply it at the time he or she is learning it. If we remember Whitehead's accomplishments as a mathematician, we will have to admit that his objections to teaching the quadratic equation must arise somewhere other than in simple math anxiety.[36] In fact, for him, the problem lies in its being such a powerful case in point of what he calls the "fatal disconnection of subjects, which kills the vitality of our modern curriculum."[37] As he puts it, "There is only one subject matter for education, and that is Life in all its manifestations. Instead of this single unity, we offer children Algebra, from which nothing follows; Geometry, from which nothing follows; Science, from which nothing follows; History, from which nothing follows; a Couple of Languages, never mastered, and lastly, most dreary of all, Literature, represented by plays of Shakespeare, with philological notes and short analyses of plot and character to be in substance committed to memory. Can such a list be said to represent Life, as it is known in the midst of the living of it?"[38] As you might have guessed, he answers his own question, "No," but takes several lines to say so. "The best that can be said of it is, that it is a rapid table of contents, which a deity might run over in his mind while he was thinking of creating a world, and has not yet determined how to put it together."[39]

Whitehead's call for educators to avoid inert ideas also leads directly to his critique of standardized, external examinations. As he sees it, assessment of learning should be entirely in the hands of the school and the individual teacher. The school should be able to develop its own exams: "No system of external tests which aims primarily at examining individual scholars can result in anything but educational waste."[40] In light of the neoliberal pressure that universities now face, we find Whitehead's way of closing his discussion of external examinations especially prescient. "Exactly the same principles apply, with the proper modifications, to universities and to technical colleges."[41]

The Students' Integrated Experience and Understanding

We come at last to the long-promised discussion of integration. In summary, Whitehead argues that what students learn should connect to what they learned before, what we call *vertical integration*. What they learn in one course should connect to what they learn in other courses (*horizontal integration*). Most urgently for Whitehead, what they learn should connect to their day-to-day lives, what we call *practical integration*.[42]

We have noted in several of our discussions in this chapter the links between Whitehead's specific complaints and integration. Education's failure to become adventure has its roots in the lack of connections between learning and life. Standardized tests fail the test because central authorities lack the teacher or professor's awareness of students' specific situations; that is, central authorities lack awareness of connections. Knowledge becomes simply inert ideas when no connections are made to students' day-to-day lives. Despite its relatively compact size, *The Aims of Education* tends to sprawl a bit. Other authors might choose other themes to try to bring this sprawling work into a more manageable form. However, we believe that Whitehead's theme that students have an integrated educational experience serves this purpose quite well.

Whitehead was not alone, in his time period, in identifying disintegration or in calling for integration. Many educators lamented what they saw as fragmentation, splintering, compartmentalization, atomization, curricular shreds and patches, artificial barriers, pigeonholing, irrelevance, the haphazard addition of subjects, triviality and isolation, and even a glut of unassimilated and unrelated ideas. Not a happy picture.[43] Many offered their laments, and several offered proposals. In 1899, not many years before Whitehead wrote, Guy Maxwell submitted a master's thesis at the Teacher's College of Columbia University entitled "The Doctrine of Correlation of Studies in the United States." He called for "the recognition of the natural relations existing among the various departments of human activity and such an arrangement of those departments for the presentation to the child that all his knowledge shall stand clearly in mind in its true relation to the whole and each in its parts."[44] A year before Maxwell presented his thesis at Columbia, Alexis Bertrand published *L'Enseignement Integral,* employing the term "integration."[45] In the first few decades of the twentieth century, when Whitehead presented the various materials that went into *Aims,* integration was clearly in the air.

We include here one expression of the concern for integration from Robert Maynard Hutchins, an educator whom we treat in some detail later in the book. Hutchins compared the modern university to "an encyclopedia. The encyclopedia contains many truths. It may consist of nothing else. But its unity can be found only in its alphabetical arrangement. The university is in much the same case. It has departments running from art to zoology but neither the students nor the professors know about the relation of one departmental truth to another, and what the relation of departmental truths to those in the domain of another department may be."[46] Without altering a word, we could attribute this citation to Whitehead. By expressing a concern for integration, Whitehead became a member of a large company.

We share Whitehead's concern. The separate parts of the student's education *should* connect with each other; we share with our students the responsibility for making and seeing those connections.[47] The parts and the whole of a student's education should also connect to life. Again, we must take some responsibility to help our students see and make those connections. Forgive us this bit of epistemic boldness if you need to, but we believe that the Christian university offers a framework—likely the only fully adequate framework—for either of those integrative tasks.

Conclusion and Questions

Whitehead called for educational reform. We have highlighted the themes of his work but have obviously skated over some of the details. As is true of the thinker-writer-authors we treat in the ten chapters that follow, Whitehead had much more to say than we can possibly treat here. A large secondary literature awaits those who wish to explore further his ideas for educational reform.[48] For that matter, the primary source we have used here runs to only 165 pages (not one of which is boring), and we recommend it to our readers. That said, Whitehead leaves us with several challenges, notably in the areas of our curriculum choices, our instruction methods, our means of assessment, our professional reading and research, and our ongoing efforts to help students connect what they learn to their other studies and to life itself.

If Paul's claim in Colossians 1 is true—that in Christ all things hold together—then we of all people should respond to Whitehead with our yes. We end with this remark from Whitehead:

> We must take it as an unavoidable fact that God has so made the world that there are more topics desirable for knowledge than any one person can possibly acquire. It is hopeless to approach the problem by the way of the enumeration of subjects which everyone ought to have mastered. There are too many of them, all with excellent title-deeds. Perhaps, after all, this plethora of material is fortunate; for the world is made interesting by a delightful ignorance of important truths. What I am anxious to impress on you is that though knowledge is the one chief aim of intellectual education, there is another ingredient, vaguer but greater, and more dominating in its importance. The ancients called it 'wisdom.' You cannot be wise without some basis of knowledge, but you may easily acquire knowledge and remain bare of wisdom.[49]

We could easily have used this citation in the context of Whitehead's discussion of the tension between breadth and depth. We present it here because we believe that Christian higher education worthy of the label demonstrates care about wisdom. We do not pretend that facts, knowledge, research—call it what you will—do not matter. But we do care about wisdom. And we believe that universities wishing to call themselves Christian must aim at nothing less than this wisdom of which Whitehead speaks.

QUESTIONS FOR REFLECTION AND DISCUSSION

- Whitehead warns his readers about the danger of inert ideas. What courses in your own teaching area might become candidates for the kind of inertia Whitehead discusses? Why?
- What departmental processes in your setting may contribute to instructional or curricular inertia?
- What resources could you draw on were you to aim at ensuring that your courses are not characterized by epistemic inertia?
- Whitehead prescribes that education be an adventure and that it be imaginative. Suggest areas where you could introduce more adventurous or imaginative approaches in some of your own courses. On your own campus, who could help you implement those approaches?
- Whitehead desires that the student's experience ultimately be an integrated, seamless whole. Most professors lack the energy or support to push for the degree of restructuring of an institution needed to facilitate students' success at realizing Whitehead's vision of integration. What changes could you make in your own design of curriculum, instruction, and assessment to increase students' opportunities to make the kinds of connections Whitehead desired?
- How might someone in the academic affairs office or teaching resources center help you learn about and implement those changes?
- What allies or supporters do you have on campus on the questions that Whitehead has raised? How can you best appropriate their support without simply participating in complaint sessions?

FOR FURTHER STUDY

Alfred North Whitehead is most noted for his work in metaphysics and mathematics, but he is also known for his work in education and theology. Books alone written by Whitehead, about Whitehead, and about his thought number in the hundreds, and the secondary scholarship continues to be vital. In the following, we offer some selected works for those who might wish to read more about Whitehead's life and ideas.

IN WHITEHEAD'S OWN WORDS (SELECTED WORKS)

Whitehead, Alfred North. *Adventures of Ideas*. Cambridge, UK: University Press, 1933.
———. *The Aims of Education: And Other Essays*. New York: New American Library, 1929.
———. *Alfred North Whitehead: An Anthology*. Cambridge, MA: Cambridge University Press, 1953.
———. *The Concept of Nature*. Cambridge, UK: Cambridge University Press, 1926.
———. *Essays in Science and Philosophy*. New York: Greenwood Press, 1968.
———. *The Function of Reason*. Louis Clark Vanuxem Foundation Lectures, 1929. Boston: Beacon Press, 1967.
———. *Modes of Thought*. New York: Free Press, 1968.
———. *The Organisation of Thought, Educational and Scientific*. Westport, CT: Greenwood Press, 1974.
———. *A Philosopher Looks at Science*. New York: Philosophical Library, 1965.
———. *Process and Reality: An Essay in Cosmology*. Gifford Lectures, 1927–28. New York: Social Science Book Store, 1929.
———. *Religion in the Making*. New York: Meridian Books, 1960.
———. *Science and Philosophy*. New York: Philosophical Library, 1948.
———. *Science and the Modern World*. Lowell Institute Lectures, 1925. New York: Macmillan, 1926.
Whitehead, Alfred North, and Bertrand Russell. *Principia Mathematica*. 2nd ed. New York: Cambridge University Press, 1927.
Whitehead, Alfred North, and Lucien Price. *Dialogues of Alfred North Whitehead, as Recorded by Lucien Price*. London: M. Reinhardt, 1954.

BIOGRAPHIES

Kuntz, Paul Grimley. *Alfred North Whitehead*. Boston: Twayne, 1984.
Lowe, Victor. *Alfred North Whitehead: The Man and His Work*. Baltimore: Johns Hopkins University Press, 1985.
Pittenger, W. Norman. *Alfred North Whitehead*. Makers of Contemporary Theology. London: Lutterworth Press, 1969.
Other Selected Works about Whitehead:
Blyth, John William. *Whitehead's Theory of Knowledge*. Brown University. Brown University Studies, vol. 7. Millwood, NY: Kraus Reprint, 1973.

Bram, Shachar, and Batya Stein. *Charles Olson and Alfred North Whitehead: An Essay on Poetry.* Lewisburg, PA: Bucknell University Press, 2004.

Brumbaugh, Robert S. *Whitehead, Process Philosophy, and Education.* SUNY Series in Philosophy. Albany, NY: State University of New York Press, 1982.

Cappon, Alexander Patterson. *Aspects of Wordsworth and Whitehead: Philosophy and Certain Continuing Life-problems.* New York: Philosophical Library, 1983.

Code, Murray. *Process, Reality, and the Power of Symbols: Thinking with A.N. Whitehead.* Basingstoke, UK; New York: Palgrave Macmillan, 2007.

Cooper, Ron L. *Heidegger and Whitehead: A Phenomenological Examination into the Intelligibility of Experience.* Athens, OH: Ohio University Press, 1993.

Eisendrath, Craig R. *The Unifying Moment: The Psychological Philosophy of William James and Alfred North Whitehead.* Cambridge, MA: Harvard University Press, 1971.

Epstein, Joseph. *Masters: Portraits of Great Teachers.* New York: Basic Books, 1981.

Fitzgerald, Janet A. *Alfred North Whitehead's Early Philosophy of Space and Time.* Washington, DC: University Press of America, 1979.

Haldar, M. K. *Studies in Whitehead's Cosmology.* Delhi: Atma Ram, 1972.

Hartshorne, Charles. *Whitehead's Philosophy: Selected Essays, 1935–1970.* Lincoln, NE: University of Nebraska Press, 1972.

Hendley, Brian Patrick. *Dewey, Russell, Whitehead: Philosophers as Educators.* Philosophical Explorations. Carbondale, IL: Southern Illinois University Press, 1986.

Hosinski, Thomas E. *Stubborn Fact and Creative Advance: An Introduction to the Metaphysics of Alfred North Whitehead.* Lanham, MD: Rowman & Littlefield, 1993.

Jentz, Arthur H. *Whitehead's Philosophy: Primary Texts in Dialogue.* Lanham, MD: University Press of America, 1985.

Jones, Judith A. *Intensity: An Essay in Whiteheadian Ontology.* 1st ed. Vanderbilt Library of American Philosophy. Nashville, TN: Vanderbilt University Press, 1998.

Kraus, Elizabeth M., and Alfred North Whitehead. *The Metaphysics of Experience: A Companion to Whitehead's Process and Reality.* New York: Fordham University Press, 1979.

Lambert, Jean Christine. *The Human Action of Forgiving: A Critical Application of the Metaphysics of Alfred North Whitehead.* Lanham, MD: University Press of America, 1985.

Lawrence, Nathaniel Morris. *Alfred North Whitehead, A Primer of His Philosophy.* Great Thinkers Series. New York: Twayne, 1974.

Leclerc, Ivor. *The Relevance of Whitehead: Philosophical Essays in Commemoration of the Centenary of the Birth of Alfred North Whitehead.* New York: Allen & Unwin; Macmillan, 1961.

Lowe, Victor. *Understanding Whitehead.* Baltimore: Johns Hopkins Press, 1962.

Mack, Robert D. *The Appeal to Immediate Experience: Philosophic Method in Bradley, Whitehead, and Dewey.* Freeport, NY: Books for Libraries Press, 1968.

Mays, Wolfe. *The Philosophy of Whitehead.* Muirhead Library of Philosophy. New York: Macmillan, 1959.

Mesle, C. Robert. *Process-Relational Philosophy: An Introduction to Alfred North Whitehead.* West Conshohocken, PA: Templeton Foundation Press, 2008.

Philipson, Sten M. *A Metaphysics for Theology: A Study of Some Problems in the Later Philosophy of Alfred North Whitehead and Its Application to Issues in Contemporary Theology.* Acta Universitatis Upsaliensis. Studia Doctrinae Christianae Upsaliensia; 22. B. Almqvist & Wiksell: NJ, 1982.

Polanowski, Janusz A., and Donald W. Sherburne. *Whitehead's Philosophy: Points of Connection.* SUNY Series in Constructive Postmodern Thought. Albany, NY: State University of New York Press, 2004.

Riffert, Franz. *Alfred North Whitehead on Learning and Education: Theory and Application.* Newcastle, UK: Cambridge Scholars Press, 2005.

Rose, Philip. *On Whitehead.* Wadsworth Philosophers Series. Belmont, CA: Wadsworth/Thomson Learning, 2002.

Schilpp, Paul Arthur. *The Philosophy of Alfred North Whitehead.* 2nd ed. Library of Living Philosophers. New York: Tudor Publishing Company, 1951.

Sieroka, Norman. "One Whitehead, Not Three." *Studies in History and Philosophy of Science* 31, no. 4 (2000): 721–730.

Stengers, Isabelle. *Thinking with Whitehead: A Free and Wild Creation of Concepts.* New York: Routledge, 2011.

Thompson, Kenneth Frank. *Whitehead's Philosophy of Religion.* Studies in Philosophy (Hague, Netherlands) vol. 20. The Hague: Mouton, 1971.

Walker, Foster N. *Enjoyment and the Activity of Mind: Dialogues on Whitehead and Education.* Amsterdam; Atlanta, GA: Rodopi, 2000.

Weber, Michel. *Whitehead's Pancreativism: The Basics.* Berlin: De Gruyter, 2006.

NOTES

[1] *The Aims of Education: And Other Essays* (New York: New American Library, 1929). Whitehead also addressed educational questions in his *Essays in Science and Philosophy* (New York: Philosophical Library, 1948). Contemporary students of Whitehead continue to offer commentary on his work, for example, George Allen's *Modes of Learning: Whitehead's Metaphysics and the Stages of Education* (Albany, NY: SUNY Press, 2013); and Adam Scarfe's edited volume, *The Adventure of Education: Process Philosophers on Learning, Teaching, and Research* (New York: Rodopi, 2009). Also see Malcolm D. Evans, *Whitehead and Philosophy of Education: The Seamless Coat of Learning* (Amsterdam: Rodopi, 1998).

[2] Cambridge: Cambridge University Press, 1927. Russell published on education as well, most notably his *Education and the Social Order* (London: George Allen and Unwin, 1932).

[3] *Shop Class as Soulcraft: An Inquiry into the Value of Work* (New York: Penguin, 2009). Crawford's more recent title is *The World beyond Your Head: On Becoming an Individual in an Age of Distraction* (New York: Farrar, Straus and Giroux, 2015). In the same vein as *Shop Class as Soulcraft*, see Richard Sennett's *The Craftsman* (New Haven, CT: Yale University Press, 2008).

[4] From an earlier version of the essay, "The Aims of Education: A Plea for Reform," in *The Organisation of Thought: Educational and Scientific* (London: Williams and Norgate, 1917), 3.

[5] *Aims*, 43–59.

[6] Ibid., 2.

[7] Ibid., 48.

[8] See José Ortega y Gasset (Chapter Nine) for a supporting argument. He simply contends that everyone has to eat, so give students the skills to do so. The question is what higher education will do *in addition*.

[9] *Aims*, 48. Related to liberal education, note this interesting secondary source, which, in fact, compares Whitehead's views of liberal education to those of Hannah Arendt, whom we treat in Chapter Three of this volume. Jean Pascal Alcantara, "On Whitehead's Thoughts concerning Teaching, Learning, and the Way of Liberal Education," in Adam S. Scarfe (ed.), *The Adventure of Education: Process Philosophers on Learning, Teaching, and Research* (New York, Brill, 2009), 127–138.

[10] *Aims* (1967 edition), 2.

[11] *Aims* (1916 edition), 3.

[12] Ibid., 3–4.

[13] Ibid., 13.

[14] R. S. Peters, *Ethics and Education* (London: George Allen and Unwin, 1966), 31–32, 43–45.

[15] Scarfe, *Adventure of Education*, 94. Although he ventures well beyond Whitehead's concept of adventure at some points, Scarfe's introductory essay to his own edited book provides a good overview of educational adventure as Whitehead understood it.

[16] *Aims*, 98.

[17] Ibid., 93.

[18] Ibid., 96.

[19] Ibid., 98.

[20] Ibid., 100.
[21] Ernest Boyer, *Scholarship Reconsidered: Priorities of the Professoriate* (Princeton, NJ: Carnegie Foundation for the Advancement of Teaching, 1990). We present our own understanding of Boyer and attempt to connect his work to Christian higher education in *Faith and Learning: A Guide for Faculty* (Abilene, TX: Abilene Christian University Press, 2014).
[22] *Aims*, 99.
[23] Ibid., 15–28.
[24] Ibid., 16–17.
[25] At this point he also sounds a bit like Montessori, whom we treat in Chapter Five.
[26] *Aims*, 17.
[27] Ibid., 33.
[28] At this point, Whitehead describes what later philosophers of education commonly called the forms of knowledge. See, for example, Paul Hirst, "Liberal Education and the Nature of Knowledge," in R. D. Archambault (ed.), *Philosophical Analysis and Education* (New York: RKP, 1965), 113–138; and D. C. Philips, "The Distinguishing Features of the Forms of Knowledge," *Educational Philosophy and Theory* 3, no. 2 (1971): 27–35.
[29] For a more detailed exploration of catalyst metaphors, see pages 62–65 in *Metaphors We Teach By*, which one of us edited with Harro Van Brummelen (Eugene, OR: Wipf and Stock, 2012).
[30] *Aims*, 26.
[31] Ibid., 1.
[32] Ibid., 3.
[33] Ibid., 4.
[34] Ibid., 5.
[35] Ibid., 5.
[36] In fact he returns to the quadratic equation later (7–9) as part of a larger discussion of the teaching of mathematics. He sounds quite like Christian Reformed philosopher Herman Dooyeweerd in his explanation that life has a quantitative aspect and therefore math is worth learning. But that warrant comes with the condition that students see the connection between the math that they are learning and their daily lives.
[37] *Aims*, 6.
[38] Ibid., 6–7.
[39] Ibid., 7.
[40] Ibid., 13.
[41] Ibid., 14.
[42] These labels now enjoy wide usage, but Whitehead's calls for integration predate the labels.
[43] Literally hundreds of observers of education have leveled criticisms along these lines. Although we will not pretend to survey that conversation here, we cannot resist including at least one Whiteheadian assessment of disintegration made by someone other than Whitehead just three years after *Aims* was published. This, from E. C. Lindeman, who writes "it is [in junior high-school] that the pupil first comes into contact with specialized teachers who know some single field or subject-matter but know practically nothing about other subjects nor about the relationship between subjects. The flood of subject-matter which now descends upon pupils in rivulets streaming from academic departments, each with its own label, and each in turn demanding a

separate loyalty begins the first of those vicious separations in our educational system which keeps learning from being an integrative experience." From "Integration as an Educational Concept," in *Integration: Its Meaning and Application*, ed. Levi Thomas Hopkins (New York: Appleton Century Crofts, 1937), 32.

[44] Maxwell cited in Edward A. Ciccorico, "Integration in the Curriculum," *Main Currents* 272 (November–December 1970): 60.

[45] Charles W. Knudsen, "What Do Educators Mean by 'Integration'?" *Harvard Educational Review* 7 (January 1937): 16.

[46] Robert Maynard Hutchins, *The Higher Learning in America* (New Haven, CT: Yale University Press, 1970), 37.

[47] And we recognize a kind of sliding scale of responsibility. The professor teaching undergraduates should expect to erect a few more signposts than we would ask of the doctoral supervisor.

[48] Several representatives of that literature are listed in the first endnote in this chapter.

[49] *Aims*, 30.

Dorothy L. Sayers

The Lost Tools of Learning (1947)

Biography and Background

IN JUNE 1893, DOROTHY LEIGH SAYERS WAS BORN IN OXFORD, INTO THE home of Helen Mary Sayers and Henry Sayers, an Anglican clergyman.[1] At the time of her birth, Church of England clergy were clearly part of the middle class, so Sayers grew up in relative comfort. As a child of four (an only child, in fact), she moved to Bluntisham, north of Cambridge, where she lived until she left for boarding school at age 16 (and where she set her 1934 novel, *The Nine Tailors*). After attending boarding school in Salisbury, she returned to Oxford to attend Somerville College, finishing her studies in language and literature in 1915, before women were granted degrees at Oxford. Five years later, in October 1920, she returned to receive both her first degree and her MA, a member of the first female graduating class from that university.

At the outset, the character of Sayers's friendship with J. R. R. Tolkien and C. S. Lewis bears mention. Many assume that Sayers was a member of the Oxford Inklings, which she was not. She enjoyed friendship with the two best-known Inklings, Lewis and Tolkien, but she actually developed a close friendship only with Charles Williams, and she carried on long correspondence with him.[2] In fact, we attribute her having endured only in small part to her connection to the Inklings, much as we might like to think that on a Tuesday afternoon at the Eagle and Child it was she who suggested to Tolkien that *Gollum* might be a scarier name than *Eric* for the loathsome character he had in mind for his trilogy. The larger reason for her having endured, in our view, is the breadth, depth, and quality of her work. She excelled in classical scholarship, translating Dante and other works, and writing theology[3] and literary criticism, besides poetry, plays, and detective fiction. In fact, she said on more than one occasion that her reason for writing detective fiction was to earn an income so that she could carry on with the important work of classical and literary scholarship.

More to the point about her having endured, her detective novels achieved great popularity in her own time and have remained popular. Those novels meet all the criteria—in spades—for the formulaic detective novel as writers and readers conceived of it at that time. But her Lord Peter Wimsey (detective) novels are also deeply thoughtful and theological, and she alludes in them to classical and historical works, literary works, and some of the burning issues of her own day. Because of her own biography, she knew intimately the details of life in Oxford, Bluntisham, Christchurch (in Dorset), Salisbury, and London. She incorporated her knowledge of places (and massive servings of careful research) into her novels. But, as Barbazon notes, there was also "a general air of literariness . . . litter[ing] the books."[4] In fact, Barbazon concludes that her habit of having Wimsey allude so frequently to his classical and literary education actually becomes a deterrent to some readers. In the Wimsey novels, she works through many of her own questions about feminism and the roles of women in society.[5] Her character Harriet Vane, novelist, detective in her own right, friend, and eventually wife of Lord Peter, has to work through her questions about women, marriage, and committing oneself to another. Especially in her 1935 novel, *Gaudy Night* (which is set in a college and involves plagiarism), Sayers has her Miss Vane agonize over these questions.

Several studies treat Sayers's life in detail, but we will focus on her contribution to the contemporary discussion of the liberal arts.[6] Stories about the new challenges facing the liberal arts circulate regularly, whether those challenges have their roots in declining institutional funding, changing societal expectations and an altered work landscape, or students' narrowed tolerance for unfamiliar or challenging ideas. Today, the liberal arts conversation has many voices, some strident, some thoughtful, some brash and unreflective. Given the concern for what Cardinal Newman called the well-being of the university (rather than just its being),[7] we want to explore this question in this chapter: What can Dorothy Leigh Sayers contribute to the contemporary conversation about the place of the liberal arts and humanities? And why Sayers? Simply, the liberal arts conversation needs calm and wise voices. So we bring her into this conversation, not out of nostalgia but out of our recognition that we urgently need wisdom, we need it now, and she has some of the wisdom we need.

Sayers and the Liberal Arts

In a general way, Sayers's own immersion in literature and history constitutes a subtle argument for the liberal arts, Barbazon's concern that Lord Peter's erudition might repel some readers notwithstanding. For example, she recounts in "A Vote of Thanks to Cyrus" how as a child she read a children's magazine called *Tales from Herodotus* and one day realized that the Cyrus of this book was the same Cyrus of the Bible. She pokes a bit of fun at herself for not realizing that the world of Greek and Roman literature connected to—was at some points the same world as—the world of the Bible. Perhaps she does have a small rebuke for those of us who write Sunday school material, for she says that in Greek and Roman literature and history, "the sun always shone so much more vividly than it did in the Bible."[8]

Throughout her work, she refers to literary works that those unfamiliar with such works will simply not understand. We might call that the *enrichment argument*. For example, Lord Peter Wimsey often purchases first editions to add to his collection. Sayers was always fastidiously accurate about the dates of these editions, although such dates were never central to the mysteries themselves. Some evenings, Wimsey would read biblical commentaries or other highbrow works, and Sayers would slip in a bit of her own assessment of the merits of his chosen reading. She wrote a series of articles in which she applied the methods of biblical criticism to deconstruct Sherlock Holmes stories. Her point was, in fact, more devious than that; she was actually deconstructing the methods themselves by demonstrating the shambles they would make of Conan Doyle's accounts of Sherlock's work.[9] Not to sound too exclusionary, but one's enjoyment of her allusions might be somewhat proportional to one's familiarity with a broad range of literature, philosophy, and theology.

At many points, Sayers addressed the question of our chapter—the liberal arts—directly as well. In "Towards a Christian Aesthetic," for example, she laments that while Christians have a tradition of thought in politics, finance, and sociology, we lack that tradition in aesthetics.[10] She puts it this way: "Oddly enough, we have no Christian aesthetic—no Christian philosophy of the arts. The church as a body has never made up her mind about the arts, and it is hardly too much to say that she has never tried.... There have, of course, been plenty of writers on aesthetics who happened to be Christians, but they seldom made any consistent attempt to relate their aesthetic to the central Christian dogmas."[11] Strong words indeed, but Sayers has something here for us who, decades later, apparently must struggle with the choice between whether we will be shaped by neoliberal values or the humanizing values of the arts and humanities. Although these are our words and not hers, it seems to us that in thinking about the place of the liberal arts, the challenge now, as then, is to choose rightly—or is that "find the right balance"?—between the values of the market and the values of the manger.

We have kept our introduction to Dorothy Sayers brief, but we will return to her later in the chapter. We leave her now, temporarily, to review the state of the liberal arts and humanities in contemporary higher education.

The Liberal Arts: Pro and Contra

That the liberal arts are under threat will not come as news to our readers. It may come as news to some that ours is not the first generation to face the question. Percy Bysshe Shelley wrote *A Defense of Poetry* in 1821.[12] Among other arguments, he claimed that poetry brings delight and satisfaction to its hearers and that it strengthens one's ability to imagine. We find it interesting that Shelley saw logic and reason as the things against which he had to defend poetry. John Locke wrote these words in 1693: "Can there be any thing more ridiculous than that a father should waste his own money and his son's time in setting him to learn the Roman language, when at the same time he designs him for a trade . . . ?" Locke continues by asking why a child should "be forced to learn the rudiments of a language which he is never to use in the course of [his] life, and neglect all the while the writing a good hand and casting accounts, which are of great advantage in all conditions of life, and to most trades indispensably necessary?"[13] The three-century gap between Locke's writing and our own does not dull the force of his words at all. The value of the liberal arts and humanities is apparently not apparent to everyone.

Of course, the conversation about the value of the liberal arts precedes Locke by millennia. The Greeks and Romans debated the same questions. Cicero complained about those who focused on dialectic so much that they ignored the public good. In his view, worthwhile education focused on rhetoric, an art useful for public service and for persuading others to worthy civic action.[14] Cicero's *Oratory* is, in fact, an extended discussion of the relative merits of practical education and theoretical education and, at points, sounds like he wrote it for last week's *Chronicle of Higher Education*. Like Martha Nussbaum (whom we treat shortly), he concludes that a broad-ranging education prepares one for citizenship. But it does more than that; in mourning the death of his own daughter, Tullia, Cicero found solace in reading and writing. For him, liberal education enriches one's life and restores the soul.[15]

As one might expect, arguments for the liberal arts have evolved over time. Traditionally, its advocates argued that it offered students insights into the perennial questions and an opportunity to deepen and broaden their own understanding of the world. It made them deeper and better people.[16] The liberal arts freed people and helped them remain free.[17] The liberal arts taught self-restraint; they allowed people to choose carefully and wisely, enabling both individuals and societies to flourish. Thus, people studied the humanities and liberal arts primarily for their own enrichment rather than to benefit the commonwealth (although that may have been a side effect; note the argument that democratic societies require educated and free people). The medieval distinction between the liberal arts and the practical arts, the *artes mechanicae*, accords with such an understanding.[18] In reality, things are a bit more complex. Recall that in the medieval university, the liberal arts were preparation for further study in medicine, law, and theology; that is, they served a practical purpose, too, one beyond personal enrichment.

Between the Medieval period and now, of course, we have experienced a sea change, with a good deal of that change happening in the last half century. Publicly available statistics reveal at least one aspect of that change. Of the 840,000 university graduates in the United States in 1971, 8 percent graduated in language and literature, while 14 percent graduated in business. By 2008, only 3.5 percent graduated in language and literature, but 22 percent graduated in business. History has it worse than languages and literature; only 2.2 percent graduated in history in 2008.[19]

One result of the recent shift away from the liberal arts and toward the view that higher education should be for job training is that a liberal arts degree may become the privilege of only the wealthy few; that is, a return to the arrangements in place before the advent of mass higher education.[20] We join with the chorus of voices expressing concern about the demise of the liberal arts.[21] We believe they do humanize, they do enrich, they do expand the horizons of those who give their academic efforts in that direction. We need the liberal arts. But we also know the financial pressures that students, families, and universities face at this juncture. The tension here is real. Facing this tension, defenders of the liberal arts have offered three reasoned justifications for the liberal arts. In this review, we will end by returning to the work of Dorothy L. Sayers.

Rationales for the Liberal Arts

The first justification we review is that we need the liberal arts because people participating in the economy will be better people. Second, we need the liberal arts for healthy democracies. Third, we need the liberal arts because people who study the liberal arts are fuller and richer people. The argument made by Dorothy Sayers fits in the final group.

First, liberal arts graduates will function better in the global economy. Expressions of this warrant for the liberal arts are easy to find. In one campus magazine, for example, we learn that the high-tech economy requires the trait of flexibility and a disposition toward lifelong learning.[22] Furthermore, the global economy requires people who can deal with diversity. A liberal arts education will produce people with these traits and dispositions. We do not single out this particular article because it provides an easy target for criticism; it is a typical expression of a standard argument. Administrators in higher education have found themselves against the economic ropes, and in response, some now offer arguments that, in one sense, are simply attempts to speak in language that the world outside the campus gates considers natural language. That is, economic justifications are the only justifications that will pass muster in a culture that speaks only economic language.

We are not so high-minded or stupid as to think that one's education should not lead to employment. In the words of George Houston, the university may have to admit that its "mission will include not only an education for life but an education that provides the skills, wisdom, and knowledge to get employed. There's nothing wrong with providing education that enables one to be hired. To work is not a sin."[23] Nevertheless, we have reviewed this argument very quickly for one simple reason: it remains a neoliberal argument, and we want something that will stand up both outside the campus gates and outside the market.

Second, we examine the argument that we need the liberal arts for healthy democracies. Many have taken this line; we will restrict ourselves to the very articulate and somewhat recent expression of the argument given by Martha Nussbaum (of the University of Chicago) in her readable volume, *Not for Profit: Why Democracy Needs the Humanities*.[24] Nussbaum argues that in the search for better national balance sheets, whole nations have begun to teach something different to their students from what they need to keep democracy alive. She claims that the liberal arts have come under attack because policymakers see them as "useless frills, at a time when nations must cut away all useless things in order to stay competitive in the global market."[25]

Nussbaum's defense is straightforward: Democracies need people capable of critical thought and reflection; such people live more responsibly in the world in which we have all found ourselves. She does not ignore the economic dimension of our lives but argues that the liberal arts are needed "to promote a climate of responsible and watchful stewardship and a culture of creative innovation,"[26] an argument quite at odds with the first cluster of arguments we reviewed above. On her account, the choice between educating for profit and educating for citizenship is a false choice. She thus presents a double argument in *Not for Profit*; first, the arts and humanities protect democracy, and second, the arts and humanities prepare people more fully for responsible participation in the economy. Read those words carefully; Nussbaum does not want simple *participation;* she wants *responsible and watchful stewardship.* Hers is not a neoliberal defense.

Not for Profit does not end on a happy note. Nussbaum asks: "What will we have, if these trends continue? Nations of technically trained people who do not know how to criticize authority, useful profit-makers with obtuse imaginations."[27] She continues on the same page: "Democracies have great rational and imaginative powers. They are also prone to some serious flaws in reasoning, to parochialism, haste, sloppiness, selfishness, narrowness of the spirit. Education based mainly on profitability in the global market magnifies these deficiencies, producing a greedy obtuseness and a technically trained docility that threaten the very life of democracy itself, and that certainly impede the creation of a decent world culture."[28] Nussbaum's comments need no commentary; she has made her views clear. We end this brief treatment of the first two kinds of defense of the liberal arts by noting that Dorothy Sayers voiced nearly the same complaints about five decades before Martha Nussbaum.

The third rationale we review for the liberal arts and humanities is that they humanize. Such arguments cannot be reduced to economic terms. Sayers is not alone in offering such arguments; many before and after have argued along the same lines. We will not take time here to review the range of voices in this conversation.

Dorothy Sayers and Her Rationale for Liberal Arts

Within a few sentences of beginning her essay "The Lost Tools of Learning,"[29] Sayers writes that "if we are to produce a society of educated people, fitted to preserve their intellectual freedom amid the complex pressures of our modern society, we must turn back the wheel of progress some four or five hundred years, to the point at which education began to lose sight of its true object, towards the end of the Middle Ages."[30] Anticipating the chilly reception such a view would likely receive, she follows her assertion by pleading with her audience not to dismiss her as a retro-grouch but to join her as she explores what she sees as the malaise of contemporary education and the larger society of which it is a part. Knowing that many intellectually nostalgic people have appropriated Sayers (and Lewis[31]) for quite conservative purposes, we make the same plea upon quoting Sayers. Please don't dismiss us quite yet; let's see where Sayers can take us.

Her original argument related to how easily her contemporaries could be persuaded of false claims in advertising and propaganda, or in meetings and on committees. And she asks in her essay whether anyone other than her has worried about how confused people can become over language used in the press and in public life. She wonders if something may be wrong with the education offered in her time given that people tend not to remember what they supposedly learned in school and that they cannot distinguish good books from bad. She also notes how school subjects remain separated forever for many people.[32] We have represented her catalogue of ills only briefly here, but she summarizes by saying "that although we often succeed in teaching our pupils 'subjects,' we fail lamentably on the whole in teaching them how to think."[33]

Sayers gives several pages to her explanation of what teaching students to think might look like, and it is this explanation from which she draws the "lost tools" of her title. In her view, which she shapes around the medieval Trivium, the tools of learning include knowing the grammar of a field so that one can work critically in that field. For her, the word *grammar* is not limited to the rules of language use, but refers both to the essential facts in any field and the ways that concepts in that field connect to each other. Thus, when one learns the grammar of a field, one can work effectively in that field. We noted above that some have appropriated Sayers and Lewis to underwrite an essentially nostalgic, classical curriculum. The middle pages of "The Lost Tools of Learning," where Sayers lays out her vision of the curriculum, have repeatedly been pressed into service for this purpose.[34] Yet, Sayers clearly calls for critical thinking. She wants students to disagree with their teachers. She wants them to take responsibility for directing a significant portion of their learning. Many readers, however, seeing the word *Trivium,* fail to notice her reasons for suggesting that it be restored: because it provided the required *tools* for other learning. Instead, they invoke her as matron saint for a very conservative program, missing, for example, that she calls for schools not to "neglect the material which is so abundant in the [student's] own daily life,"[35] a comment that could have come as easily from John Dewey's keyboard. Read differently, her essay "The Lost Tools of Learning" might just as easily encourage those who advocate inquiry learning.

Sayers on Work and Creativity

Sayers wrote enough about craft, creation, work, and aesthetics that we consider her a philosopher of aesthetics in her own right.[36] Besides writing explicitly about these topics, she also wove her views into all her fiction, drama, letters, and nonfiction. Her perspectives on these dimensions of human life were deeply theological and at some points even analogical, inasmuch as people and God share the desire to make things, the central idea she explores in *The Mind of the Maker*.[37] Of interest to anyone considering the potential for economic values to trump the liberal arts, Sayers wrote in her brief wartime essay, "Why Work?" about the likelihood that, once World War II ended, people would simply return to the consumerist ways of life they had lived before the war forced them to restrain their appetite for goods. She wrote, "And, so that the wheels may turn, the consumer—that is you and I, including the workers, who are consumers also—will again be urged to consume and waste; and unless we change our attitude—or rather unless we keep hold of the new attitude forced upon us by the logic of war—we shall again be bamboozled by our vanity, indolence, and greed into keeping the squirrel-cage of wasteful economy turning."[38] She continues a few lines later: "The habit of thinking about work as something one does to make money is so ingrained in us that we can scarcely imagine what a revolutionary change it would be to think about it instead in terms of the work done. It would mean taking the attitude of mind we reserve for our unpaid work—our hobbies, our leisure interests, the things we make and do for pleasure—and making *that* the standard of all our judgments about things and people."[39] Her words here are not Cardinal Newman's, but we cannot help but notice that, to use his words, she is distinguishing mere *being* from *well-being*, form from substance, depth, and purpose.[40]

We cite this passage at length because we believe these prescient comments fit perfectly into the contemporary argument about the purposes of a university degree and of the place of the liberal arts in that degree. Based on her views of the noneconomic value of work, Sayers would certainly have questions today were she asked to speak at a graduation ceremony where more than 20 percent of the degrees being conferred were in business. In "Why Work?" she expands her complaint about people's view of work into four propositions or implications. First, for her, focusing on payment for our work undermines our work and our own happiness. In the case of our hobbies, we love and serve our work, and we take satisfaction in a job well done. Ideally, the jobs we do to earn an income should function in the same way. When a whole society focuses only on the financial rewards of work, these inherent satisfactions are undermined.

Her second and third propositions bear directly on the questions of this chapter. Her second is that people should do the work for which they are suited. Once again, however, economic categories undermine vocational categories. Her third proposition connects closely to the second; focusing on the financial rewards of work sabotages our taking enjoyment in work. It leads us to count down the hours until we finish our work and can get to our leisure. At this point, we read Sayers this way: Imagine university students learning that earning the most money should not be the primary criterion by which they think about their own vocation. We know they need to live somewhere, and they need to eat, and that they do live in a material world where material goods have a price.[41] We understand that. But imagine, with Sayers, that they take a different perspective on their work, a less economic perspective that does not undermine their enjoyment of their work and their sense of vocation. In this picture, they might see the value of studying the liberal arts.

Fourth, Sayers proposes that a Christian view of work implies that workers would want to produce quality work. Again, we do not want to make her say what she did not say, but we believe that the contemporary worker grounded in the liberal arts and humanities would want what she describes. In fact, many young adults today explicitly do not want to become worker bees in the global economy; they do not want simply to help some multinational improve its bottom line. The payoffs they seek from work are in other than financial terms.[42] Sayers's expressed hope is that people would "fight tooth and nail, not for mere employment, but for the quality of the work.... We should clamber to be engaged in work that was worth doing, and in which we could take a pride. The worker would demand that the stuff he helped to turn out should be good stuff—he would no longer be content to take the cash and let the credit go."[43] Sayers published those words in 1949, but many younger adults today post almost those exact words on Facebook. That fact raises two more questions. First, who is demanding that education be suited only for maximizing salary? Second, are we underserving those students who fit the ideal Sayers presents and who want something other than money from life, who want to grapple with the big questions during the years they give us?

Having presented her four propositions, Sayers then provides some pointed theological commentary. She notes that it is the "business of the Church" and, we would say, of the Christian college, to help people understand a Christian view of work and vocation. Again, she uses language that, with little adaptation, could easily come out of the mouth of a young adult today: no one should be "required by economic or any other considerations to devote himself to work that is contemptible, soul-destroying, or harmful."[44] Replace "soul-destroying" with "life-sucking," and you have Facebook posts from people under 40 describing their jobs. We are not arguing here that the church should join the Occupy Movement (although it possibly should). Rather, we are arguing that the Christian college is positioned perfectly to help young adults understand vocation within a Christian framework and that the liberal arts can be central in their coming to such an understanding.

At the end of "Why Work?" Sayers argues that we should *serve the work*. By this she means something consistent with but extended from the second and third propositions we summarized above: we work because the work itself is worth doing. If we apply this principle to the study of the liberal arts, then we find Sayers in disagreement not only with those who would abolish the liberal arts because they believe an education is simply a means of increasing one's lifetime income, but also with those who believe that the liberal arts are necessary because they help preserve democracy. In arguing this way, she may have removed the median between the moral low road (abolition of the liberal arts) and the moral high road (the societal benefits of the liberal arts). In her view, these are both instrumental arguments.

Sayers ends her essay bluntly: "If work is to find its right place in the world, it is the duty of the Church to see to it that the work serves God, and that the worker serves the work."[45] On an experimental basis only, we want to alter her wording slightly: "If the liberal arts are to find their right place in the world, it is the duty of Christian colleges to see to it that the liberal arts serve God, and that we and our students serve the work."[46] Our adaptation of Sayer's language fits with Parker Palmer's argument that students should not have to go through the teacher-as-barrier to get to the subject. Rather, both teacher and student go in pursuit of what he calls the big subject. We do not mean here that professors remain ignorant or feign ignorance. Of course we bring our expertise to the class; that's why we get paid. But we are asking if the service to the work to which Sayers calls us might, in fact, be a life-giving posture for us to adopt toward our academic disciplines.

Imagine what our classes would look like if our students observed us explicitly serving the work . . . adopting a learning posture toward the materials in our courses. What would it look like to them if we continually seemed to be trying as hard as they were to understand the ideas before us? We believe that our modeling that posture would serve as a strong invitation to our students to join us on the learning journey. But we ask this as well: imagine how we might feel if we adopted the posture of learner with regard to the materials themselves, not only in front of our students, but in our offices and in our reading at home too. Especially for those introductory and core courses that we repeat year to year, would this posture enable those courses to come to life for us again? We believe it would.

Conclusion and Questions

Without doubt, the liberal arts face a challenge today, especially from neo-liberalism. Perhaps it is actually higher education that faces the challenge, and the unlucky liberal arts appeared to the market-maddened money doctors as a vestigial organ (with functions uncertain, with removal easy, with few defenders). The few who have defended the liberal arts have offered three distinct arguments. First, the global economy needs liberal arts graduates because a liberal arts education helps people become the kind of people the economy needs, people who can think clearly and who play well with others. Second, democracies need the kind of freedom-defending people that a liberal arts education helps shape. Many supporters of the liberal arts offer this second rationale; we focused here on Martha Nussbaum. Among those making the third kind of argument, we include Sayers. These defenders of the liberal arts argue that the liberal arts help people become better people, people who enjoy life more because they think and live within a richer and more robust mental frame.

We accept the arguments of Dorothy Sayers and others that the liberal arts and humanities help us become better people. We also know that such arguments ultimately will not satisfy those who live and think only in neoliberal terms; unless the liberal arts can be shown to count in economic terms, they don't count at all. So, must we and Sayers declare defeat for having failed to produce an argument that those outside the campus gates will accept? Perhaps. But there is more to our argument.

We believe that the challenge facing the liberal arts presents Christian higher educators an unprecedented opportunity. Why an opportunity? Because here is a point of difference, a site at which Christian higher educators can say that the values of the manger still trump the values of the market. Even in the face of unprecedented financial pressure, Christian higher educators can say that we still work toward an ultimately soul-enriching (albeit countercultural) mission. We will teach the liberal arts. We will educate for character. We will educate for wisdom. We will teach and live knowing that some things that count cannot be counted, that economic values are not the only values. If we take anything from Dorothy L. Sayers, let us take her wisdom about the inherent value of work and about the life-transforming practice of asking the perennial questions.

QUESTIONS

The students we teach today were born a century after Dorothy Sayers.

- How would professors and students in your own setting respond if grammar, logic, and rhetoric (broadly understood) were introduced as the foundational courses in the first degree?
- What justifications for those courses do you think might satisfy those operating within a neoliberal framework?

Sayers herself had a liberal education, as did we. We confessed to having failed to produce a noneconomic warrant for the liberal arts that would satisfy anyone who thinks primarily in market terms. We then argued that Christian higher educators may have such a warrant.

- To what degree do you think a Christian worldview provides a justification for a liberal arts education?
- What missteps, if any, can you identify that defenders of the liberal arts have made that may have led to decreased public support for the liberal arts?

Sayers located work in a context of vocation rather than in a market context. We argued that her thinking about work fits with how many contemporary younger adults view work.

- What viewpoints do you hear from your own students about the purposes of employment?

FOR FURTHER STUDY

Besides completing many translations, Dorothy L. Sayers wrote drama, poetry, fiction, and nonfiction. We do not reproduce here what is available in the many published bibliographies, but we do list a sampling of her more theological and philosophical essays. Her friendship with the Oxford Inklings has meant that many more readers have discovered the riches of her work than might have been the case otherwise. We do not count that against her; her work warrants our serious consideration regardless of who she named among her friends.

IN SAYERS'S OWN WORDS

Dorothy L. Sayers. *Are Women Human*. Grand Rapids, MI: Eerdmans, 1971.
_____. *Christian Letters to a Post-Christian World*, edited by Roderick Jellema. Grand Rapids, MI: Eerdmans, 1969.
_____. *Creed or Chaos*. New York: Harcourt, Brace, 1949.
_____. *The Lost Tools of Learning*. London: Methuen, 1948.

———. *A Matter of Eternity: Selections from the Writings of Dorothy L. Sayers,* edited by Rosamond Kent Sprague. Grand Rapids, MI: Eerdmans, 1973.
———. *The Mind of the Maker.* London: Methuen, 1941.
———. *Unpopular Opinions.* London: Gollancz, 1946.
———. "Why Work?" in *Creed or Chaos* (New York: Harcourt, Brace, 1949), 46–62.
———. *The Zeal of Thy House.* London: Gollancz, 1937.

BIOGRAPHIES

Barbazon, James. *Dorothy L. Sayers: The Life of a Courageous Woman.* New York: Scribner, 1981.

Brunsdale, Mitzi. *Dorothy L. Sayers: Solving the Mystery of Wickedness.* New York: Berg, 1990.

Reynolds, Barbara. *Dorothy L. Sayers: Her Life and Soul.* New York: St. Martin's, 1993.

Stone Dale, Alzina. *Maker and Craftsman: The Story of Dorothy L. Sayers.* Wheaton, IL: Harold Shaw, 1992.

CRITICAL STUDIES

Gilbert, Colleen B. *A Bibliography of the Works of Dorothy L. Sayers.* London: Macmillan, 1978.

Harmon, Robert B., and Margaret Burgur. *An Annotated Guide to the Works of Dorothy L. Sayers.* New York: Garland, 1977.

Simmons, Laura. *Creed without Chaos: Exploring Theology in the Writings of Dorothy L. Sayers.* Grand Rapids, MI: Baker, 2005.

Youngberg, Ruth. *Dorothy L. Sayers: A Reference Guide.* Boston: G. K. Hall, 1982.

NOTES

¹In later life, Sayers adopted her mother's maiden name, Leigh, as her middle initial because she thought it would aid in her preferred, single-syllable pronunciation of her last name (like *Sares*).

²Williams was recently called *The Third Inkling* in Grevel Lindop's 2015 book by that name (New York: Oxford University Press).

³See for example, *The Mind of the Maker* (London: Methuen, 1941); *Unpopular Opinions* (London: Gollancz, 1946); and *Creed or Chaos? And Other Essays in Popular Theology* (London: Hodder and Stoughton, 1940).

⁴James Barbazon, *Dorothy L. Sayers: The Life of a Courageous Woman* (New York: Scribner, 1981), 277. Literally hundreds of other biographical and critical studies of Sayers are available to anyone with interest, some of them difficult to distinguish from fan writing. We will not relist here what is available online and in the published bibliographies. We do note, however, *Dorothy L. Sayers: Her Life and Soul*, by Sayers scholar Barbara Reynolds (New York: St. Martin's, 1993). For those not wanting the level of detail supplied by Barbazon or Reynolds, we note the much briefer biography by Alzina Stone Dale, *Maker and Craftsman: The Story of Dorothy L. Sayers* (Grand Rapids, MI: Eerdmans, 1978). Less biographical and more theological is this volume by our own colleague from George Fox University, Laura Simmons: *Creed without Chaos: Exploring Theology in the Writings of Dorothy L. Sayers* (Grand Rapids, MI: Baker, 2005).

⁵*Are Women Human* is the best-known work where, after expressing her lack of interest in being identified with feminism and her doubts that aggressive feminism would do much good, she addresses these questions (Grand Rapids, MI: Eerdmans, 1971). Questions of feminism and women's roles run through her works and letters, at some points more directly than at others. Many secondary works examine this aspect of her thought as well, for example, *Feminist Theology: Voices from the Past*, by Ann Loades (Cambridge: Polity, 2001).

⁶In our view, three comprehensive bibliographies obviate the need for anyone but the most specialized Sayers scholar to do further bibliographic work. They are Robert B. Harmon and Margaret Burgur's *An Annotated Guide to the Works of Dorothy L. Sayers* (New York: Garland, 1977); Colleen B. Gilbert's *A Bibliography of the Works of Dorothy L. Sayers* (London: Macmillan, 1978); and Ruth Youngberg's *Dorothy L. Sayers: A Reference Guide* (Boston: G. K. Hall, 1982). Many bibliographies are available online, none of them of the quality of these three.

⁷See Chapter Six.

⁸"A Vote of Thanks to Cyrus," in *Christian Letters to a Post-Christian World*, ed. Roderick Jellema (Grand Rapids, MI: Eerdmans, 1969), 50.

⁹See, for example, "The Dates in the Red-Headed League," in *Christian Letters to a Post-Christian World*, 55–65.

¹⁰"Towards a Christian Aesthetic," in *Christian Letters to a Post-Christian World*, 69–83.

¹¹Ibid., 69.

¹²Edited by John E. Jordan (New York: Bobbs-Merrill, 1965).

¹³John Locke, *Some Thoughts concerning Education*, 3rd ed. (1695; Oxford: Clarendon Press, 2000), sec. 164.

[14] Several full-text versions of Cicero's *Oratory* are available online. We have used the Charles Duke Yonge translation from 1913, available at http://oll.libertyfund.org/titles/734.

[15] See Kate Wintrol, "The Intrinsic Value of the Liberal Arts: Cicero's Example," *Journal of the National Collegiate Honors Council* (Spring/Summer 2014): 129–134. Wintrol argues from and with Cicero that the liberal arts cannot be simply about job preparation. For her, the liberal arts help "prepare students for their future and for the suffering that they, like Cicero, will inevitably experience in their lives" (133). Her secondary argument accords with Nussbaum's: the liberal arts prepare students for life in democracy.

[16] Robert Maynard Hutchins also held this perennial view of the liberal arts. See Chapter Ten.

[17] Susan McWilliams gives an extended version of this argument in "The Liberal Arts and the Arts of Liberty," *Perspectives on Political Science* 42, no. 4 (2013): 217–221.

[18] "Artes Mechanicae," accessed November 2015, https://en.wikipedia.org/wiki/Artes_Mechanicae/. See also the Wikipedia article on the liberal arts for a compact history of the liberal arts that does not contain a single word to indicate that the liberal arts are under threat or even renegotiation.

[19] These data are available at the U.S. Department of Education's National Center for Education Statistics (http://nces.ed.gov/annuals/) and at the site of the Integrated Postsecondary Education Data System (http://nces.ed.gov/ipeds/).

[20] McWilliams notes this trend (220).

[21] Laments about the demise of the liberal arts appear regularly. See, for example, Eric Deresiewicz, "The Neoliberal Arts: How College Sold Its Soul to the Market," *Harper's Magazine* (September 2015): 25–32; Lorraine Smith Pangle, "Reclaiming the Core," *Perspectives in Political Science* 42 (2013): 207–211; and the less pessimistic volume edited by Gordon Hutner and Feisal G. Mohamed, *A New Deal for the Humanities: Liberal Arts and the Future of Public Higher Education* (New Brunswick, NJ: Rutgers University Press, 2015).

[22] Michael S. McPherson, "The Economic Value of a Liberal Arts Education," *About Campus* 3, no. 4 (September/October 1998): 13–17.

[23] "Bury the Liberal vs. Professional Debate," *Education* 117, no. 1 (1996): 13. Houston suggests that the whole question of liberal arts vs. professional training can be solved by reading two books: *The Idea of the University* by Newman (treated in Chapter Six) and *The Aims of Education* by Whitehead (treated in Chapter One). Besides raising the obvious question about the need for our own book, Houston may have clinched his own argument that we should simply dispense with the debate between whether the purpose of the university is to offer professional studies or to offer the liberal arts. Houston's solution is simple; the best preparation for a profession is a degree in the liberal arts because it offers three things: an understanding of historical events and other cultures, interaction with diverse points of view, and an understanding of the forces at work in the world today. If Houston were to suggest a third book to read, it might be *The Mission of the University* by José Ortega y Gasset, who made the same argument (summarized in Chapter Ten). Meanwhile, during our writing of this book, Ernst and Young (in the UK) stopped requiring job applicants to show evidence of their university work; that is, they wanted certain knowledge, skills, and attitudes (such as empathy and resilience) and did not care where job applicants acquired those. The move leaves the liberal arts and, for that matter, higher education, in a quandary if these are the qualities that a liberal

education was always meant to foster. See "Ernst and Young drops degree classification threshold for graduate recruitment," *Times Higher Education Supplement* (August 3, 2015), at https://www.timeshighereducation.com/news/ernst-and-young-drops-degree-classification-threshold-graduate-recruitment.

[24] Princeton, NJ: Princeton University Press, 2010.

[25] Ibid., 2. She does not put all her argumentative eggs in the citizenship basket but recognizes other arguments for liberal education, claiming at one point that education "is not just for citizenship. It prepares people for employment and, importantly, for meaningful lives" (9).

[26] Ibid., 10.

[27] Ibid., 142.

[28] Ibid., 142.

[29] Originally published in 1948 (London: Methuen), but we have used the online version, available at "Lost Tools of Learning," accessed July 19, 2016, http://www.gutenberg.ca/ebooks/sayers-lost/sayers-lost-00-h.html.

[30] Ibid., 2.

[31] Especially the final section of *The Abolition of Man* (London: Geoffrey Bless, 1967).

[32] In registering this complaint, she sounds like Alfred North Whitehead who, a few decades before Sayers, made clear his own concerns about the lack of integration or interdisciplinarity in education.

[33] "Lost Tools," 14.

[34] Ibid., 28–44.

[35] Ibid., 44.

[36] She presents her most succinct statement of her philosophy—or, more properly perhaps, her theology of aesthetics—in "Towards a Christian Aesthetic," in *Unpopular Opinions* (London: Gollancz, 1946) and reprinted in many other volumes. She gives a substantial portion of that essay to a discussion of Plato and Aristotle's views of the value of the arts, concluding that neither what the first criticized nor what the second praised were really the kind of view of artistic creation that flows from Scripture and that she expounds in the final pages of the essay.

[37] *The Mind of the Maker* (London: Methuen, 1941). Also see "Why Work?" in *Creed or Chaos* (New York: Harcourt, Brace, 1949), 46–62. Much of that essay also appeared in "Vocation in Work," in *A Christian Basis for the Post-War World*, Albert E. Baker, ed. (London: SCM, 1942), 88–103. She deals dramatically with questions of craft, creation, and creativity in *The Zeal of Thy House*, a play written for and performed at Canterbury Cathedral (London: Gollancz, 1937). Her better-known essays regularly reappear in collections such as *Christian Letters to a Post-Christian World*, Roderick Jellema, ed. (Grand Rapids, MI: Eerdmans, 1969), and *A Matter of Eternity: Selections from the Writings of Dorothy L. Sayers*, Rosamond Kent Sprague, ed. (Grand Rapids, MI: Eerdmans, 1973).

[38] *Creed or Chaos*, 51. We get the irony that this pointed criticism of consumerism comes from the pen of someone who worked in a London advertising firm for several years. She based her Lord Peter novel, *Murder Must Advertise*, on her experience from 1922–1931 at S. H. Benson's agency.

[39] *Creed or Chaos*, 51–52.

[40] We note that two authors covered in Part Two, Thorstein Veblen and Karl Jaspers, also saw a great opportunity for social change after a world war, but shared Sayers's worry that the public would settle instead for bread and circuses.

[41] We rarely agree with each other, Madonna, Adam Smith, and Karl Marx simultaneously, but we note that Christian views of the material world are more robust than those of the last three people named inasmuch as Christian views recognize another whole dimension to human life.

[42] In *No Home Like Place: A Christian Theology of Place* (Portland, OR: Urban Loft, 2014), Leonard Hjalmarson notes that many young adults now prefer to change jobs so that they can put down roots in a place rather than change cities so they can advance in their career.

[43] "Why Work?" 55.

[44] Ibid., 56.

[45] Ibid., 62.

[46] See Parker Palmer, *To Know as We Are Known: A Spirituality of Education* (San Francisco, CA: Harper, 1983), and Palmer, *The Courage to Teach* (San Francisco: Jossey-Bass, 1998).

Hannah Arendt

The Banality of Evil (1963)

Arendt's Life and Works

WE INCLUDE HANNAH ARENDT IN THIS COLLECTION BECAUSE SHE WROTE about both evil and authority, two realities that we think the Christian academy needs to take quite seriously. Although many academics—even Christians—might prefer to omit the term *evil* from the contemporary lexicon, we believe that Christian academics still need to take it seriously.[1] Additionally, we believe that, perhaps now more than ever, the academy and the Christian academy need to consider or reconsider power and authority. For these simple reasons, we give these pages to Hannah Arendt.

Arendt's biography, while fascinating, is not our main concern here. In 1906, she was born a Jew in Germany and was never a favorite of the German authorities. She completed her dissertation on Augustine under Karl Jaspers (whom we treat in Chapter Eleven). Early in WWII, she was interned at Camp Gurs in southern France[2] but, thanks to false documents provided to her by an American diplomat, was able to leave France in 1941 for the United States. There, she enjoyed a distinguished career teaching at several universities, as well as carrying on a breathtaking program of writing, speaking, and social activism—including heavy involvement in

Jewish organizations—throughout the United States and, indeed, the world. She continued working until her death in 1975.

Arendt wrote on many topics in philosophy and politics besides power, violence, and evil. She wrote prodigiously, and taken as a whole, her work constitutes a grand sweep of the history of modernity, especially how it has affected those of us who have lived in the twentieth century and, by implication, in the current century. She always eschewed the label of philosopher and much preferred to think of herself as a political scientist. Her disavowals notwithstanding, she was without doubt a philosopher. Our own interest here is more narrowly on her explorations of authority and evil and how those explorations might shed some light on our work in the Christian academy, but we want our readers to be aware that she deals with topics far beyond those on which we focus here. Arendt wrote little specifically about education,[3] but we believe that the main themes of her work apply to the academy and certainly to Christian higher education.

She is perhaps most famous for the phrase *the banality of evil*, which, interestingly, many who have not taken the time to read her work have misunderstood. As we will show later in this chapter, she did not mean that evil is not to be taken seriously; rather, she meant that it creeps into our lives in small increments for what, at the time, may look like good reasons. This understanding or misunderstanding connects to her book, *Eichmann in Jerusalem: A Report on the Banality of Evil*.[4] She did not consider this her most important work, but the fact that in it she explores the transformation of an ordinary bureaucrat into a war criminal perhaps ensured that it would become one of her two best-known books.

Among her other works, *Between Past and Future: Eight Exercises in Political Thought, Men in Dark Times, Essays in Understanding: 1930–1954,* and *On Revolution* are all well known, and (with *Eichmann in Jerusalem*) *The Human Condition* is her other best-known work.[5] She has written much that reaches beyond philosophy and political science, for example, short biographies, obituaries, book reviews, and literary criticism.[6] While we have no desire to identify a single work as the apex of her effort, we do note *The Origins of Totalitarianism* (1951) and *Eichmann in Jerusalem* (1963) as most important for our task here. She issued a new edition of *Origins* in 1958 because much new material had become available about Hitler's

Germany and, more to her point, about Stalin's rule in the Soviet Union. She revised it again in 1966 (the edition we have used here). This title bears on the two questions she connected and we have elected to follow here: power and evil. Finally, because we also treat Jaspers in this volume, we note that she coauthored with him three volumes, all with publication dates of 1962: on Kant, on Plato and Augustine, and on Socrates, Buddha, Confucius, and Jesus.

As we noted, we want to use an Arendtian lens to explore two aspects of our work in the academy. First, we want to ask about power relations—about how authority works—in the academy, especially about the relationships between ourselves and our students, between ourselves and our departmental colleagues, and between ourselves and those to whom we report. Second, we want to ask about how evil creeps into our work as academics. Let us be clear at the outset that we do not compare what happens in academic departments to the Holocaust or to Stalin's murderous rule over the Soviet Union. To do so would be unthinkable. But we do think that evil creeps in, and in small increments we make accommodations in the same way that Eichmann made accommodations to the Nazi regime, so these will be our applications of Hannah Arendt's work to our own work in the academy.

Power and Authority

We begin by exploring power and authority. Arendt deals with power throughout her works, but especially in *The Human Condition* and *On Violence*. In these books, she sets power in the context of dialogue among interested parties. That is, we talk, we agree on a course of action, and that produces a kind of power. In *On Violence*, she writes this way:

> *Power* corresponds to the human ability not just to act but to act in concert. Power is never the property of an individual; it belongs to a group and remains in existence only so long as the group keeps together. When we say of somebody that he is "in power" we actually refer to his being empowered by a certain number of people to act in their name. The moment the group, from which the power originated to begin with (*potestas in*

populo, without a people or group there is no power), disappears, "his power" also vanishes. In current usage, when we speak of a "powerful man" or a "powerful personality," we already use the word "power" metaphorically; what we refer to without metaphor is "strength."[7]

Arendt's definition is clear. Power resides in the collective. Significantly, by defining *power* in this way, she parts company with many in the political science and sociology traditions.[8] For example, Max Weber defined power with reference to one's being in a position to compel other people to carry out one's will. Thus, Arendt calls power what many in political science and sociology have called legitimacy or moral authority.[9] She takes pains to make clear that where force is used, authority has failed.[10]

Arendt illustrates her definition with reference to the student riots in the late 1960s, stating that such events illustrate how a relatively small group of people acting together can change an institution's policies. Once the group disperses, however, power vanishes, which explains the sagacity of the adage "divide and conquer." Arendt accordingly agrees that the reduction of the population's political force is, to a large extent, due to individuals who purposely isolate themselves from the majority of the group, a matter to which we will return shortly.

As it turns out, Arendt uses the word *authority* almost as a synonym for power. She continues in On Violence to say this about authority:

> *Authority,* relating to the most elusive of these phenomena and therefore, as a term, most frequently abused, can be vested in persons—there is such a thing as personal authority, as, for instance, in the relation between parent and child, between teacher and pupil—or it can be vested in offices, as, for instance, in the Roman senate . . . or in the hierarchical offices of the church (the priest can grant valid absolution even though he is drunk). Its hallmark is unquestioning recognition by those who are asked to obey; neither coercion nor persuasion is needed. A father can lose his authority either by beating his child or by starting to argue with him, that is, either by behaving to him like

a tyrant or by treating him as an equal. To remain in authority requires respect for the person or the office.[11]

We need not dig further into Arendt's unconventional assignment of meanings to the key terms in the discussion of power and authority. She may use her words differently from some, but her thinking about power and authority runs parallel to most in the sociological, philosophical, and social science traditions.

To locate Arendt's understanding of authority more properly in the larger conversation about authority, we turn to Max Weber, where almost all contemporary discussions of authority begin. Weber identified what he called *charismatic authority,* where someone is recognized as an authority due to his or her obvious abilities or outstanding character.[12] Weber's second category, *traditional authority,* related to those persons whose legitimacy derived from their representing traditions. Weber also identified what he called *legal* or *rational* authority, which some today refer to as *constituted* or *contractual* authority. Because an organization or jurisdiction has the policies or laws it has, this person has the authority to hold a certain office and to exercise the authority accorded to the holder of that office. By definition, professors with valid teaching contracts have the third kind of authority. They may also have the first or second kind, depending on a large number of factors, large and small.

Weber's three-part schema may be the start of most conversations about authority, but it is certainly not the end. In his conception of charismatic authority, he did not nuance very carefully—some critics say he ignored—the largely inseparable concepts of moral authority (the goodwill of those answering to the one in authority) and consent (legitimacy, or the permission to exercise authority). If we understand authority as consent or to rest on consent, we see that those granting the consent, by definition, willingly submit to the authority. And a kind of perverse corollary comes into view: when those ruled withdraw their consent, the one in authority must rely on coercion or power, and by power we mean raw power, not the collective agreement that Arendt suggested.[13]

We explore Hannah Arendt's understanding of authority because we observe that the contemporary academy is experiencing two simultaneous shifts in how people view authority. On the one side, students today do not grant professors the same epistemic authority they once did. Second, as neoliberal views of education have become more prominent—even in Christian colleges—professors have lost some of the influence they traditionally have enjoyed in the governance of their institutions. To word this most bleakly, we have seen our authority eroded on both sides. We will return to both these questions shortly.

Theory of the New Class

We have no doubt that Hannah Arendt can, in a sense, stand on her own two philosophical feet. In fact, she has done so quite admirably for several decades. However, to complement her perspectives on power, we want to introduce into this discussion two other illuminating strains of thought. The first of these comes from the work of Alvin Gouldner and what is now commonly called *new class theory*. The second arises out of observations we have made about contemporary culture, specifically about how technology affects epistemology, or what we have begun to call *e-pistemology*.

We turn first to Gouldner, whose theory of the new class may shed some genuinely new light on our understanding of authority in the academy.[14] In just over 100 pages, Gouldner offers his analysis of the group, or perhaps better, the "culture," to which we and most of our readers belong—intellectuals.[15] He works independently from most of the then-extant literature on intellectuals[16] but lists sixteen separate theses, all of which contribute to the single argument that intellectuals think and talk in essentially different ways from most other people.

We will not review Gouldner's entire project in this chapter, but a couple of his ideas bear mentioning. On his account, intellectuals feel most at home in the "culture of careful and critical discourse," when functioning within the "the grammar of rationality."[17] By *careful and critical discourse*, Gouldner means to recognize the presence of several distinguishable features, the first of which is that intellectuals are concerned with language use itself and prefer precise speech, speech characterized by self-editing.[18] This mode of speech appeals to reason, not to the authority or status of the speaker. Those who speak in this mode desire to elicit the voluntary consent of those addressed, based on the arguments on offer. In Gouldner's own words, "The New Class gets what it wants, then, primarily by rhetoric, by persuasion and argument through publishing or speaking."[19] On that point, he accords completely with Arendt's conception of authority, which arises out of a group's shared convictions.

Such speech has consequences, typically including a rupture between members of the new class and the public. Because of its adherence to a doctrine of rationality and justification of claims instead of acceptance of authority, the new class often becomes alienated from those whose interests it implicitly attacks or seems to attack.[20] Professing autonomy from political, business, and ecclesiastical interests, intellectuals sense a freedom or even a duty to require that all statements and claims be justified, thereby periodically finding themselves in conflict with administrators, bureaucrats, and managers.[21] Whether or not he referred particularly to academics in this next comment is unclear, but Gouldner noted at one point that members of the new class sometimes complain that their power and income do not match their possession of culture (or their high self-regard).[22] We think that complaint sounds familiar, especially in Christian higher education.

Finally, Gouldner divides the new class internally into "humanistic" and "technocratic" streams.[23] The technocratic stream earns more money; the humanistic stream (among whom we would number ourselves) gains prestige but feels rejected because, while it holds what he calls the *keys* to the culture, it is, to a degree, never allowed to drive.[24] Jacques Barzun pointed out long ago that intellectuals are "despised and rejected" by the public but still enjoy a great level of public trust. Barzun wondered aloud if that mixed message may be a difference between respect for intellect and disrespect for intellectualism.[25]

We noted several features or effects of the culture of critical discourse. No claim enjoys immunity from being made problematic. No topic or position is closed to discussion. A speaker's social position does not trump other considerations in the judgment of claims. This mode of speech becomes implicitly subversive and possibly divisive when intellectuals confront institutions running primarily along lines of constituted authority. On the other hand, the culture of critical discourse acts as a common bond between members of the new class, even between those on the humanistic side and those on the technocratic side.[26] In fact, Gouldner argues that this common language is so important to members of the new class that bonds between them will likely be stronger than the bonds they form with other people they meet day to day in the workplace or in their other various associations. Thus, it is inherently alienating regarding the public, even while being a unifying factor with regard to one's colleagues.[27]

We want to explore—or better, imagine—Gouldner's thesis from the point of view of two different people who are not intellectuals: a business owner serving on the board of a faith-based college and a senior manager in a government agency who chairs a committee on which one or two professors serve. To the intellectual, questioning is a natural form of speech, likely rooted in a desire to do the right thing in the right way. To the college board member, persistent questions may appear as rebellion, stalling, inaction, elitism, ingratitude, or plain bullheadedness. Worse, when combined with the busyness of academic life—real or perceived—and the consequence that some academics spend less time doing what some nonacademics consider *real work* in the community, such questioning may lead to the impression that intellectuals always talk but never do anything. Consider the same patterns of critical discourse, the same kinds of questions asked in the hypothetical government committee where academics have been invited to contribute their perspective to the development of a new policy. The academics wonder why the rest of the committee does not immediately see the brilliance of their ideas and then implement those ideas by Friday. They wonder this with no apparent awareness of the need for staff buy-in, of the realities of budgets, of the approvals process in government, or of myriad other details involved in shaping and implementing a new policy.[28] Of course, members of the new class see their questions as a contribution. Inasmuch as they express their thoughts in speech, talking is what they do.[29] Unfortunately, when we make what we think is our vital contribution to the commonwealth, others may consider us simply an expensive source of pain.

E-pistemology

We turn now to some observations about contemporary culture that we believe complement Arendt's perspectives on power and Gouldner's theory of the new class. In short, we have observed that our living with and our nearly ubiquitous use of certain technologies have changed the way we think and know. We recognize of course that the term e-pistemology is clever,[30] but we use it not just to appear clever; we believe it catches the shift we have noticed far better than the unhyphenated word *epistemology*. And it does so at two levels. First, we have become completely at home with the letter *e-* as a prefix for words such as -mail, -report, -article, -submission, and other such nouns. Most of us no longer give such usage a second thought. Second, we believe that it is our daily use of specific technologies that has led to this shift in epistemology. A subset of this second observation is that contemporary students, or most of them, have adopted e-pistemological patterns of thinking more thoroughly than have most of their teachers and professors.

Let us illustrate our e-pistemological thesis by pointing to several everyday phenomena. First, consider Amazon's recommendation algorithm and how the company uses it to invite us to buy more than we bargained for when we signed on to its website. We have found the book or other item we wanted when across our screen comes Amazon's message that other people who bought what we are about to buy also bought these other things. All our readers have seen this encouragement. It is just advertising, and we are used to seeing advertising nearly everywhere we go physically and, to our point here, everywhere we go digitally. Our concern is not that Amazon is advertising; after all, it's Amazon's site. Our point is that Amazon tells us that other people who are like us in an important sense—erudite and articulate people who like to read the kinds of thoughtful books that we read—also bought these other books. To gloss the writer of Hebrews, therefore since we are surrounded by so great a cloud of purchasers, let us lay aside our shopping hesitations, and the Visa bill that comes so quickly, and let us put another item in our cart. We are part of a crowd—a cloud of witnesses—and we should trust that crowd to know what is worth reading. For us, the scariest part is that the crowd is so often right.

Or consider this: On a recommendation, we type a search string into YouTube, and then we must select from several videos that, to us, look identical. One video has only a few hundred thousand views while another has nearly half a billion views. Most of us, almost invariably, conclude that the video with the half-billion views is the one we should watch. This must be the *right one*. Note the epistemological shift here. We take as true what the crowd has taken as true. We let them vote for us. It is sort of a democratization of what we used to call truth. At the moment, we see this more as interesting than sinister. But if we begin to conclude that what other people think or want is the proper basis for what we take to be knowledge, will we possibly begin to think the same way about the virtues? Will our screens begin to say, "Others who tell small lies about why they miss conference sessions also do such and such"? Will our smartphones eventually tell us "Others checking email during this lecture also do X"? We are not sure whether this is just a line on all our screens or really an epistemological shift, but we think it warrants our attention.

We will briefly mention Facebook as another shaper of e-pistemology. When dozens of people have checked that they "Like" what someone has posted, we may feel pressure to like it as well, wondering what the person who posted the story or picture will think of us if we don't. Again, we have the pressure of the crowd; our thinking has already been shaped by crowds. Facebook users also check who "Liked" items they have posted; that is, they check for validation. We need to be clear that we do not think the sky is falling; we are saying simply that we think epistemology is changing and that this change connects to Arendt's concerns about authority. Specifically, as professors, we perhaps now work in a different epistemic ethos than professors worked in only a few decades ago. As do we, our students may have begun to judge what is true and what is worthwhile on grounds quite different from the grounds traditionally discussed in Philosophy or Ethics 100 courses.

Professorial Authority

We return from this excursion into new class theory and e-pistemology to Arendt by asking this simple question: where do we think professorial authority now roots itself? Arendt believed authority had its roots in group consensus. Gouldner argued that intellectuals talk and think using a differentiated linguistic variant. We have argued that our society and our students have adopted new ways of knowing. Bringing these threads together, we conclude that now more than ever before, professors can teach only by their students' consent. They have to bring something to the classroom other than their expertise, their employment contract, possibly a sense of humor, and the widespread assumption that they get to use the remote control for the projector. From the thousands of studies on quality teaching in K–12 and higher education, one could assemble a list of more than one hundred qualities and characteristics that students, instructors, and evaluators have identified. Such a comprehensive list holds less interest for us than does the list of five elements that show up more often than any others: caring, fair, prepared, subject-area expertise, and teaching expertise.

Now tie this back to our discussion of authority. On one side, we have Arendt's definitions of power and authority in the context of the discussion of those two concepts in the wider fields of philosophy, sociology, and political science. On another side, we have Gouldner describing not just us but also many of our students, who want us to justify our claims just as we want others to justify theirs.[31] And because we all sit in front of screens so much, we have an emerging e-pistemology. Where do these threads come together? In our view, these threads force us to admit that the context we now work in operates with a dramatically different understanding of authority than was in place even thirty years ago. We will fall on our faces if we fail—or refuse—to recognize this shift. In this new context, we need to work *with* our students; we must not ever lord it over them (which we should have understood from Scripture anyway).[32] We need to understand that they will not give us respect automatically; we have to earn it. One of us takes tea and a carafe of boiling water to class, not as a cynical or calculating way to gain the freedom to teach, but to build community;[33] the increased room to move follows. We will not go on at length here, but students demand to see evidence that we care. When most students see that, they will grant their professors enough authority to execute the most challenging of classroom programs.

The Banality of Evil

No claim or words of Hannah Arendt's stirred more controversy than her phrase *the banality of evil*. Many inferred from her words the rather facile meaning that she did not take evil seriously enough. Others, even including some who read *Eichmann in Jerusalem,* understood her to have let Eichmann off the moral hook by claiming that he was not necessarily a moral monster, indicating perhaps that she did not take war crimes seriously enough. In fact, she travelled to Jerusalem to witness Eichmann's war-crimes trial firsthand. And she concluded that he was, in many senses, just an ordinary bureaucrat who wanted to take the right steps to ensure his own career progress, a rather normal human motivation. During the war, he hoped that after the war he would become the chief of police in some small city in Germany, and at trial, he presented this desire as his reason for obeying orders so meticulously, even for finding more efficient ways to do his most gruesome, morally abhorrent job. This perhaps is why Arendt wrote that the "trouble with Eichmann was precisely that so many were like him, and that the many were neither perverted nor sadistic, that they were and still are, terribly and terrifyingly normal."[34] We should not be surprised that Arendt managed to offend with words like these, because they seem to leave us all as potential Eichmanns. On her account, any one of us could slide from where we are today to a place we cannot now imagine, simply by obeying authority and keeping quiet, while somehow compartmentalizing our ethics.

Eichmann's initial involvement with what was then called *the Jewish question* entailed removing Jews from Austria, mostly by forcing them to emigrate to other countries. Hardly a benign policy, it nevertheless did not initially involve genocide. Arendt does not deny this. In fact, this is her point: that Eichmann carried out the functions of the functionary that he was. And when those to whom he reported raised the ante, finally (in the 1940s) seeking efficient ways to work Jews to death in camps or simply gas them upon arrival, Eichmann acceded to the new demands, or should we say sank to the new pogrom priorities. Arendt is clear; Eichmann knew what he was doing all along. He even quoted Kant's categorical imperative by asking how the Reich could possibly function if every soldier thought himself justified in disobeying whichever orders he objected to on moral grounds. And as he himself famously said at trial, some of his best friends were Jews. But he had a job to do, and he did it. And he cared about his life insurance, his family, his pension, and that police chief post.[35] Our normal human response—our ethical response—is likely along the lines of, "Excuse me, life insurance and a pension pale compared to genocide!" But Arendt wants us to understand that the banality of evil lies in its very ability to cause us to allow our pension and our insurance to trump the terrifyingly large moral questions that stare us in the face and should stop us in our tracks.

We accept Arendt's argument that it was by small steps that Eichmann moved from midlevel government bureaucrat to whatever he became. We disagree with her that he was not a moral monster. He may not have started out that way and might never have intended to become a moral monster, but a moral monster he became.[36] And it is the small steps that, as Christians in the academy, we find so fascinating.

We bring Arendt's appraisal of evil into this book because we know that as Christian academics we care that justice be done. But sometimes we think about our pension and our insurance, and one issue at a time, we decide that there are things just not worth fighting about in the department. We know that a colleague is abusing his or her professorial authority with regard to students, but we think about how acrimonious department meetings might be were we to register our concerns. Honestly, it is simpler just to keep quiet. Or we have a colleague who harangues the department month to month about some pet concern. We, and perhaps a majority of our colleagues, believe that we would be insane to agree to this colleague's demands. But how else can we get this colleague to be quiet than to agree to the proposal? Or perhaps, somewhere up the food chain from us, we see a supervisor abusing power. We may know it is wrong, and we may know that many of our colleagues also know it is wrong. But the possibility that speaking out might sabotage our career prospects—or simply our peace of mind—in this place, the prospect of finding a post in a different place, the thought of moving, our imaginings about what people might say about us were we to leave . . . these things combine to keep us quiet.[37] Few of our readers aspire to become the chief of police in a quiet German town after this chapter of our career. But like us, most of our readers need to function amicably in a department. Many of our readers need to undergo periodic promotion and tenure reviews. Why make things difficult for ourselves by speaking against an idea that does not affect us directly? Arendt's point about the banality of evil comes home to us right at this point: these ideas about which we remain silent do affect us. It is by small decisions and by small steps—all of which look completely reasonable at the time—that evil grows.

On Arendt's account, however, our being quiet about this or that for the moment, our focus on our pension instead of on the justice issue in front of us, leads in directions that, were we to consider them more carefully at the time, we would know we did not want our departments, our institutions, or our souls to go. She notes in *The Origins of Totalitarianism* what many observers of politics in our own time have observed, that a "politically indifferent and neutral" majority of people in any society can, without meaning to do so, allow a minority to use democratic structures to impose its political vision on the whole society. In this picture, a society "could function according to rules which are actively recognized by only a minority."[38]

In *Men in Dark Times* Arendt talks about the human tendency to avoid the hard things in life by retreating into a kind of private sphere. As she puts it, people "felt very little responsibility toward the world" and searched for ways of "resisting the weird irreality of this world."[39] She continues a couple pages later with her description of this temptation to "inner emigration," to a "shift from the world and its public space to an interior life, or else simply to ignore that world in favor of an imaginary world as it ought to be or as it once upon a time had been."[40] We think she describes precisely the tendency of some to retreat to a private sphere rather than take responsibility in a situation that stares us in the face. For example, students may bring to our attention that one of our colleagues abuses his or her professorial office with regard to students. This abuse could range from demands for authorship credit for student research to nonreturn of papers, and from demands for sexual favors to missing classes without notice or good reason. We send the complaining student to the dean or to some other office, or we plead that the institutional code of ethics forbids our getting involved. Interestingly—and this bears directly on Arendt's point—we may actually be following the appropriate institutional protocols in both cases. The dean is there for a reason; our colleague reports to the dean and not to us. The code of ethics is there for a reason; complaints from any quarter should go up the chain of command, not to the nearest sympathetic ear.

Understandably, students fear what might happen to them if they voice their concerns too loudly. But we do the same. We say (to ourselves), "Hey, I have to work in this department. I don't want to get a reputation as a complainer. The colleague who has done this will quite possibly serve on my tenure or promotion committee a year from now." And so the small injustices, the half-truths, the abuses of power grow and accumulate. A department, like a business, has assets and liabilities. Most of a business's assets and liabilities show on the books. But customer goodwill, the reputation in town for supporting good causes, and the loyalty and satisfaction of staff are harder to show on the books. Academic departments (and whole universities) have or lack these off-book assets as well. And if Arendt's commentary on Eichmann's trial awakens the academy to anything, it should be to the banality of evil.

Without once referring to Arendt, Cass Sunstein and Reid Hastie illustrate her thesis in *Wiser: Getting beyond Groupthink to Make Groups Smarter*.[41] They illustrate in painful, anecdotal detail the long-term damage possible when committees, boards, and departments make decisions without considering all possible viewpoints. They show how the support for proposals cascades in meetings, meaning that once one or two people—especially males or otherwise dominant people—have voiced their support for an idea, others who speak later hesitate to speak negatively. In some cases, people fail to speak up even when they have knowledge that supports making the opposite decision.[42] Sunstein and Hastie review several reasons why people hesitate to dissent. We will not review their book here, but one point especially warrants mention: the unfortunate irony that a dissenting voice might benefit the group but apparently offers so little to the dissenter.

Our readers have all faced (or will face) the decision to bear the costs of dissent or to keep quiet. At this point, we wish we could say that Arendt's work lightens the dissenter's burden. Unfortunately, she adds to the burden; she says that we must speak up. Arendt's telling of history may give a small measure of hope to anyone who finds the themes in her work gloomy. She notes that younger generations withhold the kind of silent consent and support that others may have given to those who took charge. In many of the students we meet now, we see more willingness to voice opposition to the powers, and we trust others can see the same thing.

Conclusions and Questions

In the first part of the chapter, we examined Arendt's understanding of authority and asked how it connected to our own authority as workers in the academy. What influences the authority that the public grants us as academics? Second, how, or why, do our students grant us the authority to teach them, and how has that landscape been altered by their ubiquitous use of technology? For that matter, how do we view the authority of the administrators to whom we report? In Arendt's picture, those who would lead us or whose ideas we would all implement do so only because we have talked and have reached an agreement about our overall goals; we have legitimated their position.

Taking Arendt's lead, we must recognize in the academy generally and in the Christian academy specifically what is the true source of authority. And we must act accordingly. We cannot control how those to whom we report use their authority. But we can control how we use ours, especially with regard to our students and to our colleagues. According to Arendt (and many others who have addressed this question), we exercise our authority properly only when we do so in dialogue with those around us and by the consent of those who report to us. We know that *servant leadership* achieved cliché status decades before we wrote this book, but we think it did so for a reason. Even if the phrase has been devalued by overuse, the world and the Christian university still need leaders who will adopt the posture of servants. Jesus said that anyone wanting to be in charge had to learn to be the servant of all (Matthew 20:27-28) long before Hannah Arendt wrote the books we have examined here. Let us take our cues about leadership from him if not from her.

In the second part of the chapter, we argued that in the academy generally and in the Christian academy specifically, we must recognize small evils and stand against them before they grow to large evils and before we lose our souls. We know that all workplaces offer similar temptations to our own. As are others, those of us who work in the academy are frequently tempted toward passive evil, to the kind of moral withdrawal or internal immigration that attracts when the costs of speaking up look too high. Sometimes the costs do not look that high, but straitened institutional finances, an overbearing supervisor, or our colleagues simply wear us down. For whatever reason, we are tempted to compartmentalize our ethics and hope to go on our way.[43] Again, we underline that we would never compare departmental nastiness in the academy to the Holocaust.

Still, Hannah Arendt reminds us that the key feature of the banality of evil is the small, self-preserving accommodations that, for the very reason that they are small, look reasonable at the time.

What happens over time is another matter. We make larger and larger accommodations. We form habits and fail to notice. And while we do not wake up one morning at a trial in Jerusalem (or Nuremberg), we nevertheless may find ourselves slip-sliding away from both the mission of our institution and from our own vocation. Arendt's warning may be stronger than we need. But she reminds us that even if the curricular stakes and budget stakes of a given meeting seem pedestrian, the moral stakes are always high.

QUESTIONS

Arendt argues that authority emerges from shared discourse where the participants agree on a direction and authorize someone to lead them in that direction.

- To what extent would you say your department works in that model of authority? Your university or college?
- List and describe the sources of your own authority in your classroom. What combination of your expert knowledge/contract and student consent or goodwill works best for you?

We have argued that technology has produced an e-pistemology that has changed the landscape for professors.

- Without reference to whether or not students send texts in class, what changes have you seen in students' understanding of what is true, honorable, just, and commendable?
- In what ways has your own understanding of knowledge (or authority) changed because of your access to and constant use of technology?

We noted that many people misunderstand Arendt's phrase, *the banality of evil*.

- How do you understand *the banality of evil*?
- What decisions or actions can you recall from the last couple years where you kept quiet despite your conviction that something morally wrong (not just unwise) was afoot? What reasons did you list to yourself in that situation or those circumstances?
- With reference to Jesus's teaching that we should get the log out of our own eye before worrying about the speck in our neighbor's eye, can you recall decisions or actions you promoted in the last couple years that colleagues or students would have identified as wrong? What changes need to be made, and what apologies need to be extended?

FOR FURTHER STUDY

Hannah Arendt considered herself a political theorist rather than a philosopher, but as you can see from the selections below, her scholarly interests range across both spheres, particularly regarding the nature of power, direct democracy, authority, and totalitarianism.

IN ARENDT'S OWN WORDS (SELECTED WORKS)

Arendt, Hannah. *Between Past and Future: Six Exercises in Political Thought.* London: Faber and Faber, 1961.
———. *The Burden of Our Time.* London: Secker & Warburg, 1951.
———. *Eichmann in Jerusalem: A Report on the Banality of Evil.* Rev. and enl. ed. New York: Viking Press, 1964.
———. *The Human Condition.* Collector's ed. Charles R. Walgreen Foundation Lectures. Chicago: University of Chicago Press, 1969.
———. *Hannah Arendt: The Last Interview and Other Conversations.* Last Interview Series. Brooklyn, NY: Melville House, 2013.
———. *The Life of the Mind.* 1st ed. New York: Harcourt Brace Jovanovich, 1978.
———. *Men in Dark Times.* Harvest Book. San Diego: Harcourt, Brace & Company, 1995.
———. *On Revolution.* Pelican Books. Harmondsworth, England: Penguin, 1973.
———. *The Human Condition.* Collector's ed. Charles R. Walgreen Foundation Lectures. Chicago: University of Chicago Press, 1969.
———. *The Origins of Totalitarianism.* 2nd ed. New York: Meridian Books, 1958.

———. *Totalitarianism*. New York: Harcourt, Brace & World, 1968.
Arendt, Hannah, P.R. Baehr, and D. Rogers. *The Portable Hannah Arendt*. Penguin Classics. New York: Penguin Books, 2003.
Arendt, Hannah, and Heinrich Blücher. *Within Four Walls: The Correspondence between Hannah Arendt and Heinrich Blücher, 1936-1968*. 1st U.S. ed. New York: Harcourt, 2000.
Arendt, Hannah, and Melvyn A. Hill. *Hannah Arendt, the Recovery of the Public World*. New York: St. Martin's Press, 1979.
Arendt, Hannah, Karl Jaspers, Lotte Köhler, and Hans Saner. *Hannah Arendt/Karl Jaspers Correspondence, 1926-1969*. 1st Harvest ed. San Diego: Harcourt Brace, 1993.
Arendt, Hannah, Jerome Kohn, and Ron H. Feldman. *The Jewish Writings*. New York: Schocken Books, 2007.
Arendt, Hannah, Mary McCarthy, and Carol Brightman. *Between Friends: The Correspondence of Hannah Arendt and Mary McCarthy, 1949-1975*. 1st ed. New York: Harcourt Brace, 1995.

BIOGRAPHIES

Allen, Amy. *Hannah Arendt*. International Library of Essays in the History of Social and Political Thought. Aldershot, England: Ashgate, 2008.
Heller, Anne Conover. *Hannah Arendt: A Life in Dark Times*. Boston: New Harvest, Houghton Mifflin Harcourt, 2015.
Kristeva, Julia. *Hannah Arendt*. European Perspectives. New York: Columbia University Press, 2001.
May, Derwent. *Hannah Arendt*. Lives of Modern Women. New York: Penguin Books, 1986.
Nordquist, Joan. *Hannah Arendt*. Social Theory; No. 14. Santa Cruz, CA: Reference and Research Services, 1989.
Swift, Simon. *Hannah Arendt*. Routledge Critical Thinkers. New York: Routledge, 2009.

OTHER SELECTED WORKS ABOUT ARENDT

Arnett, Ronald C. *Communication Ethics in Dark Times: Hannah Arendt's Rhetoric of Warning and Hope*. Carbondale, IL: Southern Illinois University Press, 2013.

Aschheim, Steven E. *Hannah Arendt in Jerusalem*. Berkeley, CA: University of California Press, 2001.
Benhabib, Seyla. *The Reluctant Modernism of Hannah Arendt*. Modernity and Political Thought, Vol. 10. Thousand Oaks, CA: Sage Publications, 1996.
Bergen, Bernard J. *The Banality of Evil: Hannah Arendt and "the Final Solution."* Lanham: Rowman & Littlefield Publishers, 1998.
Bernstein, Richard J. *Hannah Arendt and the Jewish Question*. 1st MIT Press ed. Cambridge, MA: MIT Press, 1996.
Bowen-Moore, Patricia. *Hannah Arendt's Philosophy of Natality*. New York: St. Martin's Press, 1989.
Bowring, Finn. *Hannah Arendt: A Critical Introduction*. Modern European Thinkers. London: Pluto Press, 2011.
Canovan, Margaret. *Hannah Arendt: A Reinterpretation of Her Political Thought*. 1st pbk. ed. Cambridge, England: Cambridge University Press, 1994.
———. *The Political Thought of Hannah Arendt*. Everyman's University Library. London: Dent, 1974.
Court, Anthony. *Hannah Arendt's Response to the Crisis of Her Times*. SAVUSA Series. Amsterdam: Rozenberg Publishers, 2008.
Ettinger, Elzbieta. *Hannah Arendt/Martin Heidegger*. New Haven, CT: Yale University Press, 1995.
Garrity, Lyn. *Action and "Public Happiness": Hannah Arendt's Restoration of the Political*. Portland, OR: Reed College, 1982.
Geller, Sam. *Arguing Violence: Hannah Arendt and 1968*. Portland, OR: Reed College, 2011.
Greene, Wade Chester. *Hannah Arendt's Theory of Action and Two Historical Cases*. Portland, OR: Reed College, 1967.
Gordon, Mordechai. *Hannah Arendt and Education: Renewing Our Common World*. Boulder, CO: Westview Press, 2001.
Gottsegen, Michael G. *The Political Thought of Hannah Arendt*. Albany, NY: SUNY Press, 1994.
Gunter, Helen. *Educational Leadership and Hannah Arendt*. Critical Studies in Educational Leadership, Management and Administration Series. New York: Routledge, 2014.
Hinchman, Lewis P., and Sandra Hinchman. *Hannah Arendt: Critical Essays*. SUNY Series in Political Theory. Contemporary Issues. Albany, NY: SUNY Press, 1994.
Honig, Bonnie. *Feminist Interpretations of Hannah Arendt*. University Park, PA: Pennsylvania State University Press, 1995.
Horowitz, Irving Louis. *Hannah Arendt: Radical Conservative*. New Brunswick, NJ: Transaction Publishers, 2012.

Hull, Margaret Betz. *The Hidden Philosophy of Hannah Arendt*. Routledge Curzon Jewish Studies Series. New York: Routledge/Curzon, 2002.
Kateb, George. *Hannah Arendt, Politics, Conscience, Evil*. Philosophy and Society. Totowa, NJ: Rowman & Allanheld, 1984.
King, Richard H. *Arendt and America*. Chicago: University of Chicago Press, 2015.
Knott, Marie Luise, and Nanne Mayer. *Unlearning with Hannah Arendt*. New York: Other Press, 2015.
Kristeva, Julia, and Frank Collins. *Hannah Arendt: Life Is a Narrative*. Alexander Lectures, 1999. Toronto, ON: University of Toronto Press, 2001.
Maier-Katkin, Daniel. *Stranger from Abroad: Hannah Arendt, Martin Heidegger, Friendship, and Forgiveness*. 1st ed. New York: Norton, 2010.
May, Larry, and Jerome Kohn. *Hannah Arendt: Twenty Years Later*. Studies in Contemporary German Social Thought. Cambridge, MA: MIT Press, 1996.
McCarthy, Michael H. *The Political Humanism of Hannah Arendt*. Lanham, MD: Lexington Books, 2012.
McGowan, John. *Hannah Arendt: An Introduction*. Minneapolis, MN: University of Minnesota Press, 1998.
Nixon, Jon. *Hannah Arendt and the Politics of Friendship*. London: Bloomsbury Academic, 2015.
Pirro, Robert Carl. *Hannah Arendt and the Politics of Tragedy*. DeKalb, IL: Northern Illinois University Press, 2001.
Robinson, Jacob, and Mazal Holocaust Collection. *And the Crooked Shall Be Made Straight: The Eichmann Trial, the Jewish Catastrophe, and Hannah Arendt's Narrative*. New York: Macmillan, 1965.
Sharpe, Barry, and Mazal Holocaust Collection. *Modesty and Arrogance in Judgment: Hannah Arendt's Eichmann in Jerusalem*. Westport, CT: Praeger, 1999.
Shokat, Kasra Che. *Preserving the Contradictions: Rereading Hannah Arendt's "Truth and Politics."* Portland, OR: Reed College, 2014.
Young-Bruehl, Elisabeth, and Mazal Holocaust Collection. *Hannah Arendt, for Love of the World*. New Haven, CT: Yale University Press, 1982.

NOTES

[1] We intentionally echo the sentiments of psychologist Karl Menninger, who titled his book *Whatever Became of Sin?* (New York: Hawthorn, 1973). By that title, he meant to ask why contemporary people dislike taking into account the human tendency to do bad things. In the next chapter, on Flannery O'Connor, we struggle again to find the courage to use scriptural language for this unpopular topic.

[2] In 2013, one of us (KB) spent some very sobering time at Camp Gurs while walking the Chemin de St. Jacques (the French portion of the Camino de Santiago Compestalla).

[3] There are exceptions to this claim, of course, including "The Crisis in Education," which appears in *Between Past and Future: Eight Exercises in Political Thought* (New York: Penguin, 1968), 173–196.

[4] New York, Viking, 1963, and available online at http://ir.nmu.org.ua/bitstream/handle/123456789/116873/01429edb95e875e7d5c6021da88b7cb7.pdf?sequence=1&isAllowed=y.

[5] *Between Past and Future: Eight Exercises in Political Thought*; *Men in Dark Times* (New York: Harcourt, Brace and World, 1955); *Essays in Understanding: 1930-1954*, edited by Jerome Kohn (New York: Harcourt, Brace, 1994); *On Revolution* (New York: Viking, 1963); *The Origins of Totalitarianism* (New York: Harcourt, Brace, 1951); *The Human Condition* (Chicago: University of Chicago Press, 1958).

[6] For example, in *Reflections on Literature and Culture*, which was collected and edited by Susannah Young-ah Gottlieb (Palo Alto, CA: Stanford University Press, 2007), and in *Essays in Understanding* (New York: Harcourt, Brace, 1994). Several recent secondary works are worthy of one's time. Irving Louis Horowitz, in *Hannah Arendt: Radical Conservative* (London: Transaction, 2012), sees threads running through all Arendt's work: totalitarianism, whether on the left or on the right, is usually grounded in some kind of leadership principle and always has a tendency toward empire. Totalitarianism usually follows the failure of the mechanisms of the state to function properly. Democracy is the antidote to totalitarianism. Also see Marie Luise Knott, *Unlearning with Hannah Arendt*, translated from the German by David Dollenmayer (New York: Other Press, 2013), and Simon Swift's *Hannah Arendt* (New York, Routledge, 2009).

[7] *On Violence* (New York: Harcourt, Brace and World, 1970), 44.

[8] Many note her departure from the standard distinctions between authority and power. For examples, see Jane Anna Gordon, "Hanna Arendt's Political Theology of Democratic Life," *Political Theology* 10, no. 2 (2009): 325–339; and Jürgen Habermas, "Hannah Arendt's Communications Concept of Power," translated by Thomas McCarthy, in Lewis P. Hinchman and Sandra K. Hinchman's *Hannah Arendt: Critical Essays* (Albany, NY: SUNY Press, 1994), 211–229.

[9] See "The Public and the Private Realm," in *The Human Condition*.

[10] For example, in "What is Authority?" (92–93) in her *Between Past and Future*. Brunkhorst argues that Arendt reversed her understanding of power (to what we have described here) after she completed her work on totalitarianism. See Hauke Brunkhorst, "The Productivity of Power: Hannah Arendt's Renewal of the Classic Concept of Politics," *Revista de Ciencia Política* 26, no. 2 (2006): 125–136.

[11] *On Violence*, 45.

[12] We draw this from two works by Weber: his 1947 volume, *Theory of Social and Economic Organization*, translated by A. M. Henderson and T. Parsons (London:

Collier-Macmillan); and his *Economy and Society*, translated by E. Fischoff (New York: Bedminster, 1968).

[13] Despite different language usage, Arendt agrees completely with this assessment. As Habermas puts it, she "untiringly repeats" her claim that leaders cannot replace the community's support with force (Habermas, "Hannah Arendt's Communications Concept of Power," 215, and throughout his chapter).

[14] Alvin Gouldner, *The Future of Intellectuals and the Rise of the New Class* (New York: Continuum, 1979).

[15] By equating *intellectual* with *member of the new class*, Gouldner uses *intellectual* in a wide and generous sense. We use *academic* and *intellectual* interchangeably throughout this section, recognizing three things: (1) all intellectuals do not work in academia; (2) all academics are not intellectuals (in the meritorious sense); (3) *intellectual* carries positive connotations in our own circles but negative connotations in some other circles. Jacques Barzun, whom we were unable to include in this volume, sees this transformation from *intellectual* as a positive adjective to *intellectual* as a negative noun rooted to the advent of widespread literacy. See his *House of Intellect* (New York: Harper and Row, 1959), 8.

[16] Except for a summary discussion on 6–7.

[17] Ibid., 1, 47.

[18] Ibid., 3, 29, 43–44, 59–60, 84. He notes that the language of discussion itself—its use and abuse—is frequently the focus of reflection (28, 34, 45). We perhaps might find the accusatory finger pointed our own way as well when Gouldner writes, "The culture of critical discourse must put its hands around its own throat and see how long it can squeeze" (60). Gouldner and Arendt both found discourse interesting, in her case because it figured so centrally in how groups give authority.

[19] Peter Nettl makes much the same observation: bureaucrats tend to operate by using power and intellectuals by using influence, "the essence of intellectual activity." Persuasion "defines the sphere or object of intellectual activity." When we persuade someone to do something, they now do it because they prefer it to what they preferred before. Peter Nettl, "Power and the Intellectuals," in Conor Cruise O'Brien and William Dean Vanech, *Power and Consciousness* (New York: NYU Press, 1969), 18–19. Also see Nettl's "Ideas, Intellectuals, and Structures of Dissent," in *On Intellectuals*, edited by Philip Reiff and Edward Shils (New York: Doubleday, 1969), 53–122.

[20] Ralph Dahrendorf, "The Intellectual and Society," Philip Reiff, *On Intellectuals* (Garden City, NY: Doubleday, 1969), 52. Dahrendorf believes the alienation of intellectuals is "almost inevitable" because they "have the duty to doubt everything that is obvious, to make relative all authority, to ask all those questions that no one else dares to ask."

[21] We add one specific group to Gouldner's list: the governors of faith-based colleges and universities. Throughout his volume, Gouldner expresses doubts that intellectuals are as disinterested as we insist we are. Surprise: we have agendas and we want things to go our way.

[22] Gouldner, 58, 65.

[23] By dividing intellectuals into just two streams, Gouldner aligns himself with Talcott Parsons, but departs from other schemata, such as that of Shils, who differentiates between scholarly, scientific, literary, and artistic intellectuals (omitting media and civil service). See Parsons, "'The Intellectual': A Social Role Category," in Reiff and Shils, *On*

Intellectuals, 12–13. Also see Edward Shils, *The Intellectuals and the Powers* (Chicago: University of Chicago, 1972), 9–15.

[24] Gouldner, 4, 12.

[25] Jacques Barzun, *The House of Intellect* (New York: Harper and Row, 1959), 1–2.

[26] On this account, the "two-cultures" problem is reduced somewhat. See Charles Percy Snow, *The Two Cultures* (London: Cambridge University Press, 1959). Snow argues that the lyricists and the empiricists speak two different languages, creating a gap. Gouldner argues that the two groups are similar because both prefer to use careful, critical discourse.

[27] Readers who sense more kinship with colleagues who do not identify themselves as Christian than they do with some members of their own congregation can confirm this part of Gouldner's thesis.

[28] We owe thanks to a long-time friend and director of a large mental-health agency (who wishes to remain anonymous) for leading us to what is known as implementation science. This field analyzes how shifts happen and why they do not. The national organization that focuses on implementation and its discontents is the National Implementation Research Network at http://nirn.fpg.unc.edu/. A concise introduction to the field is available at http://nirn.fpg.unc.edu/sites/nirn.fpg.unc.edu/files/resources/NIRN-MonographFull-01-2005.pdf.

[29] Charles Kadushin notes "talking" as our primary activity as well, in *The American Intellectual Elite* (Boston: Little, Brown, 1974), 322.

[30] And we thank Bruce Erickson of Tacoma, Washington, for the neologism.

[31] Of interest to us, Gouldner's description of new class speech accords with Dorothy Sayers's prescription for student speech; in *The Lost Tools of Learning*, she calls for students to push back against their professors' claims.

[32] From all three synoptic gospels (Matthew 20:25, etc.) and 1 Peter 5:3. One of us has dealt with these questions at length in another context and will not repeat here what is available elsewhere. See http://icctejournal.org/issues/v4i2/v4i2-badley/. We note Mordechai Gordon's comparison of Arendt's views to classical views of power and authority, in "Hannah Arendt on Authority Conservatism in Education Reconsidered," *Educational Theory* 49, no. 2 (Spring 1999): 161–180. He argues, contra Montessori (and our conclusion here), that Arendt wants to keep authority over the shaping of curriculum and instruction in the hands of teachers, and does not want students determining the direction of their education. In arguing thus, he takes a position directly opposite that of Wayne Veck, in "Participation in Education as an Invitation to Become Towards the World: Hannah Arendt on the Authority, Thoughtfulness and Imagination of the Educator," *Educational Philosophy and Theory* 45, no. 1 (2013): 36–48.

[33] As we do at several points in this book, we recommend Parker Palmer's discussion of classroom community. See *The Courage to Teach* (San Francisco: Jossey-Bass, 1998).

[34] Hannah Arendt, *Eichmann in Jerusalem: A Report on the Banality of Evil* (1963) rev. with new introduction by Amos Elon (New York: Penguin Classics, 2006), 276.

[35] Arendt notes these concerns of Eichmann's in *Die verborgene Tradition* [*The Babylonian Tradition*] (Frankfurt: Suhrkamp, 1976).

[36] In *The Origins of Totalitarianism*, Arendt quotes various reports of the responses of ordinary German police and soldiers who were drafted into the SS ("Protective Squadron") and required to participate in the grisly work of extermination as part

of their work. Some were keenly aware that they had become monsters, one even confessing that he could not look his wife in the face on his days off (454).

[37] Related to this, see Eugenie Samier, "The Problem of Passive Evil in Educational Administration: Moral Implications of Doing Nothing," *ISEA Journal* [International Studies in Educational Administration] 36, no. 1 (2008): 2–21. Samier provides predictable but still regrettable examples of passive evil: punishment of an innocent student, bullying of a colleague, groundless attacks on faculty by administrators. The common denominator—the passive evil—in all these is that others stand by and do nothing.

[38] *The Origins of Totalitarianism,* 312. On the opening page of "What is Authority" (*Between Past and Future,* 91–141), she also notes that when bureaucracy and hierarchy cease to function as they should, the leader's will becomes the source of policy and practice. Also see her "Authority in the Twentieth Century," in *The Review of Politics* 18, no. 4 (1956): 403–417.

[39] *Men in Dark Times,* 17.

[40] Ibid., 19.

[41] Boston: Harvard Business Review Press, 2015.

[42] Cass and Hastie review decades of research into these phenomena, going as far back as the research of Robert Thorndike, "The Effect of Discussion upon the Correctness of Group Decisions: When the Factor of Majority Influences is Allowed For," *Journal of Social Psychology* 9 (1938), 343–362.

[43] Christian college faculty have beneficially used social media to spread awareness about important causes, even to the extent that colleagues from other institutions have joined them. Though we recognize that there are inherent drawbacks in the widespread use of technology, the clear benefit is that a crowd can hear about and support a cause more quickly than in the past.

Flannery O'Connor

A Good Man Is Hard to Find (1955)

Looking in the secondary literature, you will find at least three Flannery O'Connors, perhaps four. Flannery O'Connor, the devout Roman Catholic, often appears.[1] This O'Connor writes about Christ-haunted characters whose stories contain a searing critique of contemporary nihilism.[2] A Southern novelist and short story writer—possibly Gothic—appears quite regularly as well. This Flannery O'Connor explores the fundamentalism of the rural South, with sometimes grotesque characters who exhibit a palpable contempt from below of city folk and their high-minded ways. Without much exertion, you will also find someone who, like her father before her, suffered from lupus and wrote out of that pain and disability.[3] Finally, there is a Flannery O'Connor who simply crafted great stories about people that five or six decades of readers recognize all too well but that some critics find inscrutable, despite O'Connor's repeated and explicit efforts to point her critics in the right direction.[4] Inasmuch as the critics have been trying to make sense of her—some would say *to fashion her in their own image*—for half a century already, we come a bit late to O'Connor. Not at all because we fear an argument, but because we want to let her have her own voice in this chapter, we side with none of the critical schools. Rather, we conclude that O'Connor was, to put it quite simply, complex.

She was born Mary Flannery O'Connor, on March 25, 1925, in Savannah, Georgia. Early on, she demonstrated the wry sense of humor that would later run through her writing; at age six she appeared on television because she had taught a chicken to walk backwards. She later said that this was the highlight of her life.[5] She completed her secondary and college education in her home state of Georgia, involving herself in student journalism during both those chapters.[6] She spent two years at the Iowa Writer's Workshop, as well as time at a retreat in Saratoga Springs, New York, and some years in the Redding, Connecticut, home of two people who became her dear friends and professional supporters, Robert and Sally Fitzgerald. Deteriorating from lupus, in 1951 she moved back to her family's farm at Milledgeville, Georgia, where her mother cared for her until her death in 1964 at age 39.

Much of what Flannery O'Connor wrote, she wrote while dealing with lupus. Various characters in her posthumous collection, *Everything That Rises Must Converge* (1965), also struggle with disabilities. She drew the title of that work from Pierre Teilhard de Chardin's *The Phenomenon of Man,* the source also of her concept of *diminishment,* diminishment that, on many accounts, became a driving force in O'Connor's later writing and even sustained her as she faced her own decline and death.[7] In a 1963 letter to Janet McKane, an elementary school teacher who queried O'Connor about Teilhard de Chardin's meaning of "passive diminishments," she replied that they were "the afflictions that you can't get rid of and have to bear."[8] As we noted, she wrote out of her Catholic faith, and she wrote unapologetically as a person from the South. But she also wrote out of her disability. We graciously decline the job of speculating about the exact origins of O'Connor's view—one might almost say her fascination—with sin and brokenness; many have already taken on that task and, on our reading, are not yet done. While declining the job of speculating about the exact origins, we will note again these two insuperable biographical realities. She grew up Roman Catholic. And she suffered from lupus.

Why include someone in this volume who wrote little about education? Flannery O'Connor had a profound understanding of the effects of sin on our individual and social existence. She had just as profound an understanding of grace and redemption. She reminds contemporary educators what we perhaps could have learned from Augustine or Dostoevsky that selfishness, ego, and brokenness are at work in higher education generally and surely in Christian higher education, too. In what follows, we want to explore some benefits of taking seriously the theological principle that sin is at work in ourselves and in our institutions. But recognizing that sin is at work, we focus as well on the hope that, in Christ, there is redemption, and therefore we focus on the imperative that we extend more grace to ourselves, to our students, to our superiors, and to our colleagues.

Reading Flannery O'Connor

Our purposes here are not to shed new insight on the works of Flannery O'Connor. Literally hundreds of scholars have attempted that task already. Rather, we want to appropriate the wisdom that she offers. We want to ask after the well-being of the university (a phrase from Cardinal Newman). Specifically, what insights does she offer that might make us more content professors and thereby make the university a better place? Meanwhile, we face a challenge: what should we do about the mass of secondary literature? In this chapter, we will follow the example of David Eggenschwiler, who wrote in his preface to *The Christian Humanism of Flannery O'Connor* that so much secondary scholarship was already available that he would not bother to review it to provide introductory material.[9] We agree with him. All our readers know O'Connor's name, if not her work, and we will move quite directly toward our thesis, rather than till the familiar ground of her biography and works.

We do want to review briefly a couple exemplary works from among her short stories, mainly to provide those unfamiliar with her work a taste of her approach.[10] First, in "A Good Man Is Hard to Find," she portrays an encounter between some escaped prisoners and an unfortunate family on a road trip. The family includes a particularly manipulative, petty, and obnoxious grandmother who engages toward the very end of the story in a dramatic and intense conversation with the escapee nicknamed The Misfit. By this point in O'Connor's story, readers have little sympathy left for the grandmother and none for The Misfit. She, fearing death, oozes kindness and love, even claiming that, to her, The Misfit is like a son. Alas, her flattery falls flat. To The Misfit, Jesus threw everything off balance and he himself was off balance, unable even to change course at this key point. To his companions, The Misfit says, "She would have been a good woman if it had been someone there to shoot her every minute of her life,"[11] perhaps the most widely quoted line from O'Connor. We have already spoiled the story for some but will add that O'Connor may have had The Misfit say something true not only of the grandmother but true universally: even the worst of us usually improve under the right conditions. Is there a better description anywhere of systemic evil? Admittedly, these words came from the keyboard of Flannery O'Connor, but they also came out of the mouth of a psychopathic escaped criminal known as The Misfit. In the gush of kind but specious comments that the self-righteous and pain-in-the-neck grandmother spews forth in her last moments of life, there is truth. And there is also truth in The Misfit's final (and now famous) assessment of her after he murders her.

O'Connor begins "Revelation" with Ruby Turpin, an uppity, somewhat well-do-do, self-satisfied woman surveying the trashy people with whom she is forced to share a waiting room. Ruby engages another woman in conversation about a variety of topics, including the importance of gratitude and of keeping oneself up, but the conversation turns critical as the other woman begins to talk in the third person about Mary Grace, her daughter seated next to her. Mary Grace's anger rises and she hurls her psychology textbook, *Human Development*, at Ruby and hits her above the eye. She then leaps out of her chair, physically attacks Ruby, calls her a warthog, and tells her to go back to hell where she came from. And that is just the start. The story is appropriately titled, although perhaps the plural form of "Revelation" might have suited well . . . because Ruby is not done yet. We will write only in the most general terms here, but as the story unfolds, Ruby indeed has a series of revelations about her flaws and her deep need for God's grace. For the moment of Ruby Turpin's fullest apprehension, O'Connor even puts her among pigs, a setting appropriate for revelations, familiar at least to readers of Scripture.

The stories we have summarized here both represent O'Connor's style and themes well. We see people at their rawest and most broken. And we see grace, admittedly in larger portions in "Revelation" than in "A Good Man Is Hard to Find." These stories are there for anyone to read, along with about two dozen other short stories, two novels,[12] and many essays. Literally hundreds of scholars have written about O'Connor, many of them retelling what we have told here, usually for some critical or pedagogical purpose. To our knowledge, none of the secondary scholarship has appropriated O'Connor to say what we want to say here: that her understanding of human frailty might make us more patient with those we encounter in our academic work.[13]

The Theme of Sin

We are aware that for some of our readers, our introducing this term may have the power to reawaken painful memories of guilt inducing, graceless preaching and teaching in an earlier time of life. We have no desire to reawaken those memories. In fact, we could substitute the word *brokenness, failure,* or *frailty* for *sin* throughout this chapter, but doing so might lead other readers to conclude that we were too theologically mushy about an important biblical concept. We especially might seem soft if we include mental illness and physical disabilities such as lupus in the category of brokenness. Nevertheless, we do include disabilities because we believe that in the reign of Christ there will be no lupus, no disability. Disability and lupus are part of our human experience while we live in this time of tension between the fall and the eschaton. So we will use several terms, such as *sin* and *brokenness,* interchangeably, always with the purpose of building bridges between the kind of language that might appear in an introductory theology course and the realities that we actually encounter in our work as higher educators. We admit—and we hope our readers will admit—that we see the qualities of O'Connor's characters in our own lives; we see brokenness, alienation, incompleteness, pretentiousness, pride, egoism, coveting and jealousy, narcissism, deformity, violence, suffering, bullheadedness, neediness, the grotesque, obsessions, superiority,[14] and estrangement, willful blindness, lying, and self-deception. Well, by definition, we may not see the last two, but we see these characteristics in our students and in those who report to us. And we see them in those to whom we report.

Carl Menninger, a prominent and non-Christian twentieth-century psychologist, titled a book this way: *Whatever Became of Sin?*[15] Menninger had no intention of preaching Christian theology. Rather, his purpose was simply to ask if a concept such as sin would be useful in understanding the kinds of damage to the soul and to the person that psychologists typically hear about in their offices. Whatever label one wants to put on damage—*sin, brokenness*—we need to be able to name it (and blame it?). Menninger begins his book with a story and parabolic history of the United States. The story is simple. A deranged—or possibly quite sane—man in downtown Chicago stands at a street corner, points his finger at random people, and pronounces them guilty. People react in various ways, mostly passing him by. One man turns to the source of Menninger's story and asks, "But how did *he* know?"[16] Menninger comments that many must have wondered the same thing: How *did* he know? Menninger moves from his Chicago story to quick summaries of how John the Baptist and Jesus also called people to repentance, and then he recounts the growth of the United States, including the appropriation of land from native peoples, wars with Mexico and Canada, and massive accumulation of wealth. He notes that everything was "going great" but that people eventually awoke from their dreams to the "full realization that something was wrong."[17] The next line in his book is the title of his second chapter, "What Is Wrong?" In that chapter, he recounts several stories from (then) recent U.S. news in which the word *sin* is never used to describe wrongdoing. He also notes the tendency to search for a scapegoat, for an explanation, for someone to blame. In his third chapter, he explores where the word went, and why. He suggests that its disappearance from our lexicon might connect to our wanting to shift responsibility for wrongdoing and evil away from ourselves. Still, on his account, we're left with a "vaguely uneasy" sense that something remains wrong.[18] Flannery O'Connor does not need Carl Menninger's help to write her stories. But we think he may have an insight for a whole society that sees human frailty all around and needs an explanation.[19] So, while O'Connor may not need Menninger, we admit that we do, because he offers a kind of warrant for introducing the concept of sin.

Still, does this chapter not have the potential to be a bit of a downer in comparison to all the other chapters? After all, throughout the book we try to remind ourselves and our readers of some of the big, appealing, winsome, ennobling ideas represented by significant people. Couldn't we leave sin for another day, or perhaps discuss grace but not sin?[20] Here is our solemn promise: as did Flannery O'Connor, we will treat sin unflinchingly, but we will never lose sight of grace.[21] Indeed, we think that collectively, all of us as Christian educators can fully understand our work circumstances and the people who work near us only if we maintain an unflinching understanding of sin. But we also believe that Christian educators need a robust conviction that God gives grace—if we are going to keep going back to work day after day. So, we promise to keep both concepts in view.

Sin and Brokenness in the Academy

We have argued that Flannery O'Connor could help us understand something about human beings. We turn briefly now to the kinds of human beings we meet in the course of our work in the academy. Recall that our purpose in including O'Connor in this book is to help us become more understanding of and patient with our students, our colleagues and supervisors, and ourselves. The following brief catalog of blemished, O'Connorish types is not the point of the chapter (so to speak), but it is one of our starting points.

However, before preceding to our O'Connorish catalog, we must note that many in the academy live with disabilities that are not of a moral nature. For these friends, colleagues, and students, we make accommodations and gladly support them in their work. We can frame these limitations theologically with language such as the "bondage of decay" that Paul says is part of humanity's lot (Romans 8:21). And, of course, we can frame them eschatologically and look forward to that time when all things are reconciled.

One of us (Ken), in fact, deals with a hearing impairment. Hearing a quiet student or getting one's working ear pointed toward a class participant or discussion sometimes becomes a bit of a dance, although if it serves as a reminder that one day everything will be made well, then perhaps it is a gift.

O'Connor has populated her stories with a significant number of characters who have never healed from personal hurts, and we meet some of these same people in the academy. Again, we would never trivialize pain that many endure from wounds inflicted decades before. In some cases, our students or colleagues have suffered genuine horrors. However thinking like Flannery O'Connor, we would like to ask how those in the academy should express that pain . . . or perhaps how we should keep it quiet. Some use the classroom as a bully pulpit to rail against their enemies. Others need the affirmation and even hero worship of students as psychotherapy. Still others seem to struggle just to show up and be present, stewing in the juices of their own inner conflicts and pain.

We are not psychologists, and we likewise do not intend to minimize the traumatic chapters in our students' or colleagues' backgrounds. But perhaps like some of our readers, we need new (or old) ways to understand some of the people we meet at work. And whatever the objective strengths and weaknesses of those around us, sometimes we need patience, just as they need patience with us. We included O'Connor's themes of sin and grace in this book to address those with disability as well as those with habits and personality traits that challenge those around them in the academy, what are truly nasty types.[22] So we turn now to our catalog of blemished, O'Connorish types. In each case, we deal with these briefly because we and our readers all *know the types,* so to speak, and elaboration of these categories will not serve any of us well.

First, we have the egoistic, arrogant, and pretentious; those who, like O'Connor's character Ruby Turpin in "Revelation," give themselves a perverse satisfaction by comparing themselves to the lesser beings around them, by sizing other people up.[23] Recognizably, such comparisons may be on good objective grounds; an eminent scholar likely has a long string of genuine accomplishments. But even the longest CV does not provide moral grounds for arrogance and superiority. We and our readers have met this person in faculty meetings, at conference sessions, and on committees.[24] In our more magnanimous moments, we may want to hold this person and say, "It's okay, someone loves you." Other times, we may just want to see such people find work elsewhere (to word it rather euphemistically).

Our second category populates both O'Connor's stories and the academy: those prone to coveting and jealousy.[25] We are irked by students' reports about the amazing and wonderful teaching in a colleague's class. Or three people come to our conference session (including the chair!) while a colleague's session runs out of chairs. We struggle to complete a single research paper while, for some colleagues, writing seems as natural as breathing. But these three scenarios miss an important complicating factor about our work in the academy. Unlike a hobby, where one's purposes are quite possibly entirely private (taking joy in collecting bird stamps, for example, without ever comparing one's collection to anyone else's), academic work is, by definition, public. We *want* our students to get engaged with big ideas in our classes. We *want* our publications to help people see new ways forward in their thinking and work. Inevitably, our work is a bit like figure skating; what others think of what we do matters. Is it not inevitable in these circumstances that coveting and jealousy might creep in? If your paper is more convincing than mine, is there not a sense in which I lose? We know what the Christian Scriptures have to say about coveting and jealousy, but we believe this dimension of academic work warrants a bit of digging. The line between healthy promotion of our own academic work for the sake of the kingdom and bold, barefaced self-promotion is a very fine line indeed. And from time to time, we are all prone to draw that line so that it favors ourselves. At the very least, this temptation should be acknowledged and discussed openly. Would this not be a good topic for a midyear faculty meeting: The Incivility of Self-Promotion?

O'Connor gave her readers a number of characters with a propensity toward violence and the abuse of power. We will not repeat here all that Hannah Arendt says on the topic, as we treated it in Chapter Three, but we will remind ourselves and our readers again that in the academy we see too much of this abuse. Of course, we notice it most easily in those above us in the institutional hierarchy; we see clearly when they misuse the prerogatives of their offices. We tend to miss the log in our own eye, which may express itself in snide and sarcastic remarks to students, or unjust grading practices, or the misappropriation of their ideas and work. Sadly, we see it between colleagues as well. Colleagues sabotage colleagues when they criticize other courses within students' hearing. They undermine colleagues during tenure and promotion processes. We do not need multiple examples here to make our point; we have all witnessed such abuses.

We include lying,[26] deception, and self-deception in our catalog, although O'Connor deals with the third far more frequently than she does the first two. We know that academics deceive (or try to deceive) themselves and perhaps their colleagues, students, and supervisors about the brilliance and impact of their academic work or the quality of their teaching. This deceit ranges from mild, private overestimations along the lines of "gee, but

I'm good"[27] to overt falsification of results and fraudulent publication or teaching records. Of course, we periodically hear a story such as someone being caught out for claiming that participation in a panel at Harvard was actually a teaching post at Harvard. At such times, we may be tempted to point appropriately condemnatory fingers. But we want to flag a more insidious form of academic fraud with which too many of us in the academy and the Christian academy seem to have become comfortable: inflated claims about authorship of academic papers. Collectively, academics have agreed both that research productivity counts and that we need ways to count it.[28] Having made that agreement, we then collectively developed a series of ways to game the system that we do not need to list here.[29] A number of readers of O'Connor have noted that the truly scary aspect of her characters is not their grotesqueness but their familiarity. We know them. In the case of her deceivers and self-deceived, we certainly do.

O'Connor drew characters who were bullheaded, obsessed, and willfully blind, as well as characters best described as petty and the picky. We know these colleagues as well. As we noted in our discussion of Arendt in Chapter Three, they will complain to the department month after month and year after year until we finally simply give in to their demand to include their pet course in the core or to decrease or increase this or that number. We do so hoping that now we can get on with other departmental business. Turning to the petty and the picky, some will point out a typo in front of two hundred people rather than email the report's author. For others, there is no sufficient reason ever to make an exception to a policy; after all, a compromise is a compromise. If we make an exception this time, where does it stop? Sometimes, this small-mindedness has its roots in some long-ago departmental or ideological disagreement from which one or more parties never recovered. Without reconciliation, the bleeding simply continues.[30]

With some relief, we end this catalog of negativity with four general observations. First, recall that we noted at the start of the chapter that we included Flannery O'Connor here because we believe that the plain old concept of sin would go some ways to explaining our own behavior and that of our students, colleagues, and supervisors. We believe that we might show more patience to ourselves and to each other if we understood how sin—or label it another way if you like—"is at work in [the] members" of the academic community (to gloss Romans 7:23). Second, in many cases, the types—the people—we have listed here would have been better people if someone had been there their whole life with a gun pointed at their heads. But not all. Some of the people we have cataloged did have a gun pointed at their heads inasmuch as they behaved abominably even while on probation, or even during a review year.

Third, we recognize that the people we have cataloged here have not somehow managed to cluster in the academy and avoid all other workplaces. They populate every field of endeavor we could name, likely in similar proportions. Fourth, and most soberingly, we need to recognize how our own blindness is at work in this discussion. As we wrote (and likely as you read) our catalog of bad types, particular people of our acquaintance (and likely yours) came to mind. How easy it is to see the logs in other people's eyes. We find it sobering that other people think of us, of you, when they think about these types. The greeting card should likely say, "They're called blind spots for a reason."

Grace

We can now ask what Flannery O'Connor offers us. For that matter, what does Christ's completed work offer us? We ask that for our students, our colleagues, our supervisors, and for ourselves. We believe that in God's world, and in Flannery O'Connor's world, there is grace. And we believe there is grace for the academic world as well. In a couple letters, O'Connor wrote about "stalking joy," by which she meant grace, but she noted that doing so involved going on a "dangerous quest" and that a dragon waited by the side of the road, ready to devour anyone passing by.[31] We agree with those readers of O'Connor who see her making the tension between evil and grace central to her work.[32] That tension clearly runs through the two stories we summarized earlier. And we see it in the academy.

Those of us who work in Christian higher education perhaps have an easier time making reference to sin than others. But we sometimes become inoculated to grace. Regarding the Grandmother's last gesture toward The Misfit and some people's inability to understand it, Flannery O'Connor wrote in a letter, "Our age . . . does not have a very sharp eye for the almost imperceptible intrusions of grace."[33] We, of all academics, need to keep our eyes sharp for those intrusions. Recall that in "Revelation," O'Connor has Mary Grace throw her psychology textbook at Ruby Turpin, hitting her in the forehead. We don't want to make O'Connor's story carry too much theological freight here, but we see several truths in this scene. First, sometimes we need a blow to the forehead to realize it is not someone else who needs grace (although, of course, they do); it is us. Second, grace comes from the most unexpected places. In Ruby Turpin's case, it came from a snarling teenager whose face was blue with acne. Third, grace comes. Again, those of us serving in Christian higher education need to keep our eyes peeled.

Songwriter Leonard Cohen told us that "there's a crack in everything, and that's where the light gets in."[34] St. Paul may have said the same thing in 2 Corinthians 4:7 when he wrote that it is in our human weakness—in clay jars—that the extraordinary power of God shows most clearly. In light of O'Connor, or Cohen, or the writers of Scripture, we ask then whether one of God's instruments of grace in our lives may be that overbearing supervisor who we think abuses his or her office. Could God's instrument of grace for us be that difficult colleague? Could it be that student who asked—apparently in complete innocence—to make up for the uncompleted assigned work by doing extra work? These are the O'Connor characters we know at work. We think God would have us find grace through such people.

We said we believed that we might be more patient with ourselves if we grasped the core of O'Connor's project. Could we frame our own shortcomings theologically and become more patient with ourselves? Not to flatter, but people who read this book are readers (we know that's a tautology) and are more likely the kinds of people who aim at improving their institutions and their own practices. We do not recommend complacency about our teaching, service, and research, but we do want to ask some important questions: Is there enough time in every day to do God's will? How many publications would be enough? Would it be permissible once in a while to aim at contentment rather than improvement? Would it be possible? In short, can we believe that God wants us to accept the gifts of grace? Can we believe that God wants us to enjoy life apart from work? Can we see that God calls us to be faithful, not perfect?

We write these words in the last weeks of a semester. Between us, about sixty student papers await our reading. While we might be tempted to wish for Christ's return today rather than after reading those papers, we will instead ask God for grace for today. And we will accept that grace. Given that we are at the end of the term, we may already have our minds made up about some of our students' work. We need to remember that grace can come in unexpected places (papers) and that the cracks (our end-of-term weariness) are where the light gets in.

Conclusion

Flannery O'Connor packed her fiction with truth. She painted quite an unflattering picture of human beings. She drew characters we recognize because they work down the hall, they work on the upper floor of the administration building, they sit in our classes, and they are us. For the last time in this chapter, we will use the word: we believe that if we took sin more seriously, we would be happier people.

The secular academy will need to struggle to find its own ways to account for the flaws O'Connor has helped us identify. In Christian higher education, we have an important theological concept already available for us to apply in our efforts to account for these flaws. If you accept our argument in this chapter—for that matter, if we accept our own argument—we should all be a bit more content as we carry out our God-given vocations in the academy.

We conclude with one final comment. Surely sin and grace are at work on our campuses. We hope that this chapter has made it clear that with grace there is hope, a hope that does not disappoint. However, that does not mean that we are to sit on our proverbial hands and let grace do all the work. At some moments, circumstances will compel us to step up and speak into power (part of the reason universities grant tenure), and at other times, in the face of consistent and hurtful meanness, we may have to hit the reset button and make a graceful exit. This, too, requires courage and grace. In any event, while recognizing the sewage that flows under our campuses and makes our quads so green, we remain confident that serving in Christian higher education is a high calling and one of the best places to serve on the face of the earth.

QUESTIONS FOR REFLECTION AND DISCUSSION

- Some readers of O'Connor accuse her of holding an unduly pessimistic view of human beings. If you have read Flannery O'Connor, how would you respond to this charge?
- Now that you have read our reflections on sin and grace at work on the Christian college campus, how do you respond? To what degree is our characterization accurate? If not, how so?
- What strategies and responses do you use when working with a needy or broken student? Colleague? What are some of the challenges in doing so?
- What do you see as the antidote to pride and self-promotion on your campus? Is this a concern for you?
- How do you negotiate the line between the need to make your work public and blatant self-promotion?
- We suggested that consistent, barefaced self-promotion can be an act of incivility, especially toward younger members of the faculty. To what degree do you think this assessment is accurate? Why?
- We know that we are all broken pots in one way or another. Why, then, is it easier to extend grace to a colleague or student than to ourselves?
- If you could do one thing to make your institution a more grace-filled place, what would it be?

FOR FURTHER STUDY

Flannery O'Connor's reputation was built on the strength of her fiction, although the correspondence and her occasional nonfiction pieces now collected and released have caught the attention of scholars. We list below the main collections of her own work, noting that many stories and some essays appear in more than one work. We list only a sample of the abundant secondary literature on O'Connor. We also note that in O'Connor's case, biographies and critical studies are nearly unworkable categories, although the Gooch volume listed below is clearly a biography.

IN O'CONNOR'S OWN WORDS

O'Connor, Flannery. *The Complete Stories.* New York: Farrar, Strauss and Giroux, 1971.
———. *Everything That Rises Must Converge.* New York: Farrar, Strauss, Giroux, 1965.
———. *A Good Man Is Hard to Find.* New York: Harcourt, Brace and Company, 1955.
———. *The Habit of Being,* edited by Sally Fitzgerald. New York: Farrar, Strauss, and Giroux, 1979.
———. *Mystery and Manners: Occasional Prose of Flannery O'Connor,* edited by Sally Fitzgerald. New York: Farrar, Strauss, and Giroux, 1979.
———. *The Violent Bear It Away.* New York: Farrar, Strauss, Giroux, 1960.
———. *Wise Blood.* New York: Harcourt and Brace, 1952.
———. *Flannery O'Connor: The Cartoons,* edited by Kelly Gerald. Seattle, WA: Fanagraphics Books, 2012.
O'Connor, Flannery, and Rosemary M. Magee. *Conversations with Flannery O'Connor.* Jackson, MS: University Press of Mississippi, 1987.

BIOGRAPHIES AND OTHER SELECTED WORKS ABOUT O'CONNOR

Basselin, Timothy J. *Flannery O'Connor: Writing a Theology of Disabled Humanity.* Waco, TX: Baylor University Press, 2013.
Baumgartner, Jill P. *Flannery O'Connor: A Proper Scaring.* Wheaton, IL: Harold Shaw Publishers, 1988.
Cooper, Jordan. *The Gospel According to Flannery O'Connor.* New York: Bloomsbury, 2014.
Desmond, John F. "Stalking Joy: Flannery O'Connor and the Dangerous Quest." *Christianity & Literature* 60, no. 1 (Autumn 2010): 97–111.
Eggenschwiler, David. *The Christian Humanism of Flannery O'Connor.* Detroit, MI: Wayne State University Press, 1972.
Gooch, Brad. *Flannery: A Life of Flannery O'Connor.* New York: Little Brown/ Back Bay, 2010.
Hendin, Josephine. *The World of Flannery O'Connor.* Bloomington, IN: Indiana University Press, 1970.
May, John. "The Pruning Word: Flannery O'Connor's Judgment of Intellectuals." *Southern Humanities Review* 4 (1970): 325–38.
Michaels, J. Ramsey. *Passing the Dragon: The Biblical Tales of Flannery O'Connor.* Eugene, OR: Wipf and Stock, 2013.

Niederauer, George H. "Flannery O'Connor's Religious Vision." *America* 197, no. 21 (December 24, 2007): 9–14.

Scott, Neil R. *Flannery O'Connor: An Annotated Reference Guide to Criticism.* Milledgeville, GA: Timberlane, 2002.

Sharp, Jolly Kay. *Between the House and the Chicken Yard: The Masks of Flannery O'Connor.* Macon, GA: Mercer University Press, 2011.

Wood, Ralph C. *Flannery O'Connor and the Christ-Haunted South.* Grand Rapids, MI: Eerdmans, 2004.

NOTES

[1] George H. Niederauer wrote "Flannery O'Connor's Religious Vision" while serving as Roman Catholic bishop of San Francisco. He offers what we consider a balanced assessment: she loved the Church but certainly knew its flaws and was unafraid to write about them. *America* 197, no. 21 (December 24, 2007): 9–14. Also see Joanne Halleran McMullen and Jon Parrish Peede, *Inside the Church of Flannery O'Connor: Sacrament, Sacramental and the Sacred in her Fiction* (Macon, GA: Mercer University Press, 2007).

[2] See, for example, Carolyn Michaels Kerr, "Stomaching the Truth: Getting to the Roots of Nausea in the Work of Jean Paul Sartre and Flannery O'Connor," *Christianity and Literature* 60, no. 1 (Autumn 2010): 67–96; and Ralph C. Wood, *Flannery O'Connor and the Christ-Haunted South* (Grand Rapids, MI: Eerdmans, 2004). Wood offers a worthwhile discussion of Flannery O'Connor's interaction with philosophy and theology. With great insight, Thomas Merton wrote that "she probed our very life—its conflicts, its falsities, its obsessions, its vanities." See "Flannery O'Connor: A Praise Elegy," *Raids on the Unspeakable* (New York: New Direction, 1966), 37.

[3] For example, Timothy J. Basselin, *Flannery O'Connor: Writing a Theology of Disabled Humanity* (Waco: TX: Baylor, 2013).

[4] See "Some Aspects of the Grotesque in Southern Fiction," where she asks us to frame her stories theologically instead of as instances of the grotesque. At http://www.en.utexas.edu/amlit/amlitprivate/scans/grotesque.html. By John May's count, five intellectual protagonists and one intellectual antagonist in her short stories struggle with faith, perhaps indicating something of O'Connor's prophetic gifts, inasmuch as intellectuals have struggled to make an account of—and to discount—her own faith. See "The Pruning Word: Flannery O'Connor's Judgment of Intellectuals," *Southern Humanities Review* 4 (1970): 325–38.

[5] Flannery O'Connor, and Rosemary M. Magee, *Conversations with Flannery O'Connor* (Jackson, MS: University Press of Mississippi, 1987), 38.

[6] A volume of her cartoons, including many completed while she was a student, appeared recently. *Flannery O'Connor: The Cartoons*, edited by Kelly Gerald (Seattle, WA: Fantagraphics Books, 2012).

[7] See, for example, the article based on Steven R. Watkins's 2005 doctoral dissertation, "Teilhard de Chardin's View of Diminishment and the Late Stories of Flannery O'Connor," *Global Education Journal* 2013, no. 1 (2013): 117–145. His full dissertation is available online at the University of Texas (Arlington) at https://uta-ir.tdl.org/uta-ir/bitstream/handle/10106/424/umi-uta-1153.pdf?sequence=1&isAllowed=y. Chardin was a French Jesuit and paleontologist who worked mainly in China.

[8] *Letters of Flannery O'Connor: The Habit of Being,* selected and edited by Sally Fitzgerald (New York: Farrar, Straus, Giroux, 1979), 509.

[9] David Eggenschwiler, *The Christian Humanism of Flannery O'Connor* (Detroit, MI: Wayne State University Press, 1972). We note Neil R. Scott's major bibliography of secondary O'Connor literature: *Flannery O'Connor: An Annotated Reference Guide to Criticism* (Milledgeville, GA: Timberlane, 2002).

[10] To us, it seems specious to say "spoiler alert" at this point, although we know that some of our readers will not have read the stories we review here.

[11] In *A Circle in the Fire and Other Stories*, edited by C. E. Morgan (London: Folio Society, 2013), 51.

¹² O'Connor took the title for one of those novels, *The Violent Bear It Away*, from Matthew 11:12, which reads, "From the days of John the Baptist until now the kingdom of heaven has suffered violence, and the violent take it by force" (NRSV). We will not review the many readings of this passage, but we will note that most share the view that evil still does its work. See Ralph C. Wood, "Flannery O'Connor: The Violent Bear It Away," in Robert C. Roberts, Scott H. Moore, and Donald D. Schmeltekopf, eds., *Finding a Common Thread: Understanding Great Texts from Homer to O'Connor* (South Bend, IN: St. Augustine's Press, 2013), 305–322.

¹³ We also think of Karl Jaspers (Chapter Eleven) who was asked to rebuild the University in Heidelberg in the aftermath of World War II—with colleagues who sympathized with the Nazi regime. He offered much grace to many.

¹⁴ In this regard, note Paul Blackmore's *Prestige in Academic Life: Excellence and Exclusion* (New York, Routledge, 2016).

¹⁵ New York: Hawthorn, 1973.

¹⁶ Ibid., 2.

¹⁷ Ibid., 5.

¹⁸ Ibid., 17.

¹⁹ He may also have offered an account of why some readers of O'Connor refuse even to take her own word for what themes she explores in her stories.

²⁰ One reader of Flannery O'Connor, David Eggenschwiler, argues that to ignore estrangement in O'Connor is not just to miss something in her work; it is to read her wrongly altogether.

²¹ And in the interests of full disclosure, we note that even in the O'Connor secondary literature, one will hear voices protesting that some have made too much of sin. For example, see Josephine Hendin, who believed that the doctrine of sin does make sense as a category for understanding O'Connor but that there is much it did not explain. *The World of Flannery O'Connor* (Bloomington: Indiana University Press, 1970).

²² We recognize that one can offer a theological frame for the two categories—disability and plain nastiness—that roots them in the same place: sin.

²³ Some academics, on meeting another academic at a conference, immediately do the same kind of Turpinesque assessment with reference to professorial rank, successful grant applications, and publications.

²⁴ Regarding narcissism, note this relatively new title with a rather old word, about an even older flaw: *Vainglory: The Forgotten Vice*, by Rebecca Konyndyk DeYoung (Grand Rapids, MI: Eerdmans, 2014). And we note Emily Toth's *Ms. Mentor's Impeccable Advice for Women in Academia* (College Park, PA: University of Pennsylvania Press, 2012). She describes some men's need to establish that they are the smartest one in the room at a conference. The title of one chapter, "Hello, I Have a Penis," may alarm some readers, but likely for the wrong reasons. It should alarm us all because it tells the truth about how so many men, and some women, behave. If reading the Bible or Flannery O'Connor does not help you become more patient with narcissists, we recommend searching "narcissistic personality disorder" and reading the diagnostic criteria in the American Psychological Association's *Diagnostic and Statistical Manual of Mental Disorders V*. Seriously, realizing that someone is a textbook narcissist can bring a measure of mental health.

²⁵ Regarding coveting, we note the life and corpus of work by René Girard (1923–2015) who saw the root of much violence in *mimetic desire*, people's desire to have what others

have. Girard is not alone; see the recent *Jealousy*, by Peter Toohey (New Haven, CT: Yale University Press, 2014). Toohey's book is noteworthy in part because he clarifies the differences between jealousy and envy, noting that we often use the one (as in "I'm jealous of her publishing record") when we mean the other.

[26] One can hardly call it a barrage, but new books about old flaws continue apace. See Paul Griffiths, *Lying: An Augustinian Theology of Duplicity*, originally published in 2004 (Grand Rapids, MI: Baker/Brazos).

[27] According to Stanford Ericksen, 94 percent of teachers judge themselves to be above average, and 68 percent rank themselves in the top quartile. Even in Lake Wobegon, where all the students are apparently above average, these numbers would arouse suspicion. See *The Essence of Good Teaching: Helping Students Learn and Remember What They Learn* (San Francisco: Jossey-Bass, 1984).

[28] We have argued at length in *Faith and Learning: A Guide for Faculty* (Abilene, TX: Abilene Christian University Press, 2014) that this system does not enhance the well-being of the university and that adopting the model proposed by Ernest Boyer would serve the university well.

[29] Some have argued that if all elite, international-level cyclists are doping, then true unfairness is when only one cyclist gets busted. On this account, is it not fair for all academics to inflate their publication records? One of us (Ken) has described some of these fraudulent practices in a paper called "Transgressive Co-Authorship," which has been submitted for consideration to *Christian Scholars Review*.

[30] The woman with the flow of blood (Mark 5:25–26) who wanted to be healed reminds us of so many departments and even whole institutions that simply continue to hemorrhage because they somehow cannot touch the cloak of Jesus. In some cases, a telling difference may be that she wanted to be healed.

[31] For example in her letter to "A" in *Habit of Being*, 126. See John F. Desmond, "Stalking Joy: Flannery O'Connor and the Dangerous Quest," *Christianity & Literature* 60, no. 1 (Autumn 2010): 97–111.

[32] For example, Bob Dowell, "The Moment of Grace in the Fiction of Flannery O'Connor," *College English* 27:3 (December 1965): 235–39; T. W. Hendricks, "Flannery O'Connor's 'Spoiled Prophet,'" *Modern Age* 51, no. 3–4 (Summer 2009): 202–210.

[33] *Mystery and Manners: Occasional Prose of Flannery O'Connor*, edited by Sally Fitzgerald (New York: Farrar, Strauss, and Giroux, 1979):112.

[34] "Anthem," words and music copyright, 1992 by Leonard Cohen and Sony/ATV Music.

Maria Montessori

The Montessori Method (1912)

Background and Biography

ONE MIGHT CLASSIFY THE THINKERS WE HAVE EXAMINED IN THIS BOOK in many ways, an obvious one being people we associate with higher education and people we would never connect with higher education. In Maria Montessori, we have a paradigmatic example of someone almost no one associates with higher education. After all, she focused her work on young children. And, so popular thinking has it, her concepts and methods do not suit higher education at all. If by *methods* one means sandpaper letters to help children learn the alphabet, then without doubt, popular thinking has it right. If Montessori's methods include careful study of the students we teach, or designing activities that will engage their interest in our curriculum materials, or creating an environment that will pique their curiosity, then we may need to think again about how we have classified her.

In fact, Montessori did make sandpaper letters for children to touch as they saw and said the letters of the alphabet. And she designed a host of other physical materials meant to encourage student-directed learning, to pique curiosity, and to involve more senses in the learning process than seeing and hearing. Our job in this chapter is to give you a kind of backstage tour—to get at the pedagogical principles behind the materials—and not only to suggest how those principles apply to instruction in higher education but to argue that we will actually do less than our best if we remain ignorant of them or ignore them intentionally.

Briefly, Maria Montessori lived from 1870 to 1952. She was the first woman to graduate in medicine from the University of Rome. After graduation, she worked with slum children and severely handicapped children at several locations in Italy. She experienced significant early-career success in teaching handicapped children to read and write; in some cases, her students achieved at the same levels as children of the same age without disability. This prompted her to shift her interest toward education, where she then immersed herself in the works of German educator Friedrich Froebel, Italian anthropologist Giuseppe Serge, and the French physician Jean Marc Gaspard Itard (who had made careful observations of the wild boy of Aveyron, whom he named Victor). A true interdisciplinarian from the start, she combined these various strains of thought and by 1907 was promulgating her own educational theory, which is still known as *the Montessori Method*.[1]

Maria Montessori's Themes

Montessori's method rested on a few essential principles: Children naturally want to learn; therefore, educators should be following up on students' questions rather than simply answering our own.[2] The learning environment is deeply important and must include self-correcting teaching materials to reduce teacher-centric instruction.[3] Teaching must attend to the child or student as carefully as it attends to the curriculum. Students should largely be responsible for the pacing of their learning. Learning should engage the sense of touch. One popular slogan among Montessori educators catches some of this conception of autodidactic learning: *help me to do it myself.*

Montessori believed that human development occurs on a number of distinct planes, which might be more easily understood as distinct phases, each with its own characteristics. Each of these planes is roughly six years long, implying that children to about six years of age learn in certain characteristic ways and that those ways differ sharply from how children aged seven to twelve best learn. To describe all the phases is beyond the purposes of this chapter, but we will note that Montessori said little about the fourth plane that involved the transition into adulthood that takes place from ages 18–24.⁴

Responses to Montessori

A reading of Montessori or some of the secondary literature on her, combined with a few conversations in university hallways, will reveal responses ranging from the view that she was brilliant to the view that she somehow went off the educational rails into the wild spaces of make-believe. We classify responses to her into three categories. She has experienced a degree of acceptance, in fact a fervent degree among some educators. Some have criticized her work for a wide variety of reasons. Others have actively ignored her work or simply remained ignorant of what she actually taught and practiced.

We will review some of these responses, beginning with her critics. Those critical of Montessori have raised several concerns. She has a bit of a reputation—undeserved in our view—as one in the tradition of Rousseau. On these accounts, children are essentially spiritual beings, at peace with themselves and the world, and desirous of learning when in a state of nature. In our own time, we hear various educators' names being assigned to this tradition, for example, Herbart, Pestalozzi, Froebel, Steiner, and Carl Rogers. Those who would set Montessori in this tradition ignore at least two important things, the first of which is that Rousseau and the five people just listed differed significantly in their views of the child, of learning, and of spirituality. More significant for our purposes, those who assign Montessori membership in this group ignore her orthodox Christian faith, a faith to which she constantly referred and which she explicated in printed detail at several points but especially in her book *The Child in the Church*. Anyone with doubts about the state of her Christian convictions should read this 1929 title.⁵ A healthy secondary literature related specifically to Christian education has also emerged, based on her understanding of children's spirituality and their receptivity to new learning.⁶

William Heard Kilpatrick, a prominent American educator and colleague of John Dewey, spent a year studying Montessori and published a dismissive summary of her work in 1914. Kilpatrick did not aid her acceptance in the United States by assigning her "essentially to the mid-nineteenth century, some fifty years behind the present development of educational theory."[7] In the final pages of his tract, Kilpatrick wrote this way:

> Madam Montessori hoped to remake pedagogy; but her idea of pedagogy is much narrower than Professor Dewey's idea of education. Its conception of the nature of the thinking process, together with his doctrines of interest and of education as life—not simply as preparation for life—include all that is valid in Madam Montessori's doctrines of liberty and sense-training, afford the criteria for correcting her errors, and besides, go vastly farther in the construction of educational method. In addition to this, he attacked the equally fundamental problem of the nature of the curriculum, saw it as the ideal reconstruction of the race achievement, and made substantial progress toward a methodology of its appropriation. This great problem of the curriculum, it can almost be said, Madam Montessori has, so far, not even seen. While this is no adequate recital of Professor Dewey's contributions, it suffices, in connection with what has been previously said; to show that they are ill advised who put Madam Montessori among the significant contributors to educational theory. Stimulating she is, a contributor to our theory, hardly, if at all.[8]

Kilpatrick's brush-off notwithstanding, we find it interesting that a century ago, Montessori told educators to plan instruction in view of what students already know, instead of simply moving from one point in the curriculum to the next without regard for whether one's students have understood what went before. Any recent book on instruction in higher education will underline this now commonplace view that often comes under a heading such as *scaffolding*.[9] Viewed from a century out, Kilpatrick looks like he may have been guilty of writing an apologia for Dewey rather than a clearheaded assessment of Montessori.

We noted that many educators—especially higher educators—simply do not know very much about Montessori's philosophy and practices. We illustrate this dearth of applications and connections by reporting on a search of the major educational database, Education Research Complete, which, at the time of this writing, indexed about 2,400 journals. Our search for the descriptor *Montessori* in any field and *higher education* as a subject descriptor yielded two records.[10] We would not consider this shortage so sobering if Montessori's ideas had no application to higher education. But in our view, she presented a philosophy of education, not only a philosophy of childhood education. And we have included her work in this book to address her nearly complete lack of influence in higher education.

Among the few who have seen fit to apply Montessori's ideas in higher education is a group of computer science professors at Robert Morris University in Pennsylvania. They have designed instruction in computer network security shaped in part by Montessori's findings that experience, collaboration, and directed exploration enhance learning.[11] Other than that team, we have found no higher educators reporting that they have tried to make use of Montessori's approach in higher education.

Various scholars have pointed to connections between Montessori's work and the work of other educators. Rathunde, for example, who has worked closely with Mihalyi Csikszentmihalyi (famous for his work on optimal or *flow* experiences), has pointed to similarities between Montessori's understanding of optimal learning and Csikszentmihalyi's conception of flow.[12] Another author has drawn connections between Montessori and Bloom's taxonomy,[13] and between Montessori and the educational ideas of both Tolstoy and Vygotsky.[14] Montessori's interest in Tolstoy may, in fact, have contributed to her being assigned to the romantic tradition. She had read the romantics, and she knew of Tolstoy's pedagogical discoveries when, upon the emancipation of the serfs in 1861, he began to take a direct interest in the school at Yasnaya Polyana on his estate. She concluded, as had he, that children possessed a natural desire to read, write, learn, and understand. The teacher's job was to prepare a classroom environment that is responsive to children's natural motivation to learn and conducive to self-directed learning.

Montessori and the University

We noted above that Montessori had addressed young adult learners in her "Four Planes of Education" (sometimes titled "Four Planes of Development"). In that essay, she argued that the function of higher education should be to prepare people to move from concern for the self only to concern for the human race. As she described it in "Four Planes," the university should help the individual see both the possibility and the importance of making life-giving choices among all the possibilities open to the young adult. Without using the language of *lifelong learning* that we use now, she also called for the university to impart that vision of life to its students. Montessori gave a lecture in Amsterdam in 1939 called "The Function of the University," which has been published as the closing chapter of *From Childhood to Adolescence*.[15] In this speech, she expressed with passion the concerns she had about the quality of higher education.

Readers will detect at least a little sarcasm in her assessment that the university

> is constituted in a manner that resembles the [elementary and secondary] schools. It is nothing other than a direct continuation of them. Students continue to follow lessons, to listen to teachers, and to pass examinations on which their career depends. The only difference is that the university students are not made to repeat the lessons or to do homework—which is to say that among people used to continuously controlled hard work, they work less. In addition, they have longer vacations.[16]

She went on in her speech to lament a shift that any of us might have read about in last week's *Chronicle of Higher Education*:

> The universities have become, little by little, simple professional schools where only the degree of schooling is superior to that of the other schools. But they have lost their sense of dignity and grandeur which made them a central instrument for the progress of civilization.

> The students, having as their aim only to obtain some obscure post for themselves, can no longer have the sense of mission that formerly created the "spirit of the university." The desire to work as little as possible, to pass the exams at all costs, and to obtain a diploma that will serve each person's individual interests has

become the essential motive common to the students. Thus academic institutions have become decadent as the progress of culture has transformed man's existence. True centers of progress had been established in the laboratories of the scientific researchers. They are closed places, foreign to the common culture.[17]

Her exclusive language notwithstanding, one hears in her frustration a prescient complaint. She goes on to argue that the universities should focus less on finding more efficient means of transmitting knowledge and more on how to help people. She notes that "university professors . . . will have before them ardent apostles, intelligent critics, and veritable collaborators in their students if these have developed normally. If not, they will have before them resistant, indifferent, and inert minds, respectful youths whom they will have to keep on a leash as so many young goats."[18] Higher educators may be inclined to leave rather than love such a blunt assessment. But we believe she has spoken the truth about universities, the students who attend them, and those of us who teach in them.

Potential Themes for Christian Higher Educators Today

Several possible themes from Montessori's work warrant consideration by those of us who teach in Christian higher education, the first of which is her constructivism. Because that word scares many Christians, we will refer to this theme as student-driven learning experiences. She believed that students should engage in more discovery than schools of her time allowed. We think she is right. According to some famous Harvard dropouts, everything one really needs to know today, one can discover on the Internet. But snide asides notwithstanding, Bill Gates and Mark Zuckerberg might be right when they claim that the students in our classes today did discover a great deal of what they now know on the web. For today's students, discovery is a natural mode of learning. Were Montessori alive today, she would not say "I told you so" (she was more gracious than that), but she would likely say that we ought to adjust our pedagogy in light of the way contemporary students do so much of their learning.

A second theme worthy of our attention is her advocacy of hands-on, unmediated learning experiences. She viewed physical activity as an antidote to arid lectures. In our own time, we might view activity-based learning (for example, field education, internships, labs) as an antidote to our students' highly mediated environment. Combine these first and second themes—both related to the ubiquitous presence of the Internet in our lives—and we might expect that our students have more of an e-pistemology than epistemology as we used to understand it.[19]

The third theme in Montessori's work that we consider worthy of higher educators' attention is the spirituality of the student. She believed that children—that all people—were special creations of God. This conviction may figure in some secular educators' rejection of Montessori, but it does not explain why Christian higher educators have not paid attention to her view of the student as a spiritual being.

Teaching Who They Are: The Curriculum and the Student

We want to synthesize several important aspects of Montessori's thought and practice into a single statement: *to engage students, we need to teach who they are.* By that, we mean we agree with her that we need to study our students carefully to understand who they are as learners. We also mean we agree with her that we need to view classrooms not simply as places where we deliver curriculum but as a meeting points between the curriculum and our students' life situations and interests. In what follows, we will definitely not argue that the academic disciplines and the curriculum are not important. If anything, we will argue that it is their great importance that drives us to call for Christian higher educators to pay more attention to students and their questions.

Montessori continually stressed the involvement and engagement of the learner. On her account, we must observe our students to see what catches their attention and imagination. We must help them see and make connections to the real world (for example, nature, work). In *The Discovery of the Child,* she laments that so much learning is "inert, perpetually dependent on the teacher, separated from the rest of mankind."[20] Given the mood in education in our own time, her claim that education should not "be reduced to the mere storage of knowledge necessary for practicing a profession" seems prescient.[21] In the same chapter, she directs a comment specifically to higher educators: "If the process of the children's education cannot be carried out in the confines of four walls, that of adults is still less capable of being carried out satisfactorily there."[22] We will leave off further quoting from Montessori herself at this point because we could easily give over the entire chapter to making a case that she said this or that. Instead, we will come into her work and its implication for Christian higher education from another direction altogether.

We will work our way into this conversation by noting the trend in the last couple decades of talking about what many call backward design. In this approach to curriculum, the professor's first task is to identify what students should know at the end of the course, unit, or lesson. Working backward from there, the professor identifies what kinds of assessments would demonstrate that students have learned that material, and from there, what kind of activities, including instruction by the teacher or professor, would give students the needed understanding of the material. To some higher educators, this approach—backward design—could not be more aptly named. Especially for those among us who are more heavily involved in research in our respective fields, the question must certainly arise why instruction would not begin with the academic discipline, its epistemology and structures, its canonical ideas and themes, its central concepts, its tests for truth claims and judgments of quality, and its ways of doing business.[23]

This question of where to start—with the structures of the discipline or with the ways that students learn—echoes an old debate that often goes by labels such as *student-centered versus subject-centered* (also known as "I teach subjects" versus "I teach students"), the *process versus content,* and *the logical and the psychological.* We will explore that dualism here, but we will note in advance that Montessori saw no such dualism and neither do we. As far as we can determine, John Dewey first made this distinction in 1916 when he wrote "the chronological method which begins with the experience of the learner and develops from that the proper modes of scientific treatment . . . is often called the 'psychological' method in distinction from the logical method."[24] Dewey makes it clear in *Democracy and Education* that in his view, the logical and the psychological are not opposed, but must be brought into what he called a congruence. On his account, neither the logical and epistemological categories nor the psychological and pedagogical categories can be chief. Anyone planning instruction must take both into account. So while the logical and the psychological may be a dualism, they are an unnecessary dualism, one of our own manufacture.

Given how powerfully this dualism works in higher education, it warrants our attention. Let us accept for the sake of argument (and because it is true) that in our course planning and instruction, we need to attend carefully to the logical and epistemological dimensions of the academic disciplines. We would be irresponsible to ignore them. In other words, such attention is a necessary condition for responsible higher education. We attach no caveats to that claim. But we do want to add a caution: agreeing that such attention is necessary likely does not tell us one thing about how to teach that discipline in a university classroom. If we know that disciplinary expertise always came accompanied by outstanding teaching, we would not sense any need to emphasize this caution. But disciplinary expertise does not always keep such company. So we repeat that knowing the structures of the discipline—its concepts, epistemic structure, tests, themes, canons, and so on—does not indicate how to handle that discipline in the classroom in ways that maximize student engagement and learning.

Unfortunately, some educators have gone to the other extreme, arguing that methodology is everything. We think of the colleague who claimed that professors must "teach it well or don't teach it at all." For the last several decades, constructivist educators have emphasized that when students engage in learning, they are building a cognitive structure.[25] That structure may differ from the one we would prefer they build or even the one we intend and try to make explicit in our instruction. As David Ausubel, an early participant in the logical/psychological debate worded it half a century ago,

> it should not be forgotten . . . that in addition to organized bodies of knowledge, that represent the collective recorded wisdom of recognized scholars in particular fields of inquiry, there are corresponding psychological structures of knowledge as represented by the organization of internalized ideas and information in the minds of individual students of varying degrees of both cognitive maturity and subject-matter

sophistication in these same disciplines. I am making a distinction, in other words, between the formal organization of the subject-matter content of a given discipline, as set forth in authoritative statements in generally accepted textbooks and monographs, on the one hand, and the organized, internalized representation of this knowledge in the memory structures of particular individuals, especially students, on the other.[26]

With Ausubel and many others, we are saying that good teaching entails attending to both epistemological and psychological considerations. We are not dealing just with information or just with people. We are dealing with both, and for information to become students' knowledge and for students to gain the kind of commitment to a field that their professors have, professors must attend both to the nature of the discipline and to the nature of the person. The dualism known as *the logical and the psychological* is not helpful. Both components are necessary, and we waste our time if we spend it arguing that one or the other is paramount.

We are aware that at this time Montessori can neither support nor deny our connecting her in this way to the logical/psychological dualism. But we want to address the question of *teaching who they are* from another direction.

We have spoken favorably about Montessori's call for us all to become careful observers of those we teach. We want to suggest three implications of her call that such careful observers might draw if they studied current generations of students in Christian higher education. First, we would want to understand our students' embrace of contemporary cultural forms, including lots of down-market fare, and the ways they have voluntarily agreed to be shaped by those forms. Understanding today's students may require that we explore what we might call the celebrity mind-set. We should likely ask how the constant exposure to celebrities and their lives affects some students' wishes to have their own fifteen minutes of fame. Those with such a wish may have a diminished desire to wrestle with the hard questions that life brings their way or that we may want to bring their way in our classes. In our classes, we try to raise hard questions, ones that take reading, reflection, and conversation to get sorted, and sometimes questions that cause headaches. In a culture entranced by celebrity, will our students want to join us on this journey if the travel actually entails some travail? How will our students develop the habits of thought needed to lead rich lives and to participate in our courses if they focus on keeping up with a kind of *Kardashian epistemology* (as strange as it may seem to hear those two words next to each other in a sentence)?

Teaching Who They Are: Cohort Characteristics

Second, taking seriously Montessori's mandate that we teach who they are implies the need for a deeper understanding of how our students use technology. Not to be clever, but we are less concerned here with how spy agencies invade our privacy and more concerned with how our use of technology invades our epistemology. Think about how Amazon's recommendation algorithm influences our thinking about what books to buy. Think about how getting "Likes" on Facebook influences our opinion about our own posts and those of others. Think about how we select from among similar or possibly identical YouTube videos when one has thirty thousand views and one has thirty million. As we noted in the chapter on Arendt, we take important cues from the crowd at such points and we tend to let others decide for us what is worth watching.

Have recommendation algorithms and our own habitual ways of choosing Internet content altered our ways of judging what is true, what is honorable, what is worth knowing? That is, have we—without noticing—adopted a new epistemology? We have made more space for what is often called *crowd intelligence*[27] or, as we noted earlier, a kind of e-pistemology.

Third, professors wanting to follow Montessori's advice about making a careful study and developing a disciplined understanding of the generations of students now in our courses need to take irony very seriously. That being said, we begin our exploration of irony 50 years ago, in Susan Sontag's essay "Notes on Camp."[28] In her understanding, camp mocks the qualities and dimensions of ordinary life. It is characterized by superiority and by a tongue-in-cheek posture toward almost everything. Sontag derived the name *camp* from the truly bad dress-up skits and songs young people perform at actual summer camps (which may have been bad despite the campers' best efforts or may have been bad by intention). Sontag offered a detailed picture of camp, most of which we will omit here, but let us repeat some of the key features she identified.

- Camp is more concerned with style than with beauty.
- Camp is disengaged and detached from the world it sees.
- Camp sees everything in quotation marks.
- Camp reduces being to playing roles; in camp, life is theater.
- For camp to be pure camp, it must be naïve camp.

Sontag offers us much to think about here; we will explore and illustrate just one implication of her work to illustrate our claim that if we are to teach who they are, we will need to find out who they are. That Sontag identified in 1964 what we now call air quotes (our third bullet above) warrants our attention, in part because, in our own time, air quotes serve to symbolize and even create a distance between the speaker or writer and the subject. At this time, several generations regularly use air quotes to express doubts about the sincerity of someone else's claims. In classrooms in Christian colleges, we want language to matter, and we want words to count. How will we communicate if our students have air quotes as their default setting? Will our students trust our words, whether those words are spoken, written in a textbook, or written on a syllabus? Despite having written half a century ago, Sontag has raised some good questions for Christian higher educators. If we want our courses to have gravitas but our students have too many ironies in the fire—especially with reference to epistemology—we may end up failing to connect; they will not see, grasp, or perhaps even want the gravitas we intend to offer. In these circumstances, the burden remains ours to make every effort to understand them, even as they perhaps express with their words, their hats, and their air quotes that they have less trust in the world than we had at the same age. Some of our students may feel the need to arm themselves against a hostile world. Others may want to insulate themselves from a stupid world or to distance themselves from a false and phony world. Whatever the case, Montessori calls us to study our students and to deepen our understanding of them as individuals and as cohorts. We are much more likely to engage them when we teach who they are.

Conclusions

We believe that Montessori was ahead of her time. This bad timing (if we may call it that) was combined with widespread ignorance of what she actually taught and equally widespread misinterpretation of her Christian spirituality to produce a sad result: only a minority of primary and secondary educators have adopted her approach to education. An even smaller minority of higher educators have attempted to understand or practice what she might mean for our classrooms. In this chapter, we have reviewed some of her central ideas, and we have argued that we should take seriously her call to study our students and find new ways to engage them in learning. On her account, they want to learn; why should we not take advantage of that natural desire?

We and all our readers have met students who did not want to learn. Some students would be bored in a class cotaught by Robin Williams and Jesus Christ (and, after missing a class, might email the professor the dreaded, classic, hollow question: "What did I miss?"). But those students comprise the tiniest fraction of the students we have met. Almost all the rest want to learn. They fit Montessori's account. They possess a natural hunger to make sense of their environment, implying that we must heed Montessori's call and do all we can to construct in our classrooms an ethos conducive to learning. As professors, we must listen more and talk less. We must learn how to become our students' guides so that—to some degree at least—they can do it themselves.

That summary paragraph implies a ground change in thinking about the role of the professor in higher education. We will lose some of our epistemic authority if we admit that most students could drive much—or even some—of their own learning. We may seem less essential to the process if we admit that most students actually yearn to learn. But Montessori calls us to these admissions, as have more contemporary thinkers, such as Parker Palmer.[29]

Montessori also reminded us that hands-on learning works. We believe this to be true not only in elementary education but in secondary education and, to our point in this book, in higher education. What good reason can we give for predominantly employing only two senses—seeing and hearing—in how we structure learning and teaching in the Christian college?

God gave us five senses; Montessori challenges us to use them all. Semesters abroad, internships, service projects, and labs obviously fit her vision. But listing those four experiential venues may let those of us who oversee most of the rest of the typical curriculum think the job is done, that we have answered Montessori's challenge when, in fact, the job is not done. Why should the literature class, the political science class, or the history and philosophy of higher education class (to bring the question uncomfortably close to home) not involve the sense of touch? The best professors will seek ways to introduce into students' learning what K–12 mathematics teachers now call *manipulatives*, the kinds of learning materials Montessori fabricated and used a century ago. Perhaps manipulatives are simply too much of a stretch for most university courses. Fair enough. Then we will ask why such courses cannot build upon our students' questions in addition to the canons of the respective academic disciplines.

QUESTIONS FOR REFLECTION AND DISCUSSION

As we do in each chapter in this book, we close with several questions for further reflection and discussion.

- Montessori stressed the importance of understanding our students so we could suit instruction to them for more effective learning. What are the typical characteristics of university students who demonstrate real hunger for learning? What ways can we find to structure our courses and especially our assignments that challenge and allow such students to flourish?
- Montessori believed that students could direct much of their own learning. What strategies can we develop to elicit students' questions both about life in general and about our own courses? What dispositions do we need to develop so that our courses connect with students' day-to-day lives? What curriculum materials and teaching strategies might we use to help them see our courses connect to the issues they face during any given semester?
- Montessori claimed that the learning environment was the third teacher in the classroom. Most professors teach in a variety of rooms.

Most university classrooms are just that: rooms, and those rooms host a variety of different courses in any given day. Does Montessori's point about the environment therefore not apply in higher education? The learning environment, while physical, is also social; it is a space constructed by students and professor together, largely according to the cues given by the professor. What are some ways we can shape a classroom ethos characterized by invitation and hospitality and known as a place where students must come prepared for the hard work of thinking and learning?

- What would the syllabus look like in a course where the professor envisioned such an ethos? What would the assignments be like in such courses?
- Montessori believed in self-correcting curricular materials. Can we design self-correcting curricular materials to reduce the volume of our talking?
- If we want to know who our students are, what observers might we find who could keep us abreast of what our students are watching, hearing, and thinking, and of what pressures they face? Could these be young adults from our own congregations? Websites? Magazines?

Both Tina Fey's *Bossypants* and Amy Poehler's *Yes, Please!* give great insights into our culture as a whole and are recommended readings for anyone wanting to understand our students better. But both women also talk about performing improv (improvised drama).[30] According to these two (unquestioned) experts, one of the key principles in improv is saying *yes*. The actor must follow what her partner has set up. If I point my finger at you and say it's a gun, you can't say it's my finger. It *is* a gun, and you must take the story from there. In our view, Maria Montessori has held up a mirror to higher education and implicitly said that it is boring and unengaging. Many of our students white-knuckle their way through our classes. We must give our yes to Montessori and take the story from there. We end each chapter of *Echoes of Insight* in a hopeful tone. Montessori has done her part. We believe, we hope, that we can do ours.

IN MONTESSORI'S OWN WORDS

Montessori, Maria. *The Absorbent Mind.* New York: Holt, 1995.
———. *The Child in the Church.* 2nd ed. Edited by E. M. Standing. St. Paul, MN: Catechetical Guild, 1965.
———. *The Discovery of the Child.* New York: Ballantine, 1986.
———. *Dr. Montessori's Own Handbook.* New York: Schocken, 1965.
———. "Four Planes of Education" (sometimes "Four Planes of Development"), a lecture given during the Montessori congress in 1938 in Edinburgh and of another given in London in 1939. Amsterdam: International Montessori Association, 1971.
———. *From Childhood to Adolescence.* Translated by the Montessori Educational Research Center. New York: Schocken, 1973.
———. *The Montessori Method* (with Anne E. George). New York: Schocken, 1964.
———. *The Secret of Childhood.* New York: Ballantine, 1982.
———. *To Educate the Human Potential.* Dublin, CLIO, 1989.

BIOGRAPHIES

Kramer, Rita. *Maria Montessori: A Biography.* Boston: Capo Press, 1988.
Standing, E. M. *Maria Montessori: Her Life and Work.* New York: Plume, 1998.
Tennant, S. M. *Maria Montessori.* Minneapolis, MN: Lerner, 1996.

OTHER SELECTED WORKS ABOUT MONTESSORI

Berryman, Jerome W. *The Spiritual Guidance of Children: Montessori, Godly Play, and the Future.* New York: Morehouse, 2013.
———. *Teaching Godly Play: The Sunday Morning Handbook.* Nashville: Abingdon, 1995.
Lillard, Angeline Stoll. *Montessori: The Science behind the Genius.* New York: Oxford University Press, 2005.
Lillard, Paula Polk. *Montessori Today: A Comprehensive Approach to Education from Birth to Adulthood.* New York: Schocken, 1996.
O'Donnell, Marion. *Maria Montessori: A Critical Introduction to Key Themes and Debates.* New York: Bloomsbury, 2013.
Perryman, Lucile, ed. *Montessori in Perspective.* Washington, DC: National Association of the Education of Young Children, 1971.

Rathunde, Kevin. "Montessori Education and Optimal Experience: A Framework for New Research." *NAMTA Journal* 26, no. 1 (2001): 11–43.

Schmid, Jeannine. *Religion, Montessori, and the Home: An Approach to the Religious Education of the Young Child.* 2nd ed. Cincinnati, OH: Benziger, 1969.

NOTES

¹Angeline Stoll Lillard, *Montessori: The Science behind the Genius* (New York: Oxford University Press, 2005); Paula Polk Lillard, *Montessori Today: A Comprehensive Approach to Education from Birth to Adulthood* (New York: Schocken, 1996); Marion O'Donnell, *Maria Montessori: A Critical Introduction to Key Themes and Debates* (New York: Bloomsbury, 2013); Lucile Perryman, ed., *Montessori in Perspective* (Washington, DC: National Association of the Education of Young Children, 1971); E. M. Standing, *Maria Montessori: Her Life and Work* (New York: Plume, 1998); and Florence E. Ward, *The Montessori Method and the American School* (New York: Macmillan, 1913). Also see Ginger L. Zierdt, "Women in History—Maria Montessori," *Journal of Women in Educational Leadership* 5, no. 3 (2007): 159–161. Zierdt stresses Montessori's emphasis on the importance of connecting educational activities meaningfully to life, even if those activities happen in a school building. We deliberately list publications with publishing dates as much as century apart to underline the steady supply of secondary literature on Montessori.

²Throughout her working life, Montessori argued that students naturally want to explore and make sense of their environment. See, for example, *To Educate the Human Potential* (Madras, India: Kalakshetra Publications, 1967), 7–8. Her most central work is *The Montessori Method: Scientific Pedagogy as Applied to Child Education in "the Children's Houses,"* translated by Anne E. George (New York: Frederick A. Stokes, 1912). Also see *The Absorbent Mind* (Madras, India: The Theosophical Publishing House, 1989) and *What You Should Know about Your Child* (Madras, India: Kalakshetra Publications, 1961).

³Maria Montessori, *The Discovery of the Child*, translated by M. J. Costelloe (New York: Ballantine, 1972), 135. In fact, regarding the learning environment, she says that students will learn more than we offer them if we structure the learning environment correctly.

⁴Maria Montessori's lecture, "The Four Planes of Education," is available at http://www.montessoritrainingusa.com/sites/montessoritrainingusa.com/files/The%20Four%20Planes%20of%20Education.pdf. Also see Sarah Werner Andrews' paper, "The Four Planes of Development" (Portland, OR: Montessori Institute Northwest, 2014).

⁵Maria Montessori, *The Child in the Church*, 2nd. ed., edited by E. M. Standing (St. Paul, MN: Catechetical Guild, 1965). Also see the "Religious Education" chapter in *The Discovery of the Child*, 294–301.

⁶See Jerome W. Berryman's *Teaching Godly Play: The Sunday Morning Handbook* (Nashville: Abingdon, 1995), and *The Spiritual Guidance of Children: Montessori, Godly Play, and the Future* (New York: Morehouse, 2013); Sofia Cavalletti, *The Religious Potential of the Child: Experiencing Scripture and Liturgy with Young Children* (Chicago: Liturgy Training Publications, 1992); and Jeannine Schmid, *Religion, Montessori, and the Home: An Approach to the Religious Education of the Young Child*, 2nd ed. (Cincinnati, OH: Benziger, 1969).

⁷William Heard Kilpatrick, *The Montessori System Examined* (New York: Houghton Mifflin, 1914), 63. Interesting that another writer has Montessori ahead of her time; see Britta Schill, "The Montessori System," in Lucile Perryman, ed., *Montessori in Perspective* (Washington, DC: National Association of the Education of Young Children, 1971), 31–37.

⁸Kilpatrick, 65–66.

⁹For example, see Susan A. Ambrose, Michael W. Bridges, Michele DiPietro, Marsha C. Lovett, and Marie K. Norman, *How Learning Works: Seven Research-Based Principles for Smart Teaching* (San Francisco: Jossey-Bass, 2010), especially chapters 1 and 2; M. Weimer, *Inspired College Teaching: A Career-Long Resource for Professional Growth* (San Francisco: Jossey-Bass, 2010); and K. Bain, *What the Best College Teachers Do* (Boston: Harvard University Press, 2004).

¹⁰Search conducted January 28, 2015. Rebecca Shankland, Christophe Genolini, Lionel Riou França, Julien-Daniel Guelfi, and Serban Ionescu, "Student Adjustment to Higher Education: The Role of Alternative Educational Pathways in Coping with the Demands of Student Life," *Higher Education* 59, no. 3 (2010): 353–366, dealt with how well graduates of alternative schools adjusted to university life. The second record is for one portion of a special issue of *NAMTA Journal* (North American Montessori Teachers Association) given over to the development of her method: *Maria Montessori through the Seasons of the "Method."* Paola Trabalzini, "Chapter I: From Childhood to Youth," *NAMTA Journal* 36, no. 2 (2011): 3:15.

¹¹Valerie J. H. Powell, Randall S. Johnson, Christopher T. Davis, John C. Turchek, and James C. Powell, "Designing Hands-On Network Instruction Using Virtualization," paper at the Proceedings of the IADIS International Conference on Cognition & Exploratory Learning in Digital Age, Lisbon, Portugal, December 10–12, 2008, *Proceedings*, 103–112.

¹²Kevin Rathunde, "Montessori Education and Optimal Experience: A Framework for New Research," *NAMTA Journal* 26, no. 1 (2001): 11–43.

¹³Carol S. Woods, "The Montessori Teacher and Bloom's Taxonomy," *Montessori Life* 11, no. 4 (1999): 43–45.

¹⁴Ann E. Berthoff, "Tolstoy, Vygotsky, and the Making of Meaning," *College Composition and Communication* 29, no. 3 (1978): 249–255.

¹⁵Maria Montessori, *From Childhood to Adolescence*, translated by the Montessori Educational Research Center (New York: Schocken, 1973), 129–140.

¹⁶Ibid., 129.

¹⁷Ibid., 131.

¹⁸Ibid., 133.

¹⁹For this clever linguistic contribution to our work, we thank Bruce Erickson of Tacoma, Washington.

²⁰*The Discovery of the Child*, 135.

²¹Ibid., 137.

²²Ibid., 138.

²³Historically, many have discussed the forms of knowledge and knowledge production from dramatically different viewpoints. Philosophical treatments include those by E. Hindess, "Forms of Knowledge," *Proceedings of the Philosophy of Education Society of Great Britain* 6, no. 2 (1972): 164–175; Paul Hirst, *Knowledge and the Curriculum: A Collection of Philosophical Papers* (Boston: Routledge & Kegan Paul, 1974); and D. C. Philips, "The Distinguishing Features of the Forms of Knowledge," *Educational Philosophy and Theory* 3 no. 2 (1971): 27–35. More critical views have appeared from various quarters, especially sociology or education and critical theory.

²⁴John Dewey, *Democracy and Education* (Champaign, IL: University of Illinois, 1916), 257-258.

²⁵Stephen M. Corey put this well: "In the last analysis it is the way the learner organizes his own experience that counts rather than the organization imposed by other

people upon the subject-matter the student learns." See "Psychological Foundations of General Education," in *General Education*, ed. Stanley Elam (Chicago: Rand-McNally, 1964), 222. See also David Elkind, "Montessori and Constructivism," *Montessori Life* 15, no. 1 (2003): 26–29.

[26] David P. Ausubel, "Some Psychological Aspects of the Structure of Knowledge," in *Education and the Structure of Knowledge*, ed. Stanley Elam (Chicago: Rand-McNally, 1964), 222.

[27] Many academics use citation indexes and such services as Google alerts to track the popularity of their own work. So the crowd intelligence that we caution about here may be closer to home than we in the academy naturally want to admit.

[28] Susan Sontag, "Notes on Camp," *Partisan Review* 14 (1964): 515–530.

[29] Parker Palmer, *To Know as We Are Known: Education as a Spiritual Journey* (New York: HarperOne, 1993).

[30] Tina Fey, *Bossypants* (New York: Little, Brown, 2011); Amy Poehler, *Yes, Please!* (New York: Dey Street, 2014).

PART 2

The Faculty and the Administration

Mission, Vision, and Values

John Henry Newman

The Rise and Progress of Universities (1872)

(First Published as Office and Work of Universities—1856)

JOHN HENRY NEWMAN IS THE MOST RECOGNIZABLE FIGURE COVERED in Part Two of this book, and without doubt he is also the most influential thinker about higher education. His series of lectures, published in 1852 under the title *The Idea of a University*, remains one of the most powerful and enduring arguments for the value of the liberal arts ever given in any form. He is still quoted today. And in his own time, he became a noted, albeit controversial, figure through his preaching at St. Mary's Church in Oxford, through his leadership of the Tractarian movement (also known as the Oxford movement, calling the Church of England back to its essential mission), through his much-publicized decision to leave the Anglican Church and embrace Roman Catholicism (he was raised to the College of Cardinals in 1879), through his prolific writing and speaking, and through his work to establish a Catholic university in Dublin. Even though that effort was largely a failure and a major personal embarrassment, his writings during that period have much to say to those of us who care about faith-based universities today. It is some of these writings that we will examine and discuss in this chapter, but we will first look at some of the shaping events in the life and times of John Henry Newman.

Education and Professional Life

Certainly, Newman lived an extraordinary life, yet he saw himself as simply an ordinary person trying to follow Jesus. In fact, in his sermons and speeches, his message was that one advances on the Christian pilgrimage by daily doing ordinary things in extraordinary ways. According to Lawrence Cunningham, that explains why Newman used such words as regularity, steadfastness, faith, obedience, and fidelity, to name just a few, on so many occasions.[1] As you will see in what follows, the cumulative impact of the many ordinary events in his life was indeed extraordinary.

Childhood and Boarding School

John Henry Newman was born in London on February 21, 1801. His father, John, was a banker, and his mother, Jemima, came from a papermaking family. From his mother, John Henry learned to love the Bible, having memorized several chapters by age seven and read through the entire King James Bible at age eight.[2] For all of his life, he dedicated at least an hour each day to reading the Bible and memorizing Scripture passages. From his father, he learned to love music and Shakespeare, by age ten preferring Mozart and Beethoven to Brahms and Mendelssohn—and he learned to play the violin, which he played throughout his life in good times and bad.[3]

When Newman was seven years old, his family sent him to the boarding school in Ealing, where for the next eight years, he studied, acted in Latin plays, practiced the violin, won speech contests, and edited periodicals, "for which he wrote articles in the style of Addison."[4] During his final year at Ealing, Newman found it necessary to stay at school over the holidays, and he fell seriously ill (one of the three serious illnesses he would suffer during the course of his life—each with spiritual consequences). The combination of being alone, being sick, being away from home, being worried about his father's failing business, and being influenced by his reading of Thomas Scott's *The Force of Truth* led him to what he called his first conversion, a conscious inward assent to the truth of an indwelling God that would last throughout his life. He also left Ealing with the sense that it was the will of God that he would lead a single life.[5] It was indeed a transformative holiday.

Oxford

The decision for Newman to attend Oxford[6] or Cambridge was made by Newman's father on the front doorstep of their house with a carriage waiting. The driver asked for the destination. After some hesitation, he said, "Oxford." Newman settled into Trinity College, and after a year of study as a commoner, he won a scholarship—nine years at sixty pounds a year. Nearing graduation, Newman sat for the university degree examination, hoping to receive firsts with honors. Instead, he received a lower second class in classics and a failure in mathematics. This performance was totally devastating, not to say embarrassing. Newman spent the next year trying to recover, something he talked about with remorse until the very end of his life. However, he had some years on his scholarship left, so he continued his studies and entered the competition for the Oriel Fellowship, one of the most prestigious awards in Oxford, and much to everyone's surprise (including his own), he won.

It was the day that Newman came of age; he was now a fellow of Oriel.[7] He had no other desire than to live and die a fellow at Oriel. He was ordained priest in the Church of England in 1822, appointed college tutor at Oriel, named select preacher to the university in 1826, and named vicar of St. Mary's Church in 1828. He was a popular and powerful preacher, garnering a strong following among students and colleagues alike. At the height of his Oxford career in 1832, he embarked on a continental tour with a friend and fell seriously ill in Sicily. It was a nearly fatal illness, and it led to a second deep religious experience. During his convalescence, he became convinced that God had something important in store for him to do back in England, but what it was, he did not know. It was enough for him to have light for the next step; he did not need to know the entire journey. As he embarked from Sicily on an orange-boat sailing for Marseilles, Newman penned a poem, "The Pillar of the Cloud," to that effect. The first line read "Lead, Kindly Light," and it became one of the most beloved hymns in the English-speaking world:

> Lead, Kindly Light, amidst the encircling gloom,
> Lead Thou me on!
> The night is dark, and I am far from home,
> Lead Thou me on!
> Keep Thou my feet; I do not ask to see
> The distant scene; one step enough for me.

When he finally reached England, what God had in mind for his next step became clear to him in less than a week.

The very next Sunday, his friend John Keble preached a sermon that became known as "National Apostasy." It was a fiery condemnation of state interference in church matters from without and a denunciation of the liberal influences causing indifference to the traditions and spirituality from within.[8] In response, a small band of brothers came together and decided to do something about it. What resulted was a series of tracts that pressed these concerns and pushed for change. Strong and energetic preaching by Newman and others reinforced the message of the tracts. These activities became known as the Tractarian (or Oxford) movement, running from 1833–1841. Of course, this movement was not always kind to or supportive of the powers that be in church or state. Developments finally came to a head in 1841 with Newman's (in)famous Tract 90. In effect, Newman argued that the Anglican Church and the Roman Catholic Church were not all that far apart, coming from the same roots and sharing essentially the same beliefs. What resulted was a veritable firestorm. Newman, under pressure from the bishop of Oxford, stopped publication of the tracts and retired from public life. In 1843, he resigned as vicar of St. Mary's Church in Oxford and gave up his parish responsibilities to the village of Littlemore the following year, leaving his robe on the church altar. On October 9, 1845, he was received into the Roman Catholic Church. It was neither a quick nor an easy decision. He had spent the first forty-five years of his life as an Anglican; he would spend the next forty-five as a Roman Catholic.

Rome

Of course, Newman's conversion was big news in England and throughout Europe; some took the news with surprise and elation, and others with a sense of relief and a hearty "good riddance!" In spite of all his notoriety, he was a constant critic and thorn in the side for both university and church. For Newman, it was on to Rome for study and ordination, and then back to England in 1849 to establish the country's first oration house just outside of Birmingham, modeled after the one founded by St. Philip Neri in the sixteenth century. According to Cunningham, "The Oratory consists of a community of diocesan priests who take no special vows, but who live in community with the express purpose of administering the sacraments, preaching, teaching catechism, and ministering to the surrounding community. Each Oratory has its own elected superior and operates more or less independently."[9] This model of communal life, something similar to his beloved Oxford, captured Newman's imagination and energies.

He would have been happy to spend the rest of his days there, but that was not to be. In April 1851, the Irish bishops, at the suggestion of the Pope, asked for Newman's assistance in establishing a Catholic university in Ireland. He hesitantly agreed to be the founding rector, and as it turned out, his reluctance was justified. His halting steps led him directly into the path of a growing controversy that he could not evade, resolve, or ultimately survive.

Dublin

When Newman accepted Archbishop Cullen's invitation to become rector of the Catholic University in Dublin, they agreed that a series of public lectures was in order. In essence, they needed to drum up support for the establishment of the university. On the face of it, this seems rather odd. Why would a predominantly Catholic city have to be convinced that they needed a Catholic university? This is perhaps the first question that Newman should have asked. Apparently, he did not, trusting instead in the wisdom of the church hierarchy. So in 1852, Newman delivered a set of five lectures to address three fundamental questions: why have a Catholic university in Ireland; why a liberal arts education rather than professional and vocation training; and what is the relationship of secular subjects such as literature, history, and science to the religious teachings and authority of the church? These lectures were originally published as pamphlets then brought together, along with some other writings, and published in 1873 under the title *The Idea of a University*. It is this book that is most familiar to and influential among higher educators today, whether in faith-based institutions or public universities. It is Newman's lasting achievement from his time in Dublin.

The plans for a university did not fare so well. It finally opened in 1854 with only twenty students. For Newman, it was one problem after another. Archbishop Cullen did not trust Newman and often ignored his requests for assistance and direction. The bishops did not trust the archbishops, and they did not trust each other. None of the Irish church leaders trusted the English, and the Irish laity trusted neither Newman nor the church hierarchy. They were happy to send their children to Trinity. And because it was the church that held the purse strings, Newman found himself a beggar far too often. Newman complicated all of this by his basic ignorance of Irish politics and culture, his lack of administrative expertise, his hiring of fellow Englishmen for faculty positions, and his long absences from Dublin to attend to affairs back in Birmingham. During his seven years as rector, he made over sixty trips back to England. Most of these visits lasted between six weeks and three months.[10] In addition, Newman dreamed of an Oxford-style Catholic university for the entire English-speaking world, while the bishops wanted a distinctly Irish university, and the working class laity wanted vocational preparation for their children rather than an education for gentlemen destined for high society.

As you can see, all of this produced a prescription for disaster, and a disaster it became. Newman finally resigned his position in 1858 and returned to the Oratory in England, having decided that the Dublin adventure had been simply a horrible experience. Looking back, he thought "he ought never to have accepted the rectorship in the first place without the full confidence of all the Irish Archbishops, without the formal participation of the English bishops, without lay control of the finances, and without mutual agreement on the length of his annual residence in Dublin and the term of his rectorship."[11] In the end, it is doubtful that even meeting these conditions would have guaranteed success. Clearly, the Dublin project needed someone younger and more in tune with the local sentiments and church politics. And above all, it needed an Irish rector who could win the hearts and minds of the Catholic laity if they were to make a go of it. Newman confessed late in life that he felt the pope had made a serious mistake in trying to start a Catholic university in Dublin. There were other ways to proceed. All of this brought about a modification in his understanding of papal infallibility.

England

Back in England, Newman continued his engagement with the Oratory in Birmingham and remained active in church affairs and with his own writing, including the publication of *Apologia Pro Vita Sua*, a volume that received international acclaim as a theological autobiography. Late in life, honors and invitations came his way. He was made an honorary fellow of Trinity College (Oxford) in 1878 and was raised to the College of Cardinals the following year. In 1880, he returned to Oxford after a thirty-five-year absence to preach in the Jesuit church there. This was a high honor. He had often seen the spires from the train as he traveled from Birmingham to London, but he never thought that he would preach in the city again. John Henry Newman died at the Oratory on August 10, 1890.

The Rise and Progress of Universities

The "Dublin Discourses" in 1852 would eventually become *The Idea of the University*, the most prominent and enduring aspect of Newman's work in Ireland. However, as the university opened its doors in 1854, it began a small periodical called the *Catholic University Gazette*. Newman was the primary writer for this publication. In it, he wrote about the historical development of universities. These essays were gathered and published in one volume in 1856 with the title *Office and Work of Universities*, later renamed *Rise and Progress of Universities* (in the 1872 edition). Notre Dame Professor Emerita Mary Katherine Tillman writes in the introduction to the 1991 edition that *Rise and Progress of Universities* is Newman's "most engaging work on higher education." She says it is "the ingenious story of the organic growth and historical development of what may be called 'the university venture' in the West. And this story is told according to the shifting patterns and inflections of those two preemptory powers, influence and discipline."[12] We certainly agree. We will summarize six of Newman's essays in this section before we add our commentary and offer questions for reflection and discussion.

Chapter 15: Professors and Tutors

In this delightful essay, Newman picks up and expands on his primary argument: "A University embodies the principal [sic] of progress, and a College that of stability; the one is the sail, and the other the ballast; each is insufficient in itself for the pursuit, extension, and inculcation of knowledge; each is useful to the other."[13] For the university is susceptible to many evils and can easily lose its integrity. Newman argues that to avoid this undesirable result, both an energetic professorial system (lectures) and the college (residence and guidance) are needed. "I admire the Professorial, I venerate the College. The Professorial system fulfils the strict idea of a University, and is sufficient for its *being*, but it is not sufficient for its *well-being*. Colleges constitute the *integrity* of the University."[14] Interestingly, in Newman's view, it is the college that the church *uses* in a university to achieve her sacred objectives. We will discuss this view of the connections between faith and learning in the following section.

To make his case, Newman describes the dreadful and disgraceful living conditions in which students, often poor and lacking both local knowledge and common sense, live when they arrive at the university. "They lodge in garrets or cellars, or they share a room with others; they mix with the inhabitants of the place, who, if not worse, at least will not be better than the run of mankind. A man must either be a saint or an enthusiast to be affected in no degree by the disadvantages of such a mode of living."[15] Obviously, he makes a strong case for a residential system.

And for Newman, the professorial system has its own dangers. Lecturers are prone to a certain pride of intellect, poor reasoning, and the intoxication of applause. It is a heady cocktail. He notes that the professor "may suffer from the popularity of his gift, and, then, the hearer from its fascination."[16] To make his case, he tells the story of Simon of Tournay, a famous thirteenth-century Parisian professor, who "one day proved in a lecture by such powerful arguments, the divinity of Christianity, that his students burst out into admiration of his ability. On this he cried out, 'Ha, good Jesus; I could, if I chose, refute Thee quite well.' The story goes on to say that he was immediately struck dumb."[17] We could name more than one provost who would wish the same consequences for such behavior today.

Newman's second argument against a system comprised entirely of lectures is that it makes no place for the influence of the church. For him, the three vital principles of the Christian student are faith, chastity, and love, but without nurture and discipline, they easily revert to their contraries—unbelief or heresy, impurity, and enmity—which are the three great sins against God, against neighbor, and against ourselves.

Newman's argument is not that the professorial system is unnecessary but that it loses its integrity if that is all there is. It is necessarily incomplete. "I have been saying that regularity, rule, respect for others, the eye of friends and acquaintances, the absence from temptation, external restraints generally, are of first importance in protecting us against ourselves."[18] In addition, students need an intellectual and moral guide, a Sherpa for the journey. All of this can be accomplished, according to Newman, by residence in a smaller community within the university where tutors work on behalf of the church and the university.

Newman concludes his essay by cataloging the merits of living in college. "Here, his diligence will be steadily stimulated; he will be kept up to his aim; his progress will be ascertained; and his week's work, like a laborer's, measured. It is not easy for a young man to determine for himself whether he has mastered what he has been taught; a careful catechetical training, and a jealous scrutiny into his power of expressing himself and of turning his knowledge to account, will be necessary, if he is really to profit from the able Professors whom he is attending; and all this he will gain from the College Tutor."[19] In the end, of course, both professors and tutors are essential for the integrity of a university education, but if Newman were forced to choose, he would choose the formative residential experience over a system of lectures and examinations.[20] For better or for worse, higher education today is steadily moving in the opposite direction.

Chapter 16: Abelard

In the preceding essay, Newman argues that the university (with professors) is sufficient for *being* of a university, but colleges (with tutors) are needed for its *well-being*, for its integrity. In this essay, Newman uses Abelard, the best-known and perhaps the greatest intellect of the early medieval university period, as an example to drive home this point. It could have been titled "The Rise and Fall of Abelard," for rise and fall he did.

Newman tells how Abelard first studied under, and then took on and destroyed, his teacher William of Champeaux. After doing so, Abelard set up his own school, and students from around Europe flocked to hear him teach. Newman points out that Abelard was totally committed to the new learning, and this single-mindedness was an intellectual flaw: "The calm philosophical mind, which contemplates parts without denying the whole, and the whole without confusing the parts, is notoriously indisposed to action; whereas single and simple views arrest the mind, and hurry it on to carry them out.... It is not wonderful that Abelard's devotion to the new philosophy made him undervalue the Seven Arts out of which it had grown."[21] One of the results of this rush for the new, according to Newman, was that a broader appreciation—wisdom, if you will—was forfeited: "But now, another teaching was coming in; students were promised truth in a nutshell; they intended to get possession of the sum-total of philosophy in less than two or three years."[22] For Newman, there are no shortcuts based on slick techniques; learning requires time and effort.

So by Newman's account, Abelard's downfall started with a lack of respect for his teacher and mentor, and was accelerated by his single-mindedness, demonstrating a certain lack of respect for the scope and depth of the learning tradition as well. However, as Newman puts it, these are really lesser matters. The big problem for Abelard was his inability to control the twin sisters—the desire to rise in the world and blind ambition: "Now came the time of his greatest popularity, which was more than his head could bear; which dizzied him, took him off his legs and whirled him to his destruction.... His eloquence was wonderful; he dazzled his contemporaries ... by the brilliancy of his genius.... People came to him from all quarters.... (However) it was too much for a weak head and heart, weak in spite of intellectual power; for vanity will possess the head, and worldliness the heart, of a man, however gifted, whose wisdom is not an effluence of the Eternal Light."[23]

The career of so great an intellect was so miserably thrown away, according to Newman. He closes this essay by quoting the words of Grotius on his deathbed: "*Heu, vitam perdidi, operose nihil agendo.*"[24] Of course, the message threaded throughout this essay is that Abelard and all of us would be well served to attend a university with integrity, where intellectual promise and character are both nurtured. We agree.

Chapter 17: The Ancient University of Dublin

In this chapter, Newman traces the largely failed efforts to establish an ancient university in Dublin. He begins by distinguishing between primitive and medieval institutions—later institutions began to specialize in disciplines, and hospitality was offered to laity as well as clergy and to foreigners as well as locals. One result was a migration of Irish students to England and Paris. However, Irish students studying abroad encountered myriad difficulties, ongoing feuds, incessant broils, loneliness, and the dangers of travel, to name just a few. In 1311, John Lecke, archbishop of Dublin, responding to these difficulties, obtained a charter from Clement the Fifth to establish the University of Dublin. In doing so, the Holy See foresaw the following benefits: the nurture for learned sons who would "investigate the divine law, protect justice and truth, illustrate the faith, promote good government, teach the ignorant, confirm the weak, and restore the faith."[25] Unfortunately, as Newman observes, "the parties, who had originated the undertaking, had also to carry it out. . . . (Unfortunately) John Lecke fell ill and died the next year."[26] This event set initial efforts back for several decades, and the institution languished, in and out of operation, for the next several hundred years. As Newman notes, "the time has passed when Universities grew up out of the enthusiasm of teachers and the curiosity and eagerness of students."[27] Now, a steady flow of resources, both financial support and students, are requisite for sustainability. In our own time, some local churches and pastors dream of starting their own university or college, many times because they perceive a lack of commitment or even downright theological error in the established institutions around them.[28] We commend the words of Newman as a caution to them; it takes more than enthusiasm and eagerness to start a viable university today.

One question remains. Why would the rector of the fledgling Catholic University in Ireland write such a piece about the dismal record of attempts to start a Catholic institution in Ireland for the *Catholic University Gazette* in 1856? Newman concludes this essay with the observation that times have changed. Ireland is no longer under the cruelty of a foreign king; Ireland is now the center of a great Catholic movement. There is currently a worldwide missionary effort focused on Ireland, and the Holy See is taking the initiative rather than simply responding to other people's desires. In other words, now is the time, after centuries of frustration, to succeed at last. Please send funds and send your children!

Chapter 18: Colleges the Corrective of Universities

Colleges predate universities. In many respects, they are simply continuations of cathedral schools that preceded the rise of universities. And of course, long before the cathedral schools, colleges were a part of the Museum at Alexandria and the Saracen schools at Cordova, Granada, and Malaga. In essence, according to Newman, the most helpful metaphor for a college is *home,* a refuge of helpless boyhood, a providential shelter of the weak and inexperienced, a place of elementary studies, and a "place of training for those who are not only ignorant, but have not yet learned how to learn, and who have to be taught, by careful individual trial, how to set about profiting by the lessons of a teacher."[29] A truly remarkable place, indeed!

Unlike universities that have a national or international purview, colleges tend to be more local, attracting boarders who speak the same language or hail from the same region. And colleges are for the poor student, another difference from universities, which tend over time to gravitate toward and address the concerns and wishes of the rich and powerful. As such, colleges provide a counterbalance, a place where people rather than politics matter most.

Newman goes on to describe the representative daily schedule of a student at college: "He got up between four and five; from five to six he assisted at Mass, and heard an exhortation. He then studied or attended schools till ten, which was the dinner hour. The meal, which seems also to be breakfast, was not sumptuous; it consisted of beef, in small messes for four persons, and a pottage make of its gravy and oatmeal. From dinner to five p.m., he either studied, or gave instruction to other students, when he went to supper, which was the principal meal of the day, though scarcely more plentiful than dinner. Afterwards, problems were discussed and other studies pursued, till nine or ten; and then half an hour was devoted to walking or running about, that they might not go to bed with cold feet; the expedient of hearth or stove for the purpose was out of the question." Newman quickly adds, "However, poor as was the fare, the collegiate life was a blessing in many other ways far more important than eat or drink."[30] Without the college, poor students would be at the mercy of the moral evils of the town, and of their own naïveté.

Here, Newman is making a strong case for the residential college that was the centerpiece of the Catholic University in Ireland. His clientele, primarily working-class Catholics in Ireland, needed encouragement and justification for sending their children to Dublin. Newman recognized this need for encouragement and justification, and he set out to provide these in this, and the next, essay.

Chapter 19: Abuses of the Colleges

In this essay, Newman directly attacks the English universities, especially Oxford. In typical form, he first waxes eloquently about the great contrast and partnership of university and college: "The University is for the world, and the College is for the nation. The University is for the Professor, and the College is for the Tutor; the University is for the philosophical discourse, the eloquent sermon, or the well-contested disputation; and the College for the catechetical lecture. The University is for theology, law, and medicine, for natural history, for physical science, and for the sciences generally and their promulgation; the College is for the formation of character, intellectual and moral, for the cultivation of the mind, for the improvement of the individual, for the study of literature, for the classics, and those rudimental sciences which strengthen and sharpen the intellect. . . . It would seem as if an [*sic*] University seated and living in Colleges, would be the perfect institution, as possessing excellences of opposite kinds."[31] Sadly, Newman cautions, such a partnership is extremely rare . . . and does not even exist at Oxford!

Oxford colleges have large, independent endowments and influential alumni, too, reaching to every part of the country. So if the college is under attack, the alumni will quickly and forcefully rally to her side. The result is that the Oxford colleges do not yield to or care about public opinion, university regulation, or political pressure. Piling on, Newman adds: "The Colleges, left to themselves, in the course of the last century became shamefully indolent and inactive. They were in no sense any longer places of education; they were for the most part mere clubs, and sinecures, and almshouses, where the inmates did little but enjoy themselves."[32] Degrees were given without examinations. Instead, the student merely chose his examiners, invited them to dinner, and paid for the evening. And some societies and houses, without any legal standing, supported themselves by taking in incompetent, idle, and riotous students who were denied admission or expelled from other colleges. And the university could do little about it.

Thus, the essay ends with a not-so-subtle implication: better to send your children to the Catholic University in Ireland where the college culture is alive and well, but under the umbrella of the university structure. Newman knew this to be true because he personally oversaw both systems.

Chapter 20: Universities and Seminaries

The *Catholic University Gazette* was the public relations instrument for Newman's university. As such, he always had something in mind when he wrote about excesses at Oxford, Peter Abelard, or the Ancient University of Dublin. But what does Newman have in mind with this final essay on universities and seminaries? Honestly, at times it is hard to tell, but as you will see, he begins with a historical sketch and masterfully closes with an affirmation of his present work.

In Newman's own words, "Seminaries then were long in possession before Universities were imagined; and Universities rose out of them"[33] (to provide an education for the laity). And universities grew in such strength that they "drained away the life of the institution which had given them birth."[34] Young students who would previously have attended a seminary were now sent to a university where they would develop a critical, carping, curious spirit, certainly not a spirit becoming of an ecclesiastic or one that would aid in interpreting the difficulties of Scripture or the deep questions of theology.

Newman leaves this discussion for the moment and turns to another—colleges that claimed the privileges of universities; that is, they erected a university in the college. The problem is that these colleges did not have the resources to back up their claims. For Newman, "in order to teach well, more must be learned by the teacher than he has formally to impart to the pupil; that he must be above his work, and know, and know accurately and philosophically, what he does not actually profess."[35] The same holds true for institutions that claim to be more—more is then expected, too.

In closing, Newman reflects on the humble beginnings of many faithful institutions (including his own) and suggests that it is pleasant to live in a day when the tide is coming in for Catholic higher education. The church is strong enough now, he claims, to provide both resources and safeguards for her institutions. And the Catholic University in Ireland is following the faithful path of the university at Louvain, "proving its possibility by entering on its work, and presaging its future success by its triumph over the difficulties of its commencement."[36] Newman's message to the faithful is simply this: The Catholic University of Ireland has retained its religious foundations, so it will care for her students as a mother cares for her children, and although now struggling, it will one day ride the tide to full eminence as a university of the first class. To do so, however, financial support and students are needed, and needed now!

Unfortunately, by the time he wrote this, Newman was already contemplating his resignation as rector and did so less than two years later. Sadly, the idea of the Catholic University of Ireland that Newman spoke of so eloquently never became a reality. Newman returned to England for good . . . perplexed, frustrated, and brokenhearted.

Key Arguments and Corollary Implications

We trust you enjoyed reading about Newman's mid–nineteenth-century attempt at public relations and fund-raising. We are both fond of the medieval university, but to our knowledge, its history has never been used as a centerpiece of a marketing campaign and branding effort to promote the development of a fledgling university. And of course, it was not a successful one. Nonetheless, Newman raises many valuable insights in the *Catholic University Gazette*. We will highlight five of them here before we offer some questions for reflection and discussion.

Success and Failure

Scholars have debated over the years about the success of Newman's efforts in Dublin. Certainly, the fact that his writings still inform discussions about the mission and scope of universities over 150 years later indicates some sort of success for his work there. Still, the institution struggled from the very beginning and did not grow and develop as Newman envisioned, and he resigned and left with a bad taste in his mouth. In that sense, his idea did not become a reality. Was it a failure?

We offer three comments: First, perhaps to ask about success and failure is to ask the wrong question. As we see it, no president or academic leader achieves all that is dreamed or planned. Not one. Yet much importance is given to one's administrative record: buildings built, funds raised, programs started, cash accumulated, faculty hired, and students enrolled. To the extent that these are significant, we know that such results are never the doing of just one person, although we see that credit for such collective efforts is often singularly taken. Perhaps the right question is really about being faithful: faithful to the integrity of the institution, faithful to those who serve and study there, and faithful to the God in whom we live and move and have our being.

Second, the cards were stacked against Newman from the very beginning. In hindsight, he realized that he had walked into a situation where he could not succeed. He was not the first and will not be the last to do so. Sometimes in our eagerness to be faithful, we work too hard to make the pieces fit. We overlook or minimize the real difficulties that are inherent in the assignment. This is where the discerning ear of a spiritual director or a close friend or two can be so very helpful. And when we are being wooed to consider an important move or new assignment, it is easy for our egos to cloud our good judgments. Not every opportunity is a good one, no matter the status or money that may accompany it.

Finally, if you find yourself in a situation that is constantly hurtful, frustrating, or demeaning, it is time to hit the reset button and move on. Learning new strokes to swim upstream is useful; but if the stream is toxic, it is time to get out of the water and go elsewhere. To do so is not a failure.

Genius Loci—The Spirit of a Place

In classical Roman religion, *genius loci* were protective or guardian spirits. Newman had something different in mind—the prevailing character or atmosphere of a place, the college experience. While students are a bit more transient, faculty and staff tend to form a more stable body, and within this body certain beliefs, values, commitments, practices, and ways of being emerge. If you will, a wisdom community takes shape, and it shapes both long-term members and students alike. Every faith-based institution has, we observe, a distinctive wisdom community, perhaps even more than one. The local practice of hospitality, the pursuit of truth, and the embrace of covenant will shape each particular wisdom community because each wisdom community understands and practices these shaping influences differently.[37] And there is a local history of each particular institution, too, involving place, personalities, and the peculiarities of the dominant religious tradition.

Newman saw the profound effect that residence had on students, and we do, too. As mentioned earlier, he would take residence over examinations any day as an educational format. We wonder if in the attempt to be competitive, to be marketable, and to be cost effective, we have sacrificed something very important in our educational practice and promise. Even in our adult degree programs and online coursework, we believe that it is possible, in fact necessary, to rethink the idea of residency and insist upon some form of it for all our students. Of course, we realize that the answer will not be a physical residency in a dorm somewhere on campus, but residence nonetheless. Every graduate, it seems to us, should experience in one way or another the prevailing character of a particular place.[38] We believe that faith-based institutions are wise enough to figure out how to do this, and it will be a life-giving undertaking for students and faculty alike—and not to be cynical, but it will be good branding, too.

Collegiate versus Professorial Functions

What is the difference between a college and a university in the United States? Answer: not much; in most cases, the institution gets to choose the designation. In contemporary higher education, it is honestly more about branding than it is about the reality of the product or the scope or quality of the academic programs. More likely than not, the university designation will soon be applied to all four-year institutions, regardless of mission, size, or intent, leaving the college moniker for specialty and two-year institutions.

Newman argues that both are necessary for the integrity of the institution. Without the professorial (university) functions, the institution is adrift without a sail. It lacks energy, scope, innovation, and a forward lean. But while these qualities or properties are sufficient for *being* a university, they are not enough to ensure its *well-being*. For all of us, this is a significant point. Newman is advocating for a rich educational experience, one that involves not only stimulating teaching and scholarly research, but also character formation and vocational understanding. Here we use the term *vocational* to mean a sense of calling, not the pursuit of the particular trade or skill. As we like to think about it, we do not just teach; we teach, shape, and send. Such intent will require an institution with integrity, one that is university in scope and quality, and collegial in character and ethos. We truly believe that faith-based institutions are at a real advantage in this regard and that this possibility offers one of the most compelling and competitive branding strategies for institutions in today's markets. We have something very special to offer.

Professorial Pride

Honestly, we believe that being a professor is one of the most fulfilling ways to live a simple, sincere, and serene life. If you can learn to live within your means and refrain from overloads and summer teaching, it is truly one of the best jobs around. Certainly, we trade money for time, but the benefits of such a life are almost incalculable.

However, being a faculty member can have a hard side, too. Newman points out that it is possible for professors to be dizzied by student praise and popularity, intoxicated by their applause. Trouble is headed your way when you start believing your own press clippings. And Newman points out that a lack of humility and hospitality for other ideas can lead to single-mindedness, the state of mind where you believe that you are always right and all your colleagues are usually wrong (or their ideas do not matter).

Abelard suffered from this malady, and we can name a few of our own colleagues, past and present, who fit the bill. Ultimately, such behavior undermines the collegial nature of the institution. And students see it, too. While ardent followers early on, many students distance themselves from these professors as they mature in discernment and outlook. At the end of the day, humility and hospitality will remain shaping influences for students and colleagues alike.

Church and University

Newman makes it clear in *The Idea of the University* that the university is not the church. While enlightened instruction can lead a student along the path toward God, it is ultimately God who saves souls, often through the agency of the church. The ultimate goal of higher learning is wisdom. We have heard it said that the university is the church at work in higher education. While it makes for a good sound bite, we fear that it confuses the matter just a bit. Of course, religious institutions and their sponsoring church, denomination, or tradition are intimately related, but they have different missions. We once heard a university trustee say, "I don't care if our students learn anything at all, as long as they leave with a love for Jesus." While we hope that all our students leave with a deep and growing faith, we would count it a failure if they left without learning anything. As Newman points out, the mission of the university is to pursue truth, and there is certainly more to truth than faith in God, however important such faith may be.

For Newman, the university falls under the auspices of the church—the church is over the university. We know of many trustees who see this same relationship. Others understand the church and university to be equal partners, and still others see the church and university as neighbors, living close by but independent from one another.[39] Of course, there is no single correct kind of relationship for all institutions, but it is critical that the trustees and those in institutional leadership on any particular campus be clear about how the relationship works. We know of more than one institutional difficulty caused by different constituent groups who use identical language but talk past each other. In the end, an institution needs to be clear about governance, and trouble raises its ugly head when lines of authority and accountability are misunderstood.

We have highlighted five matters, all of which build toward Newman's ultimate concern for the integrity of the university, for its well-being. In response to his work and concern, we offer the following questions to spur reflection and discussion about the integrity of your institution.

QUESTIONS FOR REFLECTION AND DISCUSSION

Success and Failure

- Some have characterized Newman's academic career as a pretentious failure, and others as a glowing success. How do you appraise Newman's career? How do you define success in your own work?
- Newman realized that he simply could not do what he was charged to do in Dublin, and he eventually resigned. Is there an aspect of your work where it is time to hit the reset button? If so, can you do so without feeling like a failure?
- Newman came to understand that institutional viability requires more than a compelling "idea" and a well-written PR magazine to be viable; it needs resources and students, too. Are your institution's resources sufficient to keep the promises made by your marketing and recruitment efforts? In short, can you live up to your recruiting brochures?

Genius Loci—The Spirit of a Place

- How would you describe the genius loci, the character or atmosphere, of your institution? What might be done to articulate and focus its formative influence?
- Newman was committed to doing ordinary things in extraordinary ways. What ordinary things at your institution are done in extraordinary ways?
- Is it time to rethink residence at your institution? How might residence be creatively instituted as a part of all your academic programs, including adult and online programs?

Collegiate versus Professorial Functions
- How do you see the professorial and collegiate functions working together in your institution? Newman argued that both are necessary for institutional integrity. Do you agree? What might be done to rebalance these functions?
- We have suggested that we do not just teach; rather, we teach, shape, and send. Does this resonate with your understanding of the mission of Christian higher education and with your own academic work?

Professorial Pride
- As it turns out, John Henry Newman was a bit of a pain for the officers of his church and university, constantly challenging the current state of affairs and agitating for change, sometimes to go forward and sometimes to go back. What is the proper way to proceed if you are a member of the loyal opposition?[40] Could your institution improve the way it deals with criticism?
- What are the best ways to avoid the heady and dizzying consequences of professorial worship by students? We noted that such worship usually ends up in disillusionment. Is this a problem at your institution?

Church and University
- How is the relationship between church and university understood at your institution? Is it mutually supportive or problematic?
- When Newman wrote, "I do not ask to see the distant scene; one step enough for me," he was making a statement about the clarity of his calling—to see one step ahead was plenty. How about you? How clear is the path before you? For your institution? Is the tide coming in or going out?

FOR FURTHER STUDY NEWMAN'S OWN WORKS

Newman was such a prolific writer and a meticulous keeper of notes and records that it would be a daunting task to list here all his works; it would also be unnecessary, given the good work of various Newman scholars and centers with robust websites. For example, see the Newman Reader for access to most of Newman's writings: http://www.newmanreader.org/. We do want to highlight the following:

Newman, John Henry. *Apologia Pro Vita Sua*. London: Penguin, 1994 (originally 1873).
———. *Autobiographical Writings*. Edited by Henry Tristam. New York: Sheed and Ward, 1957.
———. *An Essay in Aid of a Grammar of Assent*, Introduction by Nicholas Lash. Notre Dame, IN: University of Notre Dame Press, 1979.
———. *Fifteen Sermons Preached before the University of Oxford*. 3rd ed. Introduction by Mary Katherine Tillman. Notre Dame, IN: University of Notre Dame Press, 1996.
———. *The Idea of the University*. Edited by Frank M. Turner. New Haven, CT: Yale University Press, 1996 (originally 1873).
———. *Lectures on the Doctrine of Justification*. 3rd ed. London: Rivingtons, 1874.
———. *Letters and Diaries of John Henry Newman*. Edited by Charles S. Dessain et al. Oxford: Clarendon Press, 1976.
———. *Loss and Gain: A Study of a Convert*. 8th ed. London: Burns and Oats, 1884.
———. *The Philosophical Notebook of John Henry Newman*. Edited by Edward Sillem. Louvain, Belgium: Nauwelaerts, 1970.
———. *The Rise and Progress of Universities*. Introduction by Mary Katherine Tillman. Notre Dame, IN: University of Notre Dame Press, 2001 (originally 1856 as *Office and Work of Universities*).
———. *The Theological Papers of John Henry Newman on Faith and Certainty*. Edited by Hugo M. de Achaval and J. Derek Holmes. Oxford: Clarendon Press, 1976.

BIOGRAPHIES

Bouyer, Louis. *Newman, His Life and Spirituality*. New York: P. J. Kennedy and Sons, 1958.
Cornwell, John. *Newman's Unquiet Grave*. London: Continuum, 2010.
Cunningham, Lawrence, ed. *John Henry Newman: Heart Speaks to Heart*. Hyde Park: New City Press, 2004.
Garnett, Emmeline. *Tormented Angel: A Life of John Henry Newman*. New York: Ariel Books, 1966.

Ker, Ian. *John Henry Newman: A Biography.* Oxford: Oxford University Press, 1988.
McCartney, Donald, and Thomas O'Loughlin, eds. *Cardinal Newman and the Catholic University.* Dublin: University College Dublin, 1990.
Moody, John. *John Henry Newman.* New York: Sheed and Ward, 1945.
Ward, Wilfred. *The Life of John Henry Cardinal Newman Based on His Private Journals and Correspondence.* 2 vols. New York: Longmans, Green, 1912.

OTHER SELECTED WORKS ABOUT NEWMAN

Aquino, Frederick D. *An Integrative Habit of Mind.* DeKalb, IL: NIU Press, 2012.
———. *Communities of Informed Judgment: Newman's Illative Sense and Accounts of Rationality.* Washington, DC: Catholic University of America Press, 2004.
Carr, Thomas K. *Newman and Gadamer: Toward a Hermeneutics of Religions Knowledge* Atlanta, GA: Scholars Press, 1997.
King, Benjamin I. *Newman and the Alexandrian Fathers: Shaping Doctrine in Nineteenth-Century England.* Oxford: Clarendon Press, 2009.
Merrigan, Terrence. *Clear Heads and Holy Hearts: The Religious and Theological Ideal of John Henry Newman.* Louvain, Belgium: Peeters Press, 1991.
Pelikan, Jaroslav. *The Idea of the University: A Reexamination.* New Haven, CT: Yale University Press, 1992.
Selby, Robin C. *The Principle of Reserve in the Writings of John Henry Cardinal Newman.* Oxford: Oxford University Press, 1975.
Turner, Frank M. *John Henry Newman: The Challenge to Evangelical Religion.* New Haven, CT: Yale University Press, 2002.

NOTES

[1] Lawrence Cunningham, ed., *John Henry Newman: Heart Speaks to Heart* (Hyde Park: New City Press, 2004), 19.

[2] John Moody, *John Henry Newman* (New York: Sheed and Ward, 1945), 6.

[3] John Cornwell, *Newman's Unquiet Grave* (London: Continuum, 2010), 18.

[4] Ian Ker, *John Henry Newman: A Biography* (Oxford: Oxford University Press, 1988), 2.

[5] Ibid., 5.

[6] It is simply impossible to do justice to Newman's Oxford years in this short bio, so we recommend that you find a good biography and add it to your summer reading list. The story of his time in Oxford alone is worthy of a movie, and certainly worth a week or two of your time, too. Among the many sources on Newman's Oxford experience, we recommend: Ian Ker, *John Henry Newman: A Biography* (Oxford: Oxford University Press, 1988); John Cornwell, *Newman's Unquiet Grave* (London: Continuum, 2010); and John Moody, *John Henry Newman* (New York: Sheed and Ward, 1945).

[7] Ker, 16–17.

[8] Cunningham, 9.

[9] Ibid., 29.

[10] Cornwell, 124.

[11] Ker, 462.

[12] John Henry Newman, *The Rise and Progress of Universities,* introduction by Mary Katherine Tillman (Notre Dame: University of Notre Dame Press, 2001), xxix, xxxviii–xxxix. (First published 1856 with the title *Office and Work of Universities.*) All page references correspond to the 1991 edition.

[13] Ibid., xix.

[14] Ibid., 182.

[15] Ibid., 184.

[16] Ibid., 185.

[17] Ibid., 187.

[18] Ibid., 189.

[19] Ibid., 190.

[20] John Henry Newman, *The Idea of the University,* ed. Frank M. Turner (New Haven, CT: Yale University, 1996), 105. (First published 1873).

[21] Newman, *Rise and Progress*, 197.

[22] Ibid., 198.

[23] Ibid., 199–200.

[24] Ibid., 202. "I have squandered my life away laboriously in doing nothing."

[25] Ibid., 207.

[26] Ibid., 208.

[27] Ibid., 210.

[28] Many times, these visionaries are better at spotting the theological errors down the road than they are at identifying the irony in their own request two to three years later for those institutions-in-error to accredit their program or accept their courses for transfer.

[29] Ibid., 214–215.

[30] Ibid., 219.

[31] Ibid., 229.

[32] Ibid., 235.
[33] Ibid., 242.
[34] Ibid., 240.
[35] Ibid., 249.
[36] Ibid., 251.
[37] For a discussion of wisdom communities, see Patrick Allen and Kenneth Badley, *Faith and Learning: A Guide for Faculty* (Abilene, Abilene Christian University Press, 2014), 220–228.
[38] The argument for residency is developed at length in J. W. Carroll, B. G. Wheeler, D. O. Aleshire, P. L. Marler, and M Blair-Loy's volume, *Being There: Culture and Formation in Two Theological Schools* (New York: Oxford University Press, 1997).
[39] We commend to our readers Stephen Leacock's witty short story, "The Rival Churches of St. Asaph and St. Osoph," one of which attempted to move (geographically and metaphorically) closer and closer to the university because it aspired to intellectual legitimacy. At http://www.online-literature.com/stephen-leacock/arcadian-adventures-with-the-i/6/.
[40] Search the string "tempered radicals" for an interesting way to frame this question.

Abraham Flexner

The American College (1908)

ABRAHAM FLEXNER WAS NOT ALWAYS A NICE MAN. NO ONE EVER ACCUSED him of being gentle, humble, or shy and retiring, not even his mother. He carried a very high opinion of his own opinions and cared little for the arguments and ideas of those who disagreed with him. He was impatient and aggressive, and sometimes an intellectual bully. His own brother, Simon, noted that Abraham was "a strong person . . . intensively egotistical, with a great capacity for self-deception. . . . He readily translates events into his own point of view. . . . He hardly ever admits mistakes or failures on his own part, although finding many faults in others."[1] One observer noted that he was "somewhat erratic and probably hasty in judgment."[2] And more recently, Michael Nevins labeled Flexner "a flawed American icon."[3]

Yet his biographer, Thomas Neville Bonner, has a kinder and gentler take on Flexner, characterizing him as "fundamentally a deeply gifted human being, warm-hearted, decent, and dedicated to his causes and extended family."[4] And upon his death in 1959, the *New York Times* observed: "No other American of his times contributed more to the welfare of his country and of humanity in general."[5]

So who was this man, and why would we include such a flawed, iconic figure in a volume about voices from the past that speak words of wisdom to Christian higher education? As you will see, he cared deeply about the undergraduate experience, writing a little-known book, *The American College,* in 1908. This book will serve as the centerpiece of this chapter—even through his peers roundly dismissed his arguments at the time of publication as unrealistic and unnecessary. Flexner, however, simply believed that he was twenty-five years ahead of this time. We do, too—maybe even a century ahead of his time. We hope that this chapter will renew some well-deserved interest in Abraham Flexner's concerns and hopes for the American college.

The Life and Times of Abraham Flexner

Before we examine Flexner's concerns about the American college, we will look at some of the ways that Flexner's childhood, education, and early professional career shaped his views of the American college experience.[6]

Early Years and Undergraduate Experience

Abraham Flexner was born on November 13, 1866, in Louisville, Kentucky, to Esther and Moritz, both Jewish German immigrants. He was the sixth of nine children, and as we shall see, his commitment to his family (like his brothers before him) would shape and complicate his own personal and professional aspirations.

Moritz Flexner started work in Kentucky as a traveling peddler of household wares. He hated that work, wanting a job that would permit him to be home with the family each evening. To that end, after several faulty starts, he established a wholesale hat business in Louisville, and it became a great success. That is until the Panic of 1873 when the family business began to struggle and ultimately failed. Moritz ended up serving as a poorly paid store clerk in a small hat store financed by his brother-in-law. Finally, Moritz confessed to his oldest son, Jacob, that he was financially ruined, and it would be impossible for him or his brothers to continue their schooling. Jacob immediately dropped out of high school and went to work in a pharmacy to help support the family.[7] Even though he was only seven at the time, this experience helped shape Abraham. He never got over seeing his father broke and his spirit broken.

Abraham was a bright boy. For his thirteenth birthday, he received the complete works of Plutarch, which by his own admission he "read assiduously."[8] Interestingly, Plutarch's characters were often greatly flawed persons, but with enormous depth and stature. To this day, some observers characterize Flexner similarly.[9]

Flexner describes his parents as "pious Hebrews, attending the synagogue regularly and observing religious feasts" all their lives, but not so the children. Flexner continues, "For us Herbert Spencer and Huxley, then at the height of their fame and influence, replaced the Bible and the prayer book."[10] Although respectful of his parents' religious practices, Abraham Flexner saw little relevance in organized religion. He would live his life as a secular Jew, comfortable with his religious heritage but seeing himself as part of something bigger and more inclusive—the American dream.

After Abraham graduated from Louisville Male High School at the age of seventeen, his oldest brother, Jacob, who was by now operating his own drugstore, offered him one thousand dollars to attend college. He was the first of the six Flexner brothers even to finish high school, let alone think of college. However, one thousand dollars was not that much, even in 1884. It would provide for only two years of room, board, and tuition. Though it was not a lot, Abraham jumped at the opportunity. Jacob told Abraham that he should attend a rather new university, the Johns Hopkins University, barely eight years old. Why? Abraham remembers it this way:

> The reason was simple. When the Johns Hopkins University was opened in 1876, a former Louisville boy, the Reverend Samuel Sale, who is still living and in good health, past eighty years of age, was the rabbi of the Reformed Jewish congregation in Baltimore. His younger brother, Lee, had a few years previously left the Louisville High School, gone to live with him in Baltimore, and taken his bachelor's degree at the John Hopkins University, after which he returned to Louisville and taught for a year or two in the high school before taking up the study of law. Through Lee Sale we had heard of the Johns Hopkins University. My brother boldly but characteristically decided that that was the place for me.[11]

So on the recommendation of a brother of a distant family friend, Abraham took the train to Baltimore.

Unfortunately, his university studies did not get off to a good start. He promptly failed the mathematics, Latin, and Greek placement exams. Fortunately, he had a letter of recommendation from Lee Sale. The Latin professor, Minton Warren, looked over his examination paper and reread the letter of recommendation. He looked directly at Flexner and said, "Your paper shows that you don't know very much Latin, but Sale says that you come from a fine family, and we are going to let you in."[12] The Greek exam was even worse. Flexner could not even begin the exam, let alone finish it. The professor, Charles Morris, obviously seeing more in Flexner than was apparent from his test results, asked how old he was (seventeen) and where he was from (Kentucky). Then he hesitantly added, "I have a class from twelve to one every day. You seem to be in earnest. Come to me promptly at one o'clock daily, and I will tell you what to study. I can't give you more than five minutes, but if you will do your work well, you can in the course of a few months learn enough Greek to join Dr. Spieker's class in Isocrates."[13] This, Flexner did diligently, and he joined Dr. Spieker's class by Thanksgiving.

In many respects, those five minutes each day with Charles Morris changed the trajectory of Abraham Flexner's life. This is why he argues so strongly for faculty involvement with undergraduate students. Sometimes, it is the little things that professors do that have the most profound impact on the lives of their students, things that professors often do not even remember or consider significant.

Flexner buried himself in his studies, doubling up on courses, taking fourteen during his first year. He even signed up for two courses scheduled at the same time. He had very few friends and almost no social life. Other than sending a daily postcard to his mother (written in German) and enjoying a few conversations with his host family each week at dinner, he did nothing but study and attend classes. It was a solitary way to live, and he was deeply homesick. However, he was determined to go home with a degree, which he earned in two years, at the age of nineteen.

That summer, with BA in hand, Flexner applied for a graduate scholarship to continue study in Baltimore, but he was denied. Heading back to Louisville, he read his Greek every day as his professor recommended and toyed with the idea of going into law. However, his family's financial situation had not improved, so when he received an offer of an assistantship to teach at his local high school for one thousand dollars a year, he jumped at the opportunity. He was going to be a teacher.

Teaching and Mr. Flexner's School

Abraham was a demanding teacher. After his first semester, he received a promotion to full professor in recognition of his good work. And with the promotion came a well-deserved raise in annual salary to twenty-five hundred dollars. Now he could contribute to the support of his family, something he would do well into midlife. He gave his entire paycheck to his mother, who gave him back what he needed for his living expenses.

Teaching came easily for Abraham. To ward off boredom, he started tutoring students who wanted to attend an Ivy League college. One day, an affluent lawyer approached Flexner, offering to pay five hundred dollars per year if he would tutor his son and get him into Princeton. Flexner saw his chance. He told the attorney that if he could find four others who would also pay five hundred dollars for his tutoring services, he would quit his job and open his own preparatory school. In less than two weeks, the other four had come forward, and shortly thereafter, Mr. Flexner's School opened for business in the fall of 1890.

Business was great. Flexner sent a steady stream of students to the finest universities in the East, and they passed their entrance exams with ease and graduated on schedule. His students were so successful that the president of Harvard, Charles Eliot, wrote to him, inquiring about his approach because the graduates of Mr. Flexner's School "were coming to Harvard younger and graduating in a shorter period of time than students from any other school."[14] Flexner shared his approach: treat students as individuals and let them go at their own pace; emphasize and build on their strengths; and press for excellence. It was a powerful formula for success, but Flexner's career was about to go in another direction—what he called a leap in the dark.[15]

Graduate School

After running Mr. Flexner's School for fifteen years, Abraham Flexner was financially set. Along the way, he married one of his students, and he diligently cared for his family. Still, he experienced an emptiness that he could not explain. Intuitively sensing his longings, his wife, a successful New York playwright, ventured into a life-changing conversation. Flexner describes the conversation:

> In the winter of 1904 my wife and I were one evening sitting before the fire and talking of things in general. "What," she asked me, "is your idea of our future?" To be honest, my thoughts had been so consumed with the responsibilities of school and family that I had not definitely planned beyond the present. "I think," she said, "that we will grow old, be comfortably well-to-do, and lead dull lives." "What do you propose?" I asked. She had thought it all out. "What would you do if you had never married?" "I should quit schoolteaching and go to Europe." "Then," she said, "that is what we will do. As our joint earnings have been pooled, we shall not be troubled by a time limit."[16]

So the Flexners were off, but before going to Europe, Abraham attended the Graduate School at Harvard for a year to study psychology. Because he was interested in how young children learn, he found the time and motion lab work frustrating and quite useless for his purposes. After one semester, he quit the lab but finished enough coursework to earn a master's degree by the end of spring term. Then, they were off to study in Germany for two years. While in Europe, he began to reflect on what he observed while at Harvard. He didn't think much of Harvard's elective curriculum, their large lecture classes, or their extensive use of assistantships. And he didn't think much of their arrogance either. So, he decided to write a book critical of Harvard's undergraduate program, offering a prescription for a more robust undergraduate experience.

His book, *The American College,* published in 1908, was the result, and in his own words, "fell quite flat."[17] Reviews of the book were dismissive, one characterizing his work as markedly pessimistic and unsparingly critical.[18] Over a hundred years after its release, however, we find *The American*

College to be both relevant and insightful, and it will provide the grist for the remainder of this chapter.

The American College

Before we discuss four themes that knit the book together, we want to share a synopsis of *The American College*. Certainly, it was a bold undertaking for someone with such meager experience in higher education.

Chapter 1: The Problem Defined

According to Flexner, the problem is that colleges are placing their emphasis in the wrong place. He quotes President Jacob Gould Schurman of Cornell to make his case: "The college is without clear-cut notions of what a liberal education is and how it is to be secured . . . and the pity of it is that this is not a local or special disability, but a paralysis affecting every college of arts in America."[19] And Schurman wrote this in 1907, not 2007!

Flexner believes that this lack of mission clarity, coupled with a lack of effective teaching and rigor, produces graduates who are soft, comparing unfavorably with their European counterparts. However, he rejects calls to return to a more traditional curriculum dominated by Latin and Greek, arguing that there is no consensus in America about their necessity, and in any case, the old way simply does not prepare students adequately for the twentieth century. Instead, what is needed is a complete rework of modern education, bringing the students' learning powers to bear and connecting them "with life,"[20] much like he did in his own prep school.

Chapter 2: The Development of the College

In this incendiary chapter, Flexner begins by reflecting on the development of the college in America and ends with a biting criticism, pointing out the disparity between what a college claims to do and what it actually does. He finds a sad incongruity. The American college, according to Flexner, is not adaptive. Rather, since colonial times, it has served the elite. By 1870, Flexner notes, colleges were perhaps "somewhat more human, somewhat more gracious, somewhat broader in scope and interest, but hardly less conservative."[21] However, two major influences now drive change for the colleges: scientific industrialization and social democracy. The needs of industry and the demands of democracy are forcing the college to move away from simply preserving the social order for a select minority. Rather, breadth and opportunity are now required, resulting in, among other things, the development and growth of graduate and professional schools. On the one hand, Flexner applauds this expansion of the mission of higher education, but he bemoans the fact that the unique mission of the undergraduate college has been clouded by all this growth and expansion. The BA, Flexner observes, now represents "simply three or four years of study in some line or lines. . . . He may have adhered closely to the traditional classical scheme; or . . . he may have made a sort of gentlemanly 'grand tour' through the capitals of the chief provinces of intellectual interest."[22]

In effect, the college now tries to do too many things and consequently has lost its way. Unfortunately, most colleges innovate by emulation. That is, newer institutions copy the older ones, squandering any opportunity to do something distinctive or creative. To make matters worse, graduate and professional schools now receive the lion's share of resources and attention. Slowly, the mission of the college is becoming inconsequential, perhaps even invisible. The disparity between what the college claims to do and what it actually does disturbs Flexner because it "fails to enlist a respectable portion of the youth's total energy in intellectual effort; either its sincerity or its pedagogical intelligence is discredited by the occupations and diversions which it finds not incompatible with its standards and expectations."[23]

Chapter 3: The College and the Secondary School

In this passionate chapter, Flexner complains bitterly about the influence that colleges have over the college preparatory school curriculum and pedagogy, forcing schools to teach to the test. In this case, the test is the entrance examination used for college admission. Once in college, however, students are ill prepared to engage thoughtfully within the freedom offered by the elective curriculum. It is a broken connection in which the college is the controlling stockholder and the high school functions as a subcontractor. In such an arrangement, students lose their way. Flexner worried about misalignment in 1908. We wonder what he would say today. Might he use the same characterization: illogical and unscientific?

Chapter 4: The Elective System

In chapter 4, Flexner takes on the elective curriculum itself. He argues that the elective system fails to understand the individual student, while ignoring the deep connections between subjects[24] and the necessity of education to serve the common good.

Flexner begins by pointing out that most college freshmen and sophomores are simply not able to make wise educational choices. For them, college is just an interlude. Most come with only modest experience, and "there is absolutely no reason to credit a college freshman with the seriousness or the knowledge required to put together a course of study which will in these days serve as introduction to his vocation."[25] They need wise and caring advisors, but he adds that professors who are trained and interested in research are not much help: "He is not as a rule qualified by his primary interests and concerns to do the delicate and tedious work of 'advising'; he has no time for it. In the end it means nothing to him."[26] Far too often, Flexner cautions, students end up taking a narrow set of courses, thus squandering the opportunity to grow and develop beyond their own narrow academic vision of reality.

Finally, the college has functions that go beyond vocational preparation for the individual student. It is to serve the common good, too, making connections between disciplines and the public square. Flexner puts it this way: "It is none the less impossible to believe that modern intellectual life is to develop in water-tight compartments; that the college does its full duty when it produces separately preliminary lawyers, doctors, chemists, artists, without common ground. . . . Society is not a mere mosaic of sharply accentuated economic units."[27] Thus, an education that is focused solely on getting a job without an appreciation for the greater good is shortsighted at best, and perhaps dangerous, too.

Chapter 5: Graduate and Undergraduate

Chapter 5 is classic Flexner—a biting, take-no-prisoners critique of the status quo. Flexner makes three arguments. First, even though most recognize that undergraduate and graduate departments have different aims and have different needs, they are too often treated as if they are the same. This results in graduates and undergraduates often finding themselves in the same classroom, which is a disaster, according to Flexner. With general undergraduates, departmental majors, and graduate students in the same classroom, it is as if "two or three targets stand side by side; with one bullet the instructor undertakes to hit the bull's eye in each."[28]

In almost every case, graduates receive the priority of time and effort (Flexner's second argument). And this is unfortunate, in Flexner's view, because undergraduate instruction has such different aims: to develop intellectual confidence and power, to harden students' fiber, to put an edge on their purposes, and to inculcate a usable basis of fundamental knowledge. And these outcomes call for a teacher with a different set of skills and inclinations, a "broadly trained and broadly minded scholar, not necessarily a first-hand investigator: a purveyor, rehandler, relator, rather than a discoverer."[29] Sadly, the dominance of the graduate department dictates the selection of faculty who can investigate and create new knowledge, and promotions are usually granted on that basis, perpetuating a flawed system.

Finally, Flexner argues that while there is certainly a place for the lecture course, it is not with first- and second-year students, and certainly not when using teaching assistants. While the undergraduate is in need of careful attention and formative relationships, the lecture keeps the professor "at arm's length from the beginner."[30] It is at best poor instructional design, "an astonishing failure in pedagogic insight!"[31]

Chapter 6: The Way Out

Given the disconnect between secondary and undergraduate study, the detrimental effects of the elective curriculum, and the predominance of the graduate over collegiate values, is there a way out for the American college? Flexner offers a straightforward solution: "The way out lies, as I see it, through the vigorous reassertion of the priority of the college as such. The point of emphasis must be shifted back. There is the meat of the whole problem."[32]

To make this happen, six initiatives are required. First, a new kind of dean is needed, one with the power and understanding to organize and work with faculty to select, map out, and teach with the requirements of the student distinctly in mind. College presidents are too removed and college deans pulled in too many directions to drive curricular and pedagogical renewal, even if they have the knowledge to do so (and most do not). What Flexner has in mind is a dean who is a first among equals—an academic who understands the teaching mission of the college and recruits and rewards faculty for that purpose. He is certainly opposed to the detached executive. He wants a dean who lives and works in the trenches.

The next step is to allow preparatory schools to reinvent themselves free from having to prepare students for restrictive entrance examinations. Preparatory schools could offer a more informed and enlightened educational program, educating students for the college experience to come. And this step would be coupled with colleges modifying the elective curriculum, offering a coherent, concise, related body of instruction. These steps would require that college professors not only *offer* courses, but that they also actually *teach* students. Here Flexner is calling for a reorientation of the teaching profession at the collegiate level, shifting the focus from research to teaching as the central activity.

And while both the secondary and college curriculums are in major renovation, Flexner boldly calls for a reconsideration of the college as a business entity:

> Finally, emphasis of the teaching motive will put an end to commercialism. On this point plain speech is necessary. Efficient teaching is utterly irreconcilable with numerical and commercial standards of success. The colleges now want numbers; they must have and keep them, more or less regardless of quality.... There arises thus a spirited competition for students. The various offices scrutinize the numbers of incoming classes as narrowly as the merchant watches his daily sales. They send out drummers who beat up recruits and the credit man at home cannot be over-squeamish about accepting and carrying business thus obtained. This is the logic of the situation, from which there is no escape. A high standard is incompatible with acute sensitiveness to the reading of the trade barometer.[33]

Flexner ends his plain speech by reminding college administrators that it is quite unfair to solicit and sell one vision of the college experience only to offer quite another.

Reconstruction and reorientation will permit different types of educational institutions to coexist and flourish. They don't all have to be alike or chase the same definition of success, but all institutions, however conceived and constructed, must stay true to their mission. At the end of the day, the American college must claim its mission, make its own space, maintain high academic standards, and live within its means. This will take wise and courageous leadership that is grounded and committed to the values and particularity of the undergraduate experience in a particular place.

Key Arguments and Corollary Implications

As we noted earlier, *The American College* fell flat. Flexner's "way out" turned out to be a cul-de-sac. It was roundly rejected as naïve, ill conceived, and unworkable. After all, Flexner had attended college for only two years at Johns Hopkins; he struggled to obtain a master's degree; he was a former prep school proprietor; he had no work experience in higher education, and at the time of publication, he didn't even have a job! He is an unlikely critic or reformer, indeed, but over a century later we believe that Flexner's book deserves renewed attention. In this section, we will highlight and discuss four of his key concerns: the college mission, the undergraduate experience, the relationship of teaching and research, and the need for a new type of institution. And we will attempt to speak as directly and boldly as did Flexner.

The College Mission

According to Flexner, the American college has lost its identity. Nearly one hundred years later, Jacques Barzun, a well-known and respected philosopher of education, noted that no one today knows what a college is or how to define it. In fact, it would be "lunacy" even to try.[34] Yet we know that without a clear articulation of the institution's mission and a deep embrace of its identity, an institution can easily lose its way. We wish to note four factors at play in the loss of the college identity: the move to university status, global mission statements, persistent emulation, and blind doctrinal protection.

In the past three decades, we have witnessed a steady migration, perhaps even a stampede, from college to university status. We know of an institution that identified itself as a bible college in July, a liberal arts college in August, and a university the very next summer. From bible college to university in twelve months! How can this be? The typical explanation is that the distinction between college and university is no longer obvious, and university status is important for branding, for international image, and for recruiting prospective students. And really, so the rationale runs, the renaming simply recognizes what has already occurred. Apparently, senior administrators looked around one morning after staff meeting and discovered that without anyone noticing, the institution had somehow metamorphosed into a university. We wonder when someone will shout, "The emperor has no clothes!"

We acknowledge that the distinction between college and university has been blurred, particularly in the United States, and the nomenclature is largely at the discretion of the institution. But in the rush to claim university status, the core idea of the college and its unique mission can be easily minimized and sadly compromised. This, it seems to us, is a real concern. Words matter. Identity matters. How we see ourselves shapes us. Ultimately, organizational structure and nomenclature must be guided by mission, not dictate it.

Also confounding the college identity is the mission statement itself. In the past, mission statements were criticized for stating essentially that the institution is just as purposeful as the next institution down the road, and not much more. In fact, we ran across a mission statement from the 1980s that read: "Not the best, but better than some."[35] Today, however, we see mission statements that promise the world—literally. Graduates are not only guaranteed that they will be changed, but also will graduate as world changers. All this and a great job and happy life, too! Mission statements have morphed from saying almost nothing to promising almost everything. Again, we recognize the power and promise of branding, but mission statements serve as a compass to guide institutional programming. In the attempt to be all things to all people, if colleges make wild promises that can be true only for a small minority of students, the integrity and credibility of the college come into serious question.

Flexner observes that colleges are not, by nature, adaptive institutions. Just look at the process for a change in general education requirements on most campuses. Faculties will take between five and ten years to complete a comprehensive GE study, and the end result is usually more of a tweak than a substantive, innovative change.[36] It is as if someone finally fires the cannon, but a BB rolls out the end. Why? Surely some of the explanation is related to departmental politics. But also at work is what Flexner calls emulation. Colleges tend to copy the established order rather than strike out on a new and innovative path. It seems to us that faith-based institutions are in a particularly strong position to promote themselves as a distinct and powerful alternative to the status quo, but sadly, it is the existing order that our institutions too often copy and the values of the research university that we too often adopt and reward. Why? We believe the unwillingness or inability to craft unique academic programs is due in large part to a collective inferiority complex among faith-based institutions, as if straying from what is currently being done in public institutions would expose some fundamental weaknesses. To the contrary, what might happen if faith-based institutions were to craft academic programs that were truly distinctive and compelling, even graceful? Rather than instruction, research, and service, what if the functions of the college were understood to be: to teach, to shape, and to send? We believe that such an approach would have appeal in any market.

Finally, the academic identity of the college is blurred when indoctrination overrides the pursuit of truth as the operative value of the institution. Flexner notes: "The schools no longer furnish asylum to ideas that cannot maintain themselves in the open."[37] We wish that were true, but unfortunately, we see faith-based institutions operating as asylums for ideas more than we would like to admit.[38] We are not saying that institutions should have no distinctive theology or spiritual commitments, but we are saying that when these ideas are not permitted to be challenged, let alone examined and discussed openly, discourse is driven underground and the institution ceases to be a college.[39] Instead, it becomes a place for indoctrination. Such institutions should be honest and forthright about their mission and how they intend to operate. When such doctrinaire institutions claim to be and claim to act like institutions of higher learning, then confusion occurs, and far too often, faculty members and students suffer the consequences.

Certainly, there are many pressures at work that blur the identity of the college, particularly when it is located within the overarching framework of a university and/or a specific community of faith. Indeed, it is a challenge to remain clear about the mission of the college and to be faithful to it, even while trying to be faithful to the community of faith that sustains it. As Flexner notes, it will take strong and courageous leadership and, we add, a lot of grace, too.

The Undergraduate Experience

Flexner's undergraduate experience at Hopkins was nothing short of life changing, and that experience shaped his views on the undergraduate college. In particular, he believes that students should live in residence. And interestingly for Flexner, residence is not about housing. Rather, it is about caring relationships, effective advising, and a supportive educational curriculum.[40]

Without doubt, the Johns Hopkins faculty had every reason to send Flexner home after he failed all of his placement exams, but they did not. Instead, they looked at his humble letter of introduction and decided to give him a chance. We really don't know why, but we do know that it made all the difference to Abraham Flexner. And we all have had faculty members who saw more in us than was evident to the naked eye. We don't know why, either, but we are glad they did. The transformative power of the undergraduate experience begins and ends with relationships. And perhaps the most powerful connection for an undergraduate is with a faculty member or two, people who give of their time, tell the truth, push hard, expect much, and hope. More often than not, students respond with their best work.

Flexner also saw the need for careful advising. In his view, freshmen are ill prepared to make good decisions about their course schedules, let alone their lives. While all undergraduates are eager to be on their own and exercise independence, most have far too little life experience to help themselves exercise that independence. Again, they are in need of wise friends. For Flexner, this implies hiring faculty members who see their primary task as teaching rather than as conducting independent research. And we see every reason to include well-trained and caring professional staff in the equation; because students need both course scheduling and personal guidance, a joint effort from our side would be most productive. According to Flexner, it is lunacy to expect students to find their own way. They need wise friends and mentors—Sherpas who take the journey with their students rather than simply pointing to the mountaintop and wishing them good luck.

Flexner also advocates a compact, understandable, manageable curriculum designed to meet the needs of students rather than to support the teaching interests of the faculty. This is an important distinction. And would residence not be further strengthened if courses were scheduled with the student in mind rather than the instructor? For example, few would seriously argue that 7:30 A.M. courses are offered with the student's schedule in mind, particularly given the nature of residential life on most campuses. Adults in midlife get up much earlier than most undergrads. Could we not address such an obvious schedule misalignment?

Teaching and Research

To be clear, Flexner is not a critic of research or the vital role it plays in the university setting, especially in graduate programs. After all, he studied in Germany and at Johns Hopkins, where graduate study and research reigned supreme. He is, however, worried that the predominance of research over teaching in the undergraduate college leads to unhealthy and unhelpful practices.

First, according to Flexner, research should not be required of all undergraduate students. It is simply not helpful for most students because they will never otherwise engage in that activity. It is a waste of their time, an unnecessary diversion from the undergraduate experience. Research should be the province of the graduate department and those professional schools where students are in need of such training.

Second, the ability to conduct original research and publish should not be the primary criteria for selecting faculty for the undergraduate college. It will lead to faculty who are neither interested nor prepared to engage with lower-division students in the ways most needed. In the college, faculty scholars should feel a call and desire to teach.

Finally, it follows that research productivity should not be the driving criteria for promotion and tenure in the undergraduate college. Putting such criteria in place will create a misalignment between what is actually needed from undergraduate faculty (teaching, synthesis, advising, mentoring) and what is actually rewarded (publications, grants, patents). It is lunacy to reward one set of activities while hoping for another. Doing so causes confusion, frustration, and alienation.[41]

Charting A New Course

In his autobiography published in 1940, Abraham Flexner looks back at the origin and first decade of his alma mater, the Johns Hopkins University, and its founding president, Daniel Coit Gilman. He asks, "Has the time passed when knowledge of educational history, imagination, courage, and funds can still produce a new 'high' in American education?"[42] We consider that a powerful question.

Honestly, we think the time is ripe for the Christian college to become something special, to reach a new high; not by emulation, not by trying to imitate a research university, and not by trying to be all things to all people, but by faithfully embracing the distinctive mission of Christian higher education and by boldly claiming its own territory in the higher education landscape. We believe that the Christian college is not called to be an R1 institution, but rather to be a T1 institution, an institution where we encourage and reward work that leads to student transformation, an institution where teaching, shaping, and sending are the core activities.[43] Because place and purpose are such defining factors, what a given T1 institution will look like will depend largely on its unique campus setting. But we believe an extraordinary journey awaits the Christian college willing to marshal the needed knowledge of educational history, imagination, courage, and funds.

QUESTIONS FOR REFLECTION AND DISCUSSION

Abraham Flexner's concerns about the undergraduate college and the undergraduate experience prove to be relevant and challenging to all of us who care about the future of Christian higher education. We end this chapter with some questions for reflection and discussion.

The College Mission
- Flexner argues that the undergraduate college should have first lien on university resources because it is so foundational to what any

university tries to do. Do you agree, and to what extent is this true in your institution?
- How important is the Christian faith in the life of your institution? In your work?
- In some way or another, we are all trying to live up to our recruiting brochures. What part of the recruiting process at your institution gives you the most pause? What part gives you the most satisfaction?
- To what degree would you characterize your institution's mission as unique, distinctive, or just like the institution down the road (with a little Jesus thrown in)?
- Why are the values of the larger academy so pervasive in our institutions?
- To what degree does your institution furnish asylum to ideas that cannot maintain themselves in the open? How free are faculty to discuss openly, perhaps even disagree with, various theological and doctrinal stances of your college? Are the fault lines clearly marked?

The Undergraduate Experience
- Flexner argues that relationships with professors are the most formative aspect of college life for students. What weight do you assign to such relationships? Why?
- At your institution, do students have too much freedom or not enough? How is the delicate balance between support and freedom negotiated in your institution? In your classes?
- How would you rate the quality of student advising on your campus? Is there an intentional relational component?
- Is your institution's general education program compact and concise or all over the road?
- When you look at the course schedule, to what degree would you say it is designed with the needs of students in mind compared to the convenience of faculty?
- Could a vital residence program be possible if all students lived off campus? How?

Teaching and Research
- Should every undergraduate student, regardless of major, be taught laboratory and research methods? Why or why not?
- Flexner argues that undergraduate faculty should be hired with an allegiance to teaching. Do you agree or disagree? What is the practice at your institution?
- Is research productivity considered to be a higher value than excellent teaching at your institution?

Charting a New Course
- At your institution, would the undergirding values and reward structure for faculty reflect an R1 or T1 orientation?
- Of the following, what do you consider to be the most important for leading campus change: knowledge of educational history, imagination, courage, or funds? What is lacking at your institution?
- In what ways does your institution operate humanely and gracefully? In what ways does it operate like a cold, calculating business? Who wins out, people or numbers? Can a Christian college actually do both—love people and operate with a healthy bottom line?
- What is the most interesting or provocative idea from Flexner? Why?

FOR FURTHER STUDY

Flexner is best remembered as a major force for medical education reform in the United States, but he is also known for his commentaries on the mission and function of universities in the United States, England, and Germany, and as the founding director of the Institute for Advanced Study. He was also a biographer of several influential leaders in higher education, and published reports on such varied subjects as prostitution in Europe, the policies of philanthropic foundations, and the qualifications for a discipline to call itself a profession. He also wrote two autobiographies. For those interested in reading more about Abraham Flexner, we recommend the following:

THREE HELPFUL WEBSITES

Abraham Flexner Papers (span dates: 1865–1989). Manuscript Division, Library of Congress, Washington, D.C. http://lcweb2.loc.gov/service/mss/eadxmlmss/eadpdfmss/2003/ms003042.pdf.

Rockefeller Foundation Repository—photos, limited correspondence and reports. http://rockefeller100.org/solr-search/results?solrq=flexner.

Abraham Flexner web page. Institute for Advanced Studies. https://www.ias.edu/scholars/flexner.

IN FLEXNER'S OWN WORDS

Flexner, Abraham. *Abraham Flexner: An Autobiography.* New York: Simon and Schuster, 1960.

———. *The American College; A Criticism.* New York: Century, 1908.

———. *Daniel Coit Gilman, Creator of the American Type of University.* New York: Harcourt, Brace and Company, 1946.

———. *Do Americans Really Value Education?* Inglis Lectures at Harvard University, 1927. Cambridge: Harvard University Press, 1927.

———. *Funds and Foundations: Their Policies Past and Present.* New York: Harper, 1952.

———. *Henry S. Pritchett, a Biography.* New York: Columbia University Press, 1943.

———. *I Remember: The Autobiography of Abraham Flexner.* New York: Simon and Schuster, 1940.

———. "The Importance of 'Useless' Knowledge." *Hispania* 27, no. 1 (1944): 77–78.

———. *Is Social Work a Profession?* Studies in Social Work, No. 4. New York: New York School of Philanthropy, 1915.

———. *Medical Education: A Comparative Study.* New York: Macmillan Company, 1925.

———. *Medical Education in the United States and Canada: A Report to the Carnegie Foundation for the Advancement of Teaching.* Carnegie Foundation Bulletin No. 4. New York: Carnegie Foundation for the Advancement of Teaching 1910.

———. *A Modern College, and a Modern School.* Garden City, NY: Doubleday, Page & Company, 1923.

———. *A Modern School.* Occasional Papers (General Education Board [New York]), No. 3. New York: General Education Board, 1916.

———. *Prostitution in Europe*. Publications of the Bureau of Social Hygiene. New York: Century, 1914.
———. *Universities, American, English, German*, 2nd ed. New York: Oxford University Press, 1930.

BIOGRAPHIES

Bonner, Thomas Neville. *Iconoclast: Abraham Flexner and a Life in Learning*. Baltimore, MD: Johns Hopkins University Press, 2002.
Nevins, Michael. *Abraham Flexner: A Flawed American Icon*. New York: iUniverse, 2010.

OTHER SELECTED WORKS ABOUT FLEXNER

Batterson, Steve. *Pursuit of Genius: Flexner, Einstein, and the Early Faculty at the Institute for Advanced Study*. Wellesley, MA: K Peters, 2006.
Diller, Lawrence. "100 Years Later, the Flexner Report Is Still Relevant." *The Hastings Center Report* 40, no. 5 (2010): 49.
Gardner, J. W. "Abraham Flexner, Pioneer in Educational Reform." *Science* 131, no. 3400 (1960): 594–595.
Halperin, Edward C., Jay A. Perman, and Emery A. Wilson. "Abraham Flexner of Kentucky, His Report, Medical Education in the United States and Canada, and the Historical Questions Raised by the Report." *Academic Medicine: Journal of the Association of American Medical Colleges* 85, no. 2 (2010): 203–210.
Kerr, Clark. "Abraham Flexner's Universities." *Society* 31, no. 4 (1994): 40–47.
King, D. J. "The Psychological Training of Abraham Flexner, the Reformer of Medical Education." *The Journal of Psychology* 100 (1978): 131–137.
Markel, Howard. "Abraham Flexner and His Remarkable Report on Medical Education: A Century Later." *JAMA* 303, no. 9 (2010): 888–890.
Savitt, Todd. "Abraham Flexner and the Black Medical Schools." *Journal of the National Medical Association* 98, no. 9 (2006): 1415–1424.
Strauss, L. L. "Lasting Ideals of Abraham Flexner." *JAMA* 173 (1960): 1413–1416.
Wheatley, Steven Charles. *The Politics of Philanthropy: Abraham Flexner and Medical Education*. History of American Thought and Culture. Madison, WI: University of Wisconsin Press, 1988.
Zelenka, M. H. *The Educational Philosophy of Abraham Flexner: Creating Cogency in Medical Education*. Lewiston, NY: Edwin Mellen Press, 2008.

NOTES

[1] James Thomas Flexner, *An American Saga: The Story of Helen Thomas & Simon Flexner* (Boston: Little, Brown, and Company, 1984), 120.

[2] Howard Berliner, *A System of Scientific Medicine: Philanthropic Foundations in the Flexner Era* (London: Tavistock Publishers, 1985), 104–105. Also see Howard Berliner, "A Larger Perspective on the Flexner Report," *International Journal of Health Services* 5 (1975): 573–92; and Berliner, "New Light on the Flexner Report," *Bulletin of the History of Medicine* 51 (1977): 603–609.

[3] Michael Nevins, *Abraham Flexner: A Flawed American Icon* (New York: iUniverse, 2010), 6.

[4] Thomas Neville Bonner, *Iconoclast: Abraham Flexner and a Life of Learning* (Baltimore: Johns Hopkins University Press, 2002), 308.

[5] "Abraham Flexner is Dead at 92; Revolutionized Medical Schools." *The New York Times* (September 22, 1959), 1.

[6] The following section draws heavily on Flexner's autobiography: Abraham Flexner, *I Remember* (New York: Simon and Schuster, 1940). Also, Bonner, *Iconoclast,* the most definitive biography of Flexner to date.

[7] Bonner, 12.

[8] Flexner, *I Remember,* 20–21.

[9] For example, see Nevins, *Flawed American Icon.*

[10] Flexner, *I Remember,* 13.

[11] Ibid., 45–46.

[12] Ibid., 52–53.

[13] Ibid., 54.

[14] Ibid., 81.

[15] Ibid., 94. This is the title of the chapter in Flexner's autobiography that describes these events.

[16] Ibid., 96–97.

[17] Ibid., 110.

[18] "The American College," review in *The School Review* 17, no. 4 (1909): 274–275.

[19] Abraham Flexner, *The American College* (New York: The Century Company, 1908), 7. Here Flexner quotes President Schurman from the President's Report, Cornell University, 1906–07, page 20.

[20] Ibid., 21.

[21] Ibid., 24–25.

[22] Ibid., 33. Note here the similarity to Whitehead's complaint about too much breadth and not enough depth. Similarly, Sayers complained that students learned a lot of subjects but not how to think.

[23] Ibid., 58.

[24] Again, he echoes both Whitehead and Sayers.

[25] Ibid., 126.

[26] Ibid., 120.

[27] Ibid., 133.

[28] Ibid., 161.

[29] Ibid., 185.

[30] Ibid., 198.

[31] Ibid., 197.
[32] Ibid., 216.
[33] Ibid., 230–231.
[34] Jacques Barzun, "Trim the College?—A Utopia!" *Chronicle of Higher Education* (June 22, 2001): B24.
[35] We have decided that it is best to withhold the identity of this institution. Thus, we will not provide a citation for this direct quote. We suspect that Flexner would have been more forthcoming.
[36] We have written about flexibility and the speed of innovation in educational settings in K. Badley and A. Dee, "Creating an Educational Ethos Where Innovation and Accountability Flourish: A New Model for Transparency in Educational Organizations," *The International Journal of Educational Leadership Preparation* 5:4 (October–December 2010), http://cnx.org/contents/41b35c0e-74bf-454b-9f83-0478aa650b03@2/Creating_an_Educational_Ethos_ .
[37] Flexner, *The American College*, 26.
[38] We note in this regard the careful work of Elmer Thiessen on indoctrination. See his *Teaching for Commitment: Liberal Education, Indoctrination and Christian Nurture* (Montreal: McGill-Queen's University Press, 1993); and *In Defence of Religious Schools and Colleges* (Montreal: McGill-Queen's University Press, 2001).
[39] For a discussion of the damage that occurs in academic communities when discourse is driven underground, see Patrick Allen and Kenneth Badley, *Faith and Learning: A Guide for Faculty* (Abilene, TX: Abilene Christian University Press, 2014), 51–52.
[40] Note that for Flexner, residence is something apart from where one lives. This is in keeping with his experience at Hopkins (where he took room and board from a local family) and the university experience he observed in Germany. Of course, Newman's idea of residence is much broader, encompassing where the student lives, takes meals, studies, and worships (Chapter Six). Newman would not argue with the views expressed by Flexner but would argue for an even broader undergraduate experience.
[41] We know literally hundreds of such confused, frustrated, alienated faculty members who were hired to do one thing and then told that their performance evaluations would be based on something else. For more on this topic of misaligned faculty rewards, see Allen and Badley, *Faith and Learning*, 208–209.
[42] Flexner, *I Remember*, 65.
[43] See Allen and Badley, *Faith and Learning*, 207–220.

Thorstein Veblen

The Higher Learning in America (1918)

OF ALL THE VOICES PRESENTED IN THIS VOLUME, THORSTEIN VEBLEN IS in many respects the most unlikely voice to offer words of wisdom about the future of Christian higher education. After all, his "majestic skepticism" toward all claims of epistemological certainty placed him squarely at odds with his own Lutheran tradition, and he believed that religious authority was hostile to reality in general and to his professional expertise as an economist in particular.[1]

He was a mumbling, disorganized lecturer and disliked most undergraduates with a passion. He often attacked the leadership of the institutions where he served—biting the hand that fed him. And his private life can only be described as unpredictable and uncouth. For most of their marriage, he and his first wife lived apart, and he left faculty posts at the University of Chicago and Stanford University, in both cases accused of spousal neglect and improper relationships with students. He remained silent about the accusations, choosing to resign rather than to defend himself. Although the allegations were never fully substantiated, we do know that he lived for a while in a remodeled chicken coop with a graduate student while his estranged wife took up residence literally next door.[2]

Given all this, why would we include Veblen in this volume of voices from yesterday that offer insight for Christian higher education today? Clearly, he was a thoughtful, insightful observer of American culture, coining the term "conspicuous consumption," and his book, *The Theory of the Leisure Class: An Economic Study in the Evolutions of Institutions (1899)*, is a classic in economics. As a result, Veblen gained national prominence, albeit always on the margins of his own institution. However, as we have learned over the years, it is important to pay close attention to the voices of critics on the margins. They often have much to say to us . . . if we will only listen.

This is the case, we believe, with Thorstein Veblen. In 1918, Veblen published *The Higher Learning in America: A Memorandum on the Conduct of Universities by Business Men*. It was so critical of university administrators that his own president tried to block its release. It is a frontal attack on the management of universities by businessmen, and it is a strong caution that the mission of the university must be understood and honored by those who govern and lead. The concerns and critiques he put forth in the early twentieth century form the centerpiece of this chapter. Veblen has much to say to all of us as we work to shape the future of Christian higher education.

Childhood and Career

Thorstein Veblen spent his boyhood on the family farm, totally immersed in the Norwegian cultural community in Minnesota. He rarely spoke English outside of school. When he arrived at Carleton College Academy, he was naïve about American culture and deeply suspicious of the English. That "suspicious outsider" posture would continue to be a bane and a blessing throughout his professional career.[3] In that posture, he could criticize American society and business practices, as he did when he coined the term "conspicuous consumption." However, he always remained a bit of an outcast in his own profession, desperately wanting the public recognition he felt was due him. He thought of himself as a writer in exile, identifying closely with the homeless Jews.[4]

After graduating from the academy and then Carleton College, Veblen spent a year teaching at Monona Academy in Wisconsin before matriculating as a graduate student at Johns Hopkins University to study philosophy and political economy. When financial aid failed to materialize, he moved on to Yale, earning the PhD in philosophy in 1884. He returned to the family farm in Minnesota to convalesce from a bout of malaria and remained there for the next six years, unable to find a satisfactory academic post.

In an act of desperation, he enrolled as a graduate student at Cornell University to study political economy with Laurence Laughlin. Veblen's big break came when Laughlin accepted an appointment at the University of Chicago and he took Veblen with him. Veblen worked first as a student teaching fellow and later as a faculty member. His book, *Theory of the Leisure Class* (1899), was a national success, but troubles were brewing in Chicago.

First, Veblen was neither a good teacher (students dropped his courses in droves) nor popular with the administration. President William Rainey Harper made it clear to him in 1899 that he would not object to his resignation.[5] Finally, in 1906, shortly after Harper's death, Interim President Harry Pratt Judson confronted Veblen with allegations of infidelity and spousal abandonment. Neither affirming nor disputing the allegations, Veblen simply and silently submitted his resignation, ending his twelve-year career at Chicago.

At the time, David Starr Jordon, president at Stanford University, was after Veblen. The result was a stormy three years of faculty service, culminating once again in a trip to the president's office to answer allegations of marital infidelity and neglect. Again, Veblen refused to address the allegations, tendering his resignation instead. He accepted an appointment at the University of Missouri and moved to Columbia—in exile once again.

It was during his seven years at Missouri that Veblen finished the manuscript for *The Higher Learning in America* in 1918. He had been working on it, on and off, since the summer of 1904. Veblen grew concerned about the establishment of business and commerce departments within the university as well as about the corrosive and corrupting influence of businessmen who served as university presidents and trustees. These concerns form the centerpiece of his book. We will provide a synopsis and review his main arguments, then discuss what these concerns have to say to all of us about the future of Christian higher education. We believe you will see that Veblen's analysis, now nearly one hundred years old, is remarkably and powerfully relevant for our work today, despite his personal anger and venomous cynicism.

The Higher Learning in America

To provide just a bit of context, in the late nineteenth century, universities began to introduce a top-down, corporate administrative structure that emulated business organizations, resulting in the loss of any serious faculty role in institutional governance. Veblen saw this as a serious problem. The combination of his wit, sarcasm, and penetrating insights made his book a classic in the genre that is known as the professors' literature of protest.[6] As Richard F. Teichgraeber III describes it, "*The Higher Learning in America* ultimately is a hybrid text that mutates from one generic category to another: part an essay in cultural history; part a thinly disguised autobiography; part a scathing criticism of the American university's anomalous system of governance; part a clear-eyed analysis of how American university governance actually works; and part a call to action."[7] Certainly, it is interesting reading.

Chapter 1: The Place of the University in Modern Life

Sounding more like a cultural anthropologist than an economist, Veblen observes that esoteric knowledge has existed in some form in all civilizations due to two impulsive traits of human nature: idle curiosity (the desire to know things) and the instinct for workmanship (the desire to make things—particularly tools).[8] In the modern world, it is the mission of the university to preserve, promote, and protect idle curiosity and esoteric knowledge—the higher learning. In fact, "this learning has so far become an avowed 'end in itself' that the increase and diffusion of knowledge among men is now freely rated as the most humane and meritorious work to be taken care of by any enlightened community or any public-spirited friend of civilization."[9]

For Veblen, the problem is that universities are pulled in so many directions that learning for learning's sake is easily relegated to a secondary position or lost altogether. Veblen suggests that two lines of university work are indispensable: (1) scientific and scholarly inquiry, and (2) the instruction of students. The first is an absolute must; the second is important, but only to the extent that students become apprentices, learning how to do scientific and scholarly inquiry. The university should be neither interested in practical learning nor engaged in students' moral, religious, pecuniary, domestic, or hygienic interests.[10] And there should be no set curriculum. For Veblen, the mentoring relationship between graduate student and professor is center stage.

Veblen takes pains to explain why the undergraduate college and professional schools are so detrimental to the work of the university: they shift the focus and resources from the higher learning and corrupt the values of the research university. Simply put, they are too enamored with business interests and pecuniary gain, and the result is mission drift. Veblen warns: "By virtue of this long-term idealistic drift, any seminary of learning that plays fast and loose in this way with the cultural interests entrusted to its keeping loses caste and falls out of the running."[11] Throughout his book, Veblen will challenge trustees and presidents to be mindful of this danger, and he will criticize them for not doing so.

Chapter 2: The Governing Boards

Chapter 2 begins by reemphasizing the true distinction of the university: "It is, indeed, the one great institution of modern times that works to no ulterior end and is controlled by no consideration of expediency beyond its own work."[12] At least, that is the ideal, but reality is far from it. Why? The problem can be traced back to the lay control of the governing board.

Now, the power and control rests firmly in the hands of businessmen. The problem is that they are so myopic that they spend all their time looking at the financial elements of the university and lose sight of its central mission. Their spirit is one of "quietism, caution, compromise, collusion, and chicane."[13] They have nothing in common with the higher learning; not knowing the difference, or even that there is a difference, between a college and a university.[14]

Veblen then makes the case that the inclinations, values, and training for business and for scholarly work are so distinct that they are literally worlds apart. Certainly, hiring a scholar to try to manage a business would be an instant disaster. No one should think of doing so, but the road runs both ways. In one of Veblen's best-known arguments, he writes: "Plato's classic scheme of folly, which would have the philosophers take over the management of affairs, has been turned on its head; the men of affairs have taken over the direction of the pursuit of knowledge. To anyone who will take a dispassionate look at this modern arrangement it looks foolish, of course—ingeniously foolish."[15]

He points out that governing boards derive their power and control over the academic enterprise from their ability to allocate budgets and to appoint the president. If the head of the university believes that pecuniary success is the test of his success, and he has control over where resources are allocated, these two factors ensure that business principles and methods will dominate.[16] In such an environment, little hope of change remains.

Veblen concludes this chapter with these insightful words: "The upshot of it all should be that when and in so far as a businesslike governing board delegates powers to the university's academic head *(president)*, it delegates these powers to one of their own kind, who is somewhat peremptorily expected to live up to the aspirations that animate the board. What such a man, so placed, will do with the powers and opportunities that so devolve on him is a difficult question that can be answered only in terms of the compulsion of the circumstances in which he is placed and of the moral wear and tear that comes of arbitrary powers exercised in the tangle of ambiguities."[17] In the next chapter, however, he takes dead aim at university presidents, betraying little sympathy for the complexities of the position or the tangle of ambiguities they face.

Chapter 3: The Academic Administration and Policy

According to Veblen, university presidents are captains of erudition. This is not a compliment, being lumped together with the captains of industry. In Veblen's view, these captains do not exhibit the two impulsive human traits (wanting to *know* or *make* something) but rather a less noble trait (wanting to *take* something). Just how much of his presidential contempt is personal or philosophical is difficult to determine. To be sure, though, on several accounts he is not big fan of presidents.

First, Veblen is adamant that faculty members who engage in the disinterested pursuit of knowledge need a free hand, time, and space to pursue esoteric knowledge, and that "a university can remain a corporation of learning, *de facto*, on no other basis."[18] Strong words, indeed, but Veblen points out that presidents do not share these sentiments. In fact, they view faculty as mere employees, able to be dismissed on a whim. Loyal obedience is mandatory, and criticism is unwelcome. From the president's point of view (according to Veblen), "They have eaten his bread, and it is for them to do his bidding."[19] Clearly, these two divergent views of the nature of faculty work inevitably will lead to frustration and conflict.

Second, Veblen points out that presidents love prestige. As such, the undergraduate college is the central figure in the university and receives the lion's share of resources. But of even greater concern for Veblen, the aims, activities, and sheer size and complexity of the undergraduate college leave students with the ability to be successful in business, but not as scholars. In his own words: "The mental discipline exercised by these sports and polite events greatly favors the growth of tactful equivocation and a guarded habit of mind, such as makes for worldly wisdom and success in business . . . (but) an undergraduate who does his whole duty in the way of sports, fraternities, clubs, and reputable dissipation at large, commonly comes through his undergraduate course with a scanty and superficial preparation for scholarly or scientific pursuits, if any."[20] The only recourse, according to Veblen, is a formal separation, or better yet an absolute divorce. The undergraduate college is better suited to be joined with the secondary school.

Veblen's third axe to grind with the behavior of the captains of erudition is perhaps his most insightful contribution to the professors' literature of protest. Most faculty instinctively recoil at the suggestion that the university is simply a business and should be run as such, but Veblen clearly articulates the underlying implications for faculty work. If an institution is guided by "sane business practice," it is certainly "bad business to offer a better grade of goods than the market demands, particularly to customers who do not know the difference, or to turn out goods at a higher cost than other competing concerns."[21] This approach requires a skilled labor force able to produce standardized products for customers in high volume while being employed at the lowest possible wages. Rather than the disinterested pursuit of esoteric knowledge and the formation of the next generation of scholars, the driving institutional values become marketable quality but not high quality, competitive but not adequate wages, and large-scale merchantable output. He argues that these practices destroy the very essence of faculty work and misdirect the mission of the university. For Veblen, this is the fundamental problem with the conduct of universities by businessmen.

Chapter 4: Academic Prestige and the Material Equipment

In this short chapter, Veblen takes direct aim at campus buildings. Remembering the utilitarian approach to buildings at Johns Hopkins, while watching the construction of elaborate, neo-Gothic campus facilities at Chicago and the Mission Revival buildings at Stanford, Veblen fears that such enormous, ornate, even vulgar campus buildings are a bootless waste of funds, having nothing to do with, and in some cases, actually hindering the work of the faculty. At the very least, such architectural extravagance directs funds away from more central uses. These "marketable illusions" and "conspicuous extensions of the plant"[22] become an institutional version of conspicuous consumption, a term Veblen coined with regard to the consumption behavior of the leisure class.

The chapter concludes with an insult aimed directly at the donors of such buildings: "It appears that the successful men of affairs to whom the appeal for funds is directed, find these wasteful, ornate, and meretricious edifices a competent expression of their cultural hopes and ambitions."[23] Is it any wonder that his own president tried to suppress the publication of the book?

Chapter 5: The Academic Personnel

Veblen begins this chapter by reiterating that the power of the president to select personnel will, over time, deform the faculty by packing its ranks with colleagues with a lower-school or pecuniary mentality. However, there will always be a small minority, an inner circle of heroic academics, interested only in the disinterested pursuit of esoteric knowledge. They are the true university.

However, academics are constantly being pulled away from their work, required to attend social events for prominent citizens and donors, compelled to lecture to groups of devout and well-to-do women, told to remain morally above reproach, and voluntold—even if that involves an appearance at a public ceremonies or solemn festivity. (By voluntold, we refer to the exact opposite of volunteering where a boss mandates an unpleasant assignment.) To add insult to injury, the uncertain tenure of office and low pay result in the necessity to take on other work to make ends meet. About this last requirement, Veblen complains: "No infirmity more commonly besets university men than this going to seed in routine work and extra-scholastic duties. They have entered on the academic career to find time, place, facilities, and congenial environment for the pursuit of knowledge, and under pressure they presently settle down to a round of perfunctory labor by means of which to simulate the life of a gentleman."[24] All this can be blamed on the president, whose discretion and official sanctions encourage these activities.

Chapter 6: The Portion of the Scientist

Presidents actually need a few researchers around to keep up appearances, an inner circle to lend credence to the mysterious respect and sympathy for the disinterested pursuit of esoteric knowledge that is held by the faculty (even though most do not and cannot engage in it). These few faculty stars represent the brightest memories of university life and a glimmer of hope for the future—but only a glimmer.

Next, in a moment of genuine sympathy for university presidents, Veblen recognizes that presidents are often caught between the values of the academy and the values of the board. In the end, however, he is convinced that most scholarly activities will be suppressed unless they can add instant prestige of the university. And because there is no settled code of business ethics to guide them, presidents will dismiss scholars when people of pecuniary interest raise concerns about them. He speaks from experience.[25]

At the end of the day, the challenge for faculty will be to balance the demands of the discipline and the demands of the governing board as best they can. However, as Veblen concludes, "The run of the facts is, in effect, a compromise between the scholar's ideals and those of business, in such a way that the ideals of scholarship are yielding ground, in an uncertain and varying degree, before the pressure of businesslike exigencies."[26] It is a losing effort.

Chapter 7: Vocational Training

In a true university, there is no place for "fitting schools, high-schools, technological, manual, and other training schools for mechanical engineering and other industrial pursuits, professional schools of diverse kinds, music schools, art schools, summer schools, schools of 'domestic science,' 'domestic economy,' 'home economics' (in short, housekeeping), schools for the special training for secondary-school teachers, and even schools that are avowedly of primary grade."[27] He's against them all.

And who is responsible for this invasion of lower learning and the dumbing down of the curriculum? The answer is predictable: the captains of erudition and the boards that hire them. Business proficiency and sales have replaced learning, Veblen bemoans. The university offers what the market demands rather than what students need to learn, subjecting the higher learning to the pragmatism of the marketplace. Veblen decries this as "criminally foolish."[28]

Singled out for intense criticism are schools of commerce, a recent addition to university offerings.[29] Veblen sees little to like about them. Commercial schools emphasize practicality and usefulness, pushing disinterested research and esoteric knowledge to the side. They draw little upon the results of modern science, and they contribute even less to the common good.[30] It is simply institutionalized selfishness and as such has no place in the university.

Before concluding, Veblen flags one more concern that remains an issue today. In order to attract highly paid professionals to the university, professional school salaries will need to increase. And since there are only so many resources to go around, it will be at the expense of other programs, resulting in schools and colleges with differential salaries. The ultimate losers will be the inner circle of true scholars.

Chapter 8: Summary and Trial Balance

Veblen fusses that the focus on undergraduate students makes universities appear to be large penal settlements, and the qualifications for faculty are "vendibility, volubility, tactful effrontery, and conspicuous conformity to the popular taste in all matters of opinion, usage and conventions."[31] There is certainly no place for the scholar or for esoteric knowledge in such an alien environment.

Taking dead aim once again, Veblen compares presidents to professional politicians and describes them as "a picked body of men, endowed with a particular bent . . . peculiarly open to the appeal of parade and ephemeral celebrity, and peculiarly facile in the choice of means by which to achieve these gaudy distinctions; peculiarly solicitous in appearances, and peculiarly heedless of the substance of their performance."[32] Adding yet another criticism, Veblen suggests that the two foci around which the modern university swings are notoriety and the president. With alarming insight, he suggests that in many instances, the two become one. That is to say, the president (in his own mind, at least) *is* the university. He runs it as his own and takes all public criticism of the university or internal resistance as if it were aimed solely at him. This, Veblen worries, is dangerous.

In one last swipe at presidents, Veblen calls them "an itinerant dispensary of salutary verbiage," known for the "effusion of graceful speech at all gatherings of the well-to-do for convivial deliberation on the state of mankind at large."[33] He wonders if the study of presidents isn't a study in total depravity. (Teichgraeber notes that "a study in depravity" was actually Veblen's first choice for the subtitle of his book.[34])

Given this state of affairs, what is the solution? Veblen suggests that moving graduate studies out of universities and into small research institutes would be a start. While this might look like a surrender of the university ideal, it would better than nothing. But he acknowledges that it is unlikely that such a scheme could be developed on a large enough scale to be productive, so a better solution is in order.

For Veblen, the solution is clear: "All that is required is the abolition of the academic executive and of the governing board. Anything short of this heroic remedy is bound to fail, because the evils sought to be remedied are inherent in these organs, and intrinsic to their functioning." Veblen continues, "It should be plain, on reflection, to anyone familiar with academic matters that neither of these official bodies serve any useful purpose in the university, in so far as bears in any way on the pursuit of knowledge."[35]

What Veblen has in mind is some type of loosely affiliated collection of colleges and schools along European lines, each with self-governance. And here he gives a nod to the American college by suggesting they might be able to "return to that ancient footing of small-scale parcelment and personal communion between teacher and student that once made the American college, with all its handicaps of poverty, chauvinism and denominational bias, one of the most effective agencies of scholarship in Christendom."[36]

He also estimates that about 75 percent of the administrative staff could be eliminated, and the faculty could get back to doing what they are prepared to do. Curiously, Veblen the economist does not address how such an enterprise would be funded. Perhaps he does not know. The only non-negotiable is that the graduate school must be separate and independent of the collegiate division.

In the end, Veblen holds little hope that his solution will be taken seriously, particularly given who is in control of the university, yet he presses his case one last time: "As seen from the point of view of the higher learning, the academic executive and all his work are anathema, and should be discontinued by the simple expedient of wiping him off the slate; and that the governing board, in so far as it presumes to exercise any other than vacantly perfunctory duties, has the same value and should with advantage be lost in the same shuffle."[37] All that should remain is the higher learning and those who are dedicated to that vision of the university.

Key Arguments and Corollary Implications

As we discuss Veblen's insights and concerns, you will note that we do so with a bite and a bit of angst of our own, in keeping with Veblen's own style. We are trying to replicate Veblen's arguments and emotions in the manner of the professor's literature of discontent. Please know that we mean no disrespect.

The Fragility of Mission

Veblen argues that the mission of the university is to protect, promote, and preserve esoteric knowledge, knowledge for its own sake. However, any approach to learning that excludes all other activities and programs from the university is, at best, shortsighted and self-serving. Even R1 institutions, whose primary mission it is to create new knowledge, are much more complex than a singular research institute of the kind envisioned by Veblen—and actually created by Abraham Flexner.[38]

But Veblen is on point with several observations. For example, he stresses the importance of a clearly articulated, widely understood, and broadly supported mission. A Christian college can be pulled in so many directions, with various stakeholder groups and constituencies always having something in mind but rarely the same thing in mind. The tension can make even the best leaders weary and lose heart at times, but the focus must always be on keeping first things first. And, of course, if a university loses its sense of true north, it is difficult to remember what the first things are in the first place.

We agree with Veblen that organizational complexity also complicates leadership and confounds mission. Even small colleges can be organized in almost indescribable ways. We know of colleges with more faculty committees than faculty members, and with two or three layers of administrative committees and task forces as well. All this structure results in hours and hours of mundane and often unnecessary work, stealing time and energy away from the essential tasks for which one came to the university in the first place. And in the midst of such busywork, it is easy for a person or an institution to lose its way.

Finally, Veblen worries that campus buildings and balance sheets can become more important to those in leadership than the work of the faculty, and when faculty are viewed as mere labor, their roles and wisdom are diminished. High frustration, low morale, and widespread cynicism result. No one wants to feel unimportant or invisible. Particularly in a faith-based institution, there must be a better way. Covenant and community are words that possess a moral trajectory. We have come to believe that, particularly in a Christian college, the first obligation of a leader is to care for the human spirit, and those who can't offer such care have forfeited their right to lead.

The Role of Trustees

If Veblen had his way, he would get rid of governing boards. That's probably a bit too much, but his concerns do deserve our attention as we think about the future of Christian higher education.

First, hiring the president is one of the chief responsibilities of the trustees, but a governing board dominated by businesspeople will hire a president who is just like them and then expect the president to promote their values. In effect, they hire a CEO. Academic trappings are important for public acceptance, but the real necessity is business acumen. And since the board is responsible for evaluating the president, their review is conducted with these expectations and values in mind. Academic quality and campus morale are rarely factors in the evaluation.

Veblen grants that some understanding of business is necessary for any president, and so do we. The rub comes when the values of business override the values of the academic community, and a healthy tension is lost. When this happens, academic values regarding instruction, formation, and vocation are relegated to an inconsequential position or disregarded altogether, and the institution is malformed. In a faith-based institution, this is particularly debilitating because the transformation of students is—or should be—a key distinctive. We worry about the overuse of non-tenure-track, temporary faculty and adjuncts who are asked to teach very heavy loads and, in return, are not held to any scholarly expectations or asked to perform committee work.[39] In effect, they become teaching pack mules. In our view, this is a shortsighted business practice with long-term ramifications for mission and quality.

Finally, we point out that most Christian college governing boards are comprised of individuals who collectively are the most conservative group on campus. In some regards, this is as it should be; they are, legally, the group ultimately responsible for the university. And after all, no one is interested in risky financial dealings and relentless calls for entrepreneurship. On the other hand, trustees are apt to issue institutional policy statements on any number of matters, in essence speaking for the entire academic community when no real consensus exists. Usually, there is little dialogue with faculty before such pronouncements are made. The result is a silent chasm stretching across campus that is difficult to navigate or even discuss.

The Power of Presidents

Veblen would get rid of presidents, too. After all, two presidents got rid of him. We confess that on an occasion or two, we have shared the sentiment, but Veblen is clearly reaching too far. Most presidents we know are a committed, industrious lot, and they dutifully serve at the very epicenter of institutional criticism. It is a difficult job, never being able to please everyone and sometimes no one. There are many effective presidents in faith-based institutions, and we applaud their good work.

Unfortunately, Christian colleges have their share of ineffective presidents, too, spreading uncertainty, fear, and pain across the campus like a dust storm. Good people either leave, hide, or simply quit caring, and sadly, the trustees rarely ever know. And some individuals change when they become president. The power goes to their heads, and they wield it in unnecessary and unkind ways.[40] And presidents who report to an absentee group of trustees, many of whom were personally recruited to the board by the president, literally have no accountability as long as the books balance and the campus looks good. This is one of the dirty little secrets of Christian higher education.

Veblen takes note that presidential vanity is a serious problem, especially when presidents lose the ability to differentiate the institution they are meant to serve from themselves. Trouble is brewing when presidents take criticisms, failures, and complaints personally. They begin to think and act as though they were the institution. When such narcissism rears its ugly head, blame and fear become the currency of trade. Everything becomes personal, and rational discourse goes out the window.

We know of far too many academics who, after becoming president, suddenly take on the vocabulary of the business community and see themselves as a business leader, spouting a steady stream of corporate jargon. Many times we have heard faculty, looking on in amazement, ask, "Weren't they a (insert name of academic discipline here) just last year?" Did they forget where they came from? Do they have amnesia? The simple answer is yes. They've moved to another planet and adopted another language. Veblen notes that some presidents do experience the tension of living in two worlds—the academic world and the business world. We honestly would like to see more presidents recognize and respond thoughtfully to that tension.

The Voice of Faculty

Veblen wants to keep the faculty, and if he had his way, they would run the entire institution. While he makes the case that a university run by businessmen poses a serious problem, no less serious would be the problem of a university run by professors! Again, he goes too far. Here we will discuss a concern we think he did get right, the matter of faculty voice—or shared governance.

The absence of faculty voice was an issue for Veblen and many of his contemporaries, and it has been a consistent concern for faculty members in all types of institutions for the past one hundred years. And sadly, we believe it is a concern for faculty members in most Christian colleges, too. We observe that a culture of cynicism grows on many campuses and roots itself in a collective sense of powerlessness.

Christian colleges have a tradition of strong presidents and weak faculty voice, partly due to the fact that a president is chosen as the keeper of the religious tradition as well as the leader of the institution. Boards expect presidents to "keep the faculty toeing the line." The problem for faculty is that the line seems to keep moving, so no one knows exactly where to stand. Many faculty members have been pushed out or removed for being "out of line," sometimes for good reasons and sometimes for no good reason at all.[41] Our questions are: Where is the faculty voice when these unsavory events occur? Why have faculty, by and large, been ineffective in making their concerns known? Why isn't shared governance working?

The first reason why faculty voice is weak is the severe lack of clarity about how shared governance is to be shared. As a result, faculty members spend a good deal of time watching the administration and complaining that they are not consulted about such things as the placement of the new parking lot or the color of the trim on their building, things that are clearly administrative in nature. Simply put, some faculties think that shared governance means that they must be consulted about everything. This is simply wrongheaded and counterproductive. John Millett makes a good distinction between management (administrative prerogative), governance (decisions shared by administration and faculty), and leadership (energy and direction for the two processes). Keeping these distinctions in mind certainly helps to clarify the purpose and define the territory for shared governance.[42]

Another reason for a weak faculty voice is simply a lack of effective organization, having either too little or too much. On one hand, some faculties, in the spirit of community and informality, have a small faculty council that sits with no clear authority or mandate to speak for the faculty, serving largely as an informal sounding board and social committee. When real trouble hits, there is little they can officially say or do. On the other hand, other faculties are notorious for organizational overkill. Even with a clear mandate, we know of faculty senates that are organized into so many units, each with committees, subcommittees, task forces, and study groups, that the organization implodes. So much time is spent trying to manage all the units that little if anything of substance is ever said or done. The faculty senate takes on a life of its own, and faculty voice suffers.

Perhaps the greatest impediment to faculty voice is simply courage.[43] When troubles brew on campus, most faculty members are truly upset, but the conversations go underground. There are rarely organized or public expressions of concern, even from tenured faculty. This is puzzling. Is it just human nature to drive by a burning house but not stop to offer assistance? On many Christian college campuses, there is simply and sadly a basic unwillingness to stand up to power, and when fear rules, the result is a loss of faculty voice and hope.

We offer this suggestion in closing. In Veblen's time, the American Association of University Professors was founded to protect academic freedom and faculty voice (1915). The principles of this organization have served higher education with varying degrees of success for the past one hundred years. We wonder if a similar organization might be in order today, one organized and charged to address the particular concerns of faculty serving in faith-based institutions. Perhaps a way forward is to organize, particularly given the power of a work stoppage and the promise of social media as a means of communication and social pressure, so that individuals and faculties under attack do not have to struggle in isolation.[44] Perhaps through collective action, there can be a new day for shared governance and faculty voice, for the sake of all who are dedicated to the mission of Christian higher education.

QUESTIONS FOR REFLECTION AND DISCUSSION

You cannot read Veblen's *The Higher Learning in America* without sensing the sarcasm and anger stemming from his own rollercoaster career. After all, he was pushed out of two prominent faculty positions. Obviously, these departures were painful, and at times his book is painful to read, too. He may no longer be branded as a naughty professor, but he is certainly an angry one. Even so, his book contains many astute observations and insightful commentary. We will attempt to draw on these as we pose some questions for reflection and discussion about the Christian college.

The Mission of the Christian College
- Veblen argues that the mission of the university is to promote the disinterested pursuit of esoteric knowledge. Is this a mission of the Christian college? How so?
- How would you describe the mission of your own college or university?
- How clear is the articulation and common agreement about the mission of your college or university? If it is not clear, why not?
- Veblen worried about mission drift, the movement from what is essential to other commitments. Do you sense any drift at your institution? If so, how would you describe it, and what are several specific things that can be done about it?

The Governing Board
- How would you characterize the composition of your governing board? How are trustees selected, and who does the selecting?
- To what degree do business interests dominate your governing board, and are their primary concerns financial in nature? How do they assess and support academic policy?
- Does the board evaluate the president on a regular basis, and is the evaluation open to voices other than their own? Are the results made public? Do trustees have a sense of the pulse on campus? Who evaluates the effectiveness of the board?

- We observe that governing boards are more conservative than other constituency groups on campus, yet are inclined to speak for the entire campus community. Does this characterization fit your campus, or do your trustees act in more inclusive ways?

Presidents
- To what degree would you say that wise counsel surrounds your president?
- Where would you characterize your president and senior administrators on a continuum running from closed to open to minority views and expressions of concern?
- Veblen worries that power often goes to the head of the president, who often acts in arbitrary and hurtful ways. How does your president wield power?
- Veblen also worries that trouble is brewing when presidents cannot separate themselves from the university, coming to think narcissistically that whatever happens to the university happens to them—that they *are* the university. To what degree does this characterization reflect reality on your campus?

Faculty Voice
- How strong is the cult of criticism and cynicism operative on your campus?
- How strong is the faculty voice on your campus?
- What is the major impediment to a stronger faculty voice on your campus: clarity of purpose, organizational complexity, or courage to speak up?
- Is the suggestion of a union-style organization for faculty serving in Christian colleges helpful and timely, unnecessary, or counterproductive?

General
- If this chapter spotlighted issues that are at work in your institution, what are three specific actions that you could undertake to address these concerns?

FOR FURTHER STUDY

Thorstein Veblen was certainly a well-known, influential economist in his own time, and his wide-ranging writings have sustained serious interest among scholars to the present day. There are several websites that offer most of Veblen's own works at little or no expense. We would suggest the following, but there are certainly others:

Online Books web page. http://onlinebooks.library.upenn.edu/webbin/book/lookupname?key=Veblen%2c%20Thorstein%2c%201857-1929

Veblen, Thorstein. *The Complete Works*. Kindle edition. Amazon Digital Services LLC, 2016. https://www.amazon.com/Complete-Works-Thorstein-Veblen-Economics-ebook/dp/B01BDL64PO

Below, we highlight some of Veblen's works, biographies, and other works about Veblen's life, thought, contributions, and controversies. He was certainly controversial in his own day, and as you will see, the controversies have not yet been completely settled. Enjoy learning more about Thorstein Veblen, a "Victorian Firebrand" if there ever was one.

IN VEBLEN'S OWN WORDS

Veblen, Thorstein. "Christian Morals and the Competitive System." *International Journal of Ethics* 20, no. 2 (1910): 168–185.

———. "The Barbarian Status of Women." *American Journal of Sociology* 4, no. 4 (1899): 503–514.

———. "The Beginnings of Ownership." *American Journal of Sociology* 4, no. 3 (1898): 352–365.

———. *The Higher Learning in America: A Memorandum on the Conduct of Universities by Business Men*. New York: Viking Press, 1935.

———. *The Instinct of Workmanship and the State of Industrial Arts*. New York: B.W. Huebsch, 1914.

———. *The Theory of Business Enterprise*. New York: C. Scribner's Sons, 1904.

———. *The Theory of the Leisure Class: An Economic Study of Institutions*. Library of American Civilization. LAC 10563. New York: Macmillan, 1899.

———. *Thorstein Veblen: Selections from His Work*. Major Contributors to Social Science Series. New York: Crowell, 1963.

———. *The Vested Interests and the Common Man ("The Modern Point of View and the New Order")*. New York: Viking Press, 1946.
Veblen, Thorstein, and Mitchell Wesley Clair. *What Veblen Taught: Selected Writings of Thorstein Veblen*. New York: A. M. Kelley, Bookseller, 1964.

BIOGRAPHIES

Blaug, Mark. *Thorstein Veblen (1857–1929)*. Elgar Reference Collection. Brookfield, VT: E. Elgar Pub., 1992.
Dorfman, Joseph. *Thorstein Veblen and His America*. New York: Viking, 1934.
Dowd, Douglas Fitzgerald. *Thorstein Veblen*. The Great American Thinkers Series. New York: Washington Square Press, 1964.
Edgell, Stephen. *Veblen in Perspective: His Life and Thought*. Studies in Institutional Economics. Armonk, NY: M. E. Sharpe, 2001.
Hobson, J. A. *Veblen*. New York: John Wiley and Sons, 1937.
Jorgensen, Elizabeth Watkins, and Henry Irvin Jorgensen. *Thorstein Veblen: Victorian Firebrand*. Armonk, NY: Sharpe, 1999.
Riesman, David. *Thorstein Veblen: A Critical Interpretation*. Continuum Book. New York: Seabury Press, 1975.

OTHER SELECTED WORKS ABOUT VEBLEN

Barber, William J. "Political Economy in an Atmosphere of Academic Entrepreneurship: The University of Chicago." In *Breaking the Academic Mold: Economists and American Higher Learning in the Nineteenth Century*. Edited by William J. Barber. Middletown, CT: Wesleyan University Press, 1988.
Bartley, Russell H. and Sylvia E. Bartley. "Stigmatizing Thorstein Veblen: A Study in the Confection of Academic Reputations." *International Journal of Politics, Culture and Society* 14 (Winter 2000): 363–399.
Camic, Charles, and Geoffrey Martin Hodgson. *The Essential Writings of Thorstein Veblen*. New York: Routledge, 2011.
Daugert, Stanley Matthew. *The Philosophy of Thorstein Veblen*. New York: King's Crown Press, 1950.
Diggins, John P. *Thorstein Veblen: Theorist of the Leisure Class*. Princeton, NJ: Princeton University Press, 1999.

Dowd, Douglas Fitzgerald. *Thorstein Veblen: A Critical Reappraisal; Lectures and Essays Commemorating the Hundredth Anniversary of Veblen's Birth.* Ithaca, NY: Cornell University Press, 1958.

Eby, Clare Virginia. *Dreiser and Veblen: Saboteurs of the Status Quo.* Columbia, MO: University of Missouri Press, 1998.

———. "The Two Mrs. Veblens, among Others." *International Journal of Politics, Culture and Society* 13 (1999): 353–361.

Hobson, J. A., Peter Cain, and Thorstein Veblen. *Veblen.* Collected Works of Thorstein Veblen vol. 1. London: Routledge/Thoemmes Press, 1994.

Hughey, Michael W. "The Use and Abuse of Thorstein Veblen." *International Journal of Politics, Culture and Society* 13 (1999): 347–352.

Lambert, Thomas. "Thorstein Veblen and the Higher Learning of Sport Management Education." *Journal of Economic Issues* 33, no. 4 (1999): 973–984.

Lawson, Tony. "Process, Order and Stability in Veblen." *Cambridge Journal of Economics* 39, no. 4 (2015): 993–1030.

Maynard, Tony. "Thorstein Veblen: Victorian Firebrand." *Journal of Economic Issues* 33, no. 4 (1999): 1037.

Newfield, Christopher. "Professorial Anger, Then and Now: What Thorstein Veblen Got Right." *Chronicle of Higher Education* 62, no. 9 (2015): B11.

Nilan, Roxanne, and Karen Bartholomew. "No More The Naughty Professor." *Sandstone* 31, no. 2 (2007): 13–33.

Plotkin, Sidney, and Rick Tilman. *The Political Ideas of Thorstein Veblen.* New Haven, CT: Yale University Press, 2011

Raymer, Emilie. "A Man of His Time: Thorstein Veblen and the University of Chicago Darwinists." *Journal of the History of Biology* 46, no. 4 (2013): 669–698.

Riesman, David. *Thorstein Veblen, a Critical Interpretation.* Twentieth Century Library. New York: Scribner, 1953.

Rutherford, Malcolm. "The Intellectual Legacy of Thorstein Veblen: Unresolved Issues." *Journal of Economic Issues* 32, no. 1 (1998): 244.

Tilman, Rick. *Thorstein Veblen and His Critics, 1891–1963: Conservative, Liberal, and Radical Perspectives.* Princeton, NJ: Princeton University Press, 1992.

NOTES

[1] Clare Virginia Eby, *Dreiser and Veblen: Saboteurs of the Status Quo* (Columbia, MO: University of Missouri Press, 1998), x–xi.

[2] Roxanne Nilan and Karen Bartholomew, "No More the Naughty Professor," *Sandstone* 31, no. 2 (2007): 18.

[3] J.A. Hobson, *Veblen* (New York: John Wiley and Sons, 1937), 11–12.

[4] Eby, 56.

[5] William J. Barber, "Political Economy in an Atmosphere of Academic Entrepreneurship: The University of Chicago," in William J. Barber, ed., *Breaking the Academic Mold: Economists and American Higher Learning in the Nineteenth Century* (Middletown, CT: Wesleyan University Press, 1988), 263.

[6] A designation of the genre by Richard F. Teichgraeber III in Thorstein Veblen, *The Higher Learning in America: A Memorandum on the Conduct of Universities by Business Men* (Baltimore: Johns Hopkins University Press, 2015), 7. For another example of protest literature or the literature of dissent, one that influenced Veblen's thinking, see J. McKeen Cattell, *University Control* (New York: The Science Press, 1913).

[7] Ibid., 22.

[8] In Chapter Two, we noted that Dorothy Sayers also considered this an important aspect of human nature.

[9] Ibid., 43.

[10] Ibid., 50.

[11] Ibid., 64.

[12] Ibid., 75.

[13] Ibid., 82.

[14] Ibid., 85.

[15] Ibid., 88.

[16] Ibid., 91.

[17] Ibid., 92–92.

[18] Ibid., 103.

[19] Ibid., 98.

[20] Ibid., 128.

[21] Ibid., 116.

[22] Ibid., 130–132.

[23] Ibid., 137.

[24] Ibid., 151.

[25] Here, Veblen is surely mindful of his own experiences. He was pressured to resign "voluntarily" from Chicago and Stanford, and refused to speak to the unsubstantiated accusations from his own wife that presidents shared with certain newspapers and governing board advisory groups.

[26] Veblen, *The Higher Learning*, 167.

[27] Ibid., 168.

[28] Ibid., 174.

[29] The College of Commerce and Administration opened at the University of Chicago in 1898, and the Harvard Business School in 1908. The Whitehead paper to which we referred in Chapter One was given on the occasion of the Harvard Business School getting its own building.

30 Remember that Veblen saw two noble human instincts—to know something and to make something. He fears that business schools pander to a less noble instinct—to take something for self. One of Veblen's biggest concerns about business practice is that it plays on a selfish human instinct to accumulate personal fortunes rather than serve the common good. That being so, the university should have nothing to do with it.

31 Veblen, *The Higher Learning*, 190.

32 Ibid., 204.

33 Ibid., 213.

34 Ibid., 217.

35 Ibid., 227–228.

36 Ibid., 232.

37 Ibid., 234.

38 With the assistance of a $5 million grant, Flexner founded the Institute for Advanced Study at Princeton University in 1928. It was exactly the kind of research institute that Veblen had in mind.

39 In some faith-based institutions, adjunct faculty are also held only to the barest faith expectations, sometimes only being required to agree not to teach against the Christian foundations of the university.

40 We addressed this unfortunate process in the discussion of Arendt in Chapter Three.

41 We know of one denominational college where faculty members were required to sign the sponsoring denomination's statement of faith each year with their contract. When the denomination changed its position on the timing of Christ's return, the college followed suit. One faculty member asked if the faculty were all supposed to have changed their beliefs over the summer. The answer was yes.

42 See John Millett, *Management, Governance, and Leadership* (New York: AMACOM, 1980), 17–21.

43 Compounded with this lack of courage is a widespread belief among Christians that being nice is the chief Christian virtue, and confrontation is not nice. This weakness perhaps deserves another whole book.

44 We make this suggestion recognizing that some will charge anyone leading such an effort to organize with not being nice, or possibly with violating the sense of family that ostensibly characterizes the Christian university. Must we remind anyone that universities that hire workers, give out degrees, and issue tax-deductible receipts for gifts are organizations or institutions, but not families.

José Ortega y Gasset

The Mission of the University (1930)

Introduction

JOSÉ ORTEGA Y GASSET, OR SIMPLY ORTEGA, AS HE IS KNOWN IN SPANISH and will be referred to in this chapter, was one of the most penetrating and perplexing thinkers in the first third of the twentieth century, but sadly he is now a largely forgotten voice. Even though he is known to scholars of higher education as a key figure in discussions about the mission and purposes of the university from the early thirties until shortly after World War II, his biography in *Contemporary Authors—2003* (over 6,300 words) did not give even one word to his thinking about higher education, and his classic, *Mission of the University,* gets only a mention in the list of his writings.[1]

Oh, how we wish we could have attended the university-wide lecture series he gave at the invitation of the Spanish Students' Union Federation at the University of Madrid in late 1930.[2] At that time, Ortega served as a senior member of the faculty, holding an appointed chair as professor of metaphysics, and he was enormously popular with students. Even though he was small in stature, there was a certain Spanish fire and flair about him. In Ortega's university office hung a photo of him courageously staring down a bull. As it turns out, it was a very small bull, but a bull nonetheless. Sadly, staring down bulls is an apt metaphor for his professional life, too.

But on this evening in Madrid, words did not fail him. The students were expecting a spirited defense of the freedoms of the university and a scathing criticism of the government and the university. They heard both—and much more. Not only did the administration take it on the chin, so did the faculty and the students. Ortega told the students that he came to them with great enthusiasm, but with small faith. Why? In 1930, Spain was on the cusp of something hopeful, perhaps even a second republic. The monarchy was crumbling and the military dictatorship was showing signs of weakness. It was a time for action, for renewal, for new possibilities. Why then, with so many reasons for enthusiasm, did Ortega express so little faith? Ortega told the students in the clearest possible terms that his faith had shriveled in the face of their laziness. He urged them to have a tempered spirit of reform, which in his view implied a flaming passion for action tempered with logic and precision. They took the critique well.

This lecture series was first printed in the Madrid newspapers and subsequently compiled and released as a book, *Mission of the University* (in Spanish in 1930 and in English in 1946). It is now considered one of the classics in the philosophy of higher education. The questions and challenges that we can take from Ortega are particularly pertinent as Christian colleges and universities face uncertain times. In this chapter, we will look first at José Ortega y Gasset, the person—his biography, his intellectual influences, his careers (he had five concurrently), and his major ideas related to higher education. We will then examine his classic work, *Mission of the University*, clarifying some of his foundational concerns and proposals. We will close the chapter by mining some of Ortega's key ideas, reframing them through a Christ-centered lens, and offering some questions for discussion and reflection. We believe that you will find Ortega interesting, challenging, and helpful—and a bit irritating, too. His colleagues certainly did.

The Life and Times of José Ortega y Gasset
Early Years and Intellectual Influences
Ortega was born and died in Madrid. When he was baptized, his mother requested that there be a special consecration to the Most Holy Virgin.[3] Beyond that early act, there is very little to suggest any formal engagement with the Catholic Church, particularly in his adult years. In fact, on his

deathbed, several priests came to his home and offered him the opportunity for final confession. Irritated, Ortega sent them away.

From an early age, Ortega's parents knew that he was bright, describing him as their "precocious child."[4] At age seven, they offered to buy him a toy horse if he could memorize the first chapter of *Don Quixote*. He did so in three hours.[5] Ortega attended a rigorous Jesuit boarding school where he received a solid classical education, but what he described as the self-righteousness and intellectual arrogance of his Jesuit teachers offended him deeply, and he looked back at his time there with "sadness and pain."[6] We find no evidence that Ortega was ever comfortable with the authoritarian nature of the church or the government. For him, life meant inventing, invigorating, and creating new alternatives, not toeing any party line—church or state.[7]

Ortega grew up in an enlightened and influential upper-class family. His grandfather owned and published a major newspaper in Madrid, and his father was a noted journalist and novelist. Growing up in a house full of intellectuals, where dinner conversations about Spanish culture, the actions (or inaction) of the government, the monarchy, and local politics were commonplace events, obviously shaped Ortega's interest in writing, politics, public speaking, and teaching. He would often quip that he was born "on a rotary press."[8] He certainly knew his way around the business, and effectively used his family's publishing apparatus to promote his own ideas and views. Like so many in his generation, he wanted Spain to recapture both the vitality and the culture that had been lost, and to join with the rest of Europe in crafting a new and bright future. As you might imagine, however, this was easier said than done.

Ultimately, he was truly a creative, independent, eclectic thinker, difficult to place squarely in any particular philosophical camp. After earning an MA in arts and letters (1902) and a PhD in philosophy (1904) from the Central University of Madrid, Ortega embarked four times for postgraduate study in Germany—Leipzig (1905), Berlin (1906), and Marburg (1906–07 and 1911). While there, he studied neo-Kantianism and Edmund Husserl's phenomenology, but existentialists such as Kierkegaard, Nietzsche, Bergson, and Heidegger would ultimately serve as his primary influences.[9] Diego Sevilla points out that Ortega "was impressed by the efficiency and organization of the German people and by the strength of their thought and culture, but he was wary of the excessive importance of collective and military influences on German society at the time."[10] As events would reveal, he had good reason to be wary.

Public Life and Parallel Professions

Ortega accepted an appointment to the chair of metaphysics in the Central University of Madrid in 1910. There he served with distinction for twenty-five years, and it was from this post that he delivered the six lectures in 1930 that would become *The Mission of the University*. However, this was only one of his five careers—parallel careers, actually. In addition to his career as a professor, he was also an essayist, publisher-editor, philosopher, and politician.[11] He was a prolific writer and a public figure, a newspaper and literary journal publisher, a political party founder and organizer, the representative of the province of Leon to the Parliament of the Second Spanish Republic, and the founder of the League for Political Education. He certainly lived an active, prophetic life. Robert McClintock, in a major work on Ortega and his public political mission, puts it this way: "Ortega's public power was that of a *cleric,* he was a man of the world who continually confronted his people with worthy standards and the woeful gap between these ideals and human achievement."[12] In true existentialist fashion, he argued that each person was "a substantial emigrant on a pilgrimage of being"[13] and that one's mission was an activity that one *had to do*.[14] Ultimately, Ortega came to believe that "if you shy away from life (task), you fall in insincerity," echoing themes that Europe would hear repeatedly from the postwar French existentialists, Sartre and Camus.[15] Sadly, some critics suggest that shying away from life is precisely what Ortega did. We will say more about this as we close the chapter. Here we simply say that living in word *and* deed is a challenge for all of us.

Ortega's Philosophical Convictions

Ortega was not a systematic, orderly thinker. Prolific, yes, but not organized. A collection of his complete works would total more than 6,000 pages,[16] a veritable "seedbed of ideas."[17] However, in nearly all his major writings, Ortega consistently repeated four fundamental convictions. They all have to do with life, the *individual human life*: (1) it is the "root reality" that frames all other realities; (2) it is essentially a problem to be solved or a task to be done; (3) it is a fundamental decision to be made about who you will become; and (4) it is a series of circumstantial possibilities—not limitless but plural—that one must face. Indeed, life is a journey of becoming and of making courageous choices within the circumstances life presents.

> Clearly, on Ortega's account, each of us is on a mission. McClintock puts it this way: According to Ortega, a person's mission was an activity that he *had to do* in the double sense that the person had certain things he could do, for they were within his sphere of possibilities, and that he not only had them to do, but he had to do them, he was obligated to do them, on the pain of voluntarily falsifying his best self. . . . Each man had a mission, which each had to find in his circumstances. . . . Ultimately, the quality of *life* in any community was the function of the degree to which its members freely aspired to fulfill their missions, their destinies.[18]

We quote at length from McClintock because we believe that he captures powerfully the very essence of Ortega's idea of mission—in this case, personal mission[19]—and we will return to this idea as Ortega explains his vision for the mission of the university. The two missions, as we will see, are intimately related.

At the end of the day, Ortega was a passionate voice for the renewal of Spain. In his daily paper, *El Sol,* he wrote these words in August 1926, at which time Rivera was in firm control of the country: "I firmly believe in the possibility—note, in the possibility—that Spain will now begin a new historic ascent. I firmly believe that in a few years we can make of Spain, not the richest or the most learned country, but the healthiest one, politically and socially, of all Europe."[20] And he believed that the university must play a vital role if it were to live up to its mission.

Criticisms and Concluding Comments

Before we conclude this section of the chapter and begin an examination of *Mission of the University* in some detail, it is only fair to note that Ortega made just about everyone angry at some point or another. Ceplecha says that "the majority were opposed—often violently—to more than one page of his almost endless writing." Even worse, he was called "a purveyor of myths," helping the elite class in Spain to believe what they want to believe, thus sustaining their elitist attitudes and their privileged behaviors.[21] A milder complaint was that he was "frequently guilty of leaving his works unfinished."[22] And finally, there is the criticism that in the end, Ortega did not live out his convictions and embrace his circumstances, but rather fled the country and lived in self-imposed exile for a silent decade. This, it seems to us, is also a fair criticism.

We include these criticisms because we feel that it is important to see Ortega as a real human being—a brilliant, inspiring visionary, and a broken pot, too; imperfect, like the rest of us. Perhaps the most balanced assessment of Ortega's work and life comes from Ouimette: "Ortega y Gasset possessed a greatness of mind that became a historical fact in twentieth-century Spain. He has been accused, often with reason, of superficiality and intellectual vanity, yet the fact remains that he opened the doors of Spain, as he intended, to ways of thinking that might otherwise never have penetrated the Peninsula."[23]

Mission of the University

Mission of the University is a rewrite and compilation of a lecture series Ortega gave at the request of the Spanish Students' Union Federation at the University of Madrid in 1930 on "some topic related to the reform of higher education." Although their instructions to Ortega were not very specific, the students were hoping for an impassioned criticism of the university and the state, as well as a way forward for reform. The result of these six lectures is a classic work, joining the ranks of John Henry Newman, Karl Jaspers, Robert Maynard Hutchins, Hannah Arendt, Dorothy L. Sayers, and Alfred North Whitehead (among others) as an essential source for any serious consideration of the enduring mission of the university and the purpose of higher education in any century, including the twenty-first century. As we shall see in the final portion of this chapter, those who serve in faith-based institutions can appropriate much that is good from Ortega.

We will briefly introduce and then consider each lecture in turn. You will see that Ortega returns time and again to four distinct missions that encompass his vision for the university: the teaching of the learned professions, scientific research and the preparation of scientific investigators, training for political leaders, and the transmission of culture. His *Mission* is truly a marriage of his existential experiences (circumstances) and his philosophical and political convictions.

The First Lecture: A Tempered Spirit of Reform

Ortega begins his opening remarks with a setup: "I come with great enthusiasm, but with small hope."[24] He explains that it is possible to have enthusiasm about uncertain things, and in fact, having too much self-assurance is not very helpful. He points to Germany's overconfidence of victory in World War I as a primary reason for their defeat, and he identifies as a grave concern the resolute belief that technology and social organizations are capable of solving their own problems. Interestingly, Sevilla points out that Ortega was among the first in Spain to recognize that the modern era was coming to an end and the postmodern era was dawning.[25]

To be sure, Ortega tells his audience, he has enthusiasm for certain reforms already underway. The university is better than it used to be, but it is not yet what it needs to be. There is still much work to be done. He quotes Sancho Panza, who advised on more than one occasion that even if you are given a cow, you still have to carry the rope.[26] Are there possibilities? Yes. Did he have new faith? No, not yet. Why? Ortega tells his students straightaway that he sees no group yet capable of realizing such reforms. Why? To put it bluntly, they are lazy—slovenly. Slovenliness, he fears, permeates the entire Spanish culture from top to bottom, the fundamental ailment of Spain. It is surely a crime, perhaps not as horrific as the crimes of the state, but a crime nonetheless. Sadly, he points out, slovenliness "grows accustomed to its own presence; it finds itself pleasantly comfortable, and tends to spread and perpetuate itself. Thus, it permeates everything."[27] And that would include all of student life on campus—and, to bring it home to us and our readers, to faculty meetings as well.

Students, he insists, need to be *in form*. To illustrate, Ortega uses the analogy of an athlete in training. We all know the difference between athletes when they are in form and when they are not. They are certainly capable of doing things that at other times they could only imagine. In effect, they are two different people. It is the result of regular discipline, steadfast resolve, purpose, and time. This applies equally to organizations as well. They must be in form or they will accomplish very little. When you are in form, Ortega told the students, you have *cool passion,* giving a nod to Hegel. The result will be "a fire supported with the constancy of clear understanding and a calm will . . . a passion with cool logic and an iron will lodged within it." [28] Such a fire cannot easily be extinguished. It is a tempered spirit of reform.

Ortega assures his students that he did not come to the auditorium that evening to dissuade them from taking part in the reform of the university, but to urge them to do it *in form*. He ends with these words: "A generation *in form* can accomplish what centuries failed to achieve without form. And there, my young friends, lies a challenge."[29] Indeed, what Ortega offered that night comes as a challenge to all of us.

The Second Lecture: The Fundamental Question

In this lecture, Ortega first poses and then forcefully answers these questions: what is the university for, and what must it be consequently? He quickly notes that true reform must be about new usages, not merely the correction of abuses. It is important to correct abuses, he concedes, but if you want reform, corrections in and of themselves will never do. Far too many faculty members confuse adjustments and tweaking of the curriculum or pedagogy with doing something new and vital, and according to Ortega, imitation is even worse. The kiss of death is to try to copy some other university's program or curriculum. He presses the argument even further by suggesting that "because of their willingness to imitate and to evade thinking through the questions for themselves, our best professors (he is speaking here of his own colleagues at the University of Madrid) live in all respects in a spirit fifteen or twenty years behind the times, except that they are up to date in the details of their field . . . the fate of people who try to save themselves the effort of being authentic and forming their own convictions."[30]

Currently, the university has two stated missions: the teaching of the professions and research. Of course, these missions are fine, but Ortega fears that they have squeezed out the teaching of general culture—and that is unacceptable because "culture is what saves human life from being a mere disaster."[31] What the university offers now for general education is simply "a mere miserable residue" of ages past, an ornamental knowledge.[32] Such an approach leads to the training of a new barbarian, someone who has professional knowledge without culture. Surely professional knowledge is critical, but we expect and need more from those who have been privileged with a university education. To ensure that his listeners understood his argument, Ortega finished with one more example: "Civilization has had to await the beginning of the twentieth century, to see the astounding spectacle of how brutal, how stupid, and yet how aggressive is the man learned in one thing and fundamentally ignorant in all else,"[33] something he refers to as the barbarism of specialization in his best-known work, *The Revolt of the Masses,* which appeared a year before these lectures.[34] John Henry Newman (Chapter Six) expressed these same sentiments about professional education eighty years earlier, as did Maria Montessori (Chapter Five) in her lecture in Amsterdam eight years after Ortega. Over eighty years later, we share his sentiments.

It is important, Ortega concludes, to "make your life a vital influence, in harmony with the height of the times."[35] The key to the reform of a university is to make the transmission of culture central to the university's mission, not a mere add-on or a set of requirements to get out of the way, but as *the* fundamental mission to which all other missions must give support. Only a firm resolution to turn the university on its head in this way will bear fruit.

The Third Lecture: The Principle of Economy in Education

We note that lectures three to six are much shorter than the first two lectures. Ortega was in his late forties at the time, so it was certainly not due to old age. However, he did complain about the condition of the lecture hall and was in ill health at the time, so perhaps the combination of the two took their toll and he simply ran out of gas. Or, like many lecture series, perhaps he delivered his main points and concerns early on, leaving the remaining lectures for commentary. Honestly, we do not know, but we want to point out this fact and assure the reader that we are bringing a careful abridgment of the later lectures as well.

Ortega begins his third lecture by pointing out that the basis of all economic activity is scarcity, and the economic principle of scarcity applies to education, too—the scarcity of the capacity to learn. That is, students can learn only so much, and surely they cannot learn everything there is to know about any subject, or everything that we want them to know, or even everything that they might want to know. Simply put, you can't learn everything. Given this principle, and noting the "tropical underbrush of subject matter"[36] currently required of students, Ortega argues that the curriculum requires a thorough pruning. And how to decide what gets trimmed? Curricular trimming is to be guided by two questions: what does "life" require that a student know, and what can a student reasonably learn? At the close of the lecture, Ortega harks back to the medieval university in Bologna by suggesting that another key to renewal is to return the control of the university to the students. We will say more about the implications of doing so in our discussion of the last three lectures, but it is clear that Ortega has a flair for the dramatic, even if his solutions are largely impractical. As you might imagine, his faculty colleagues were not at all sure that he was on the right track, but his proposals were well received by his students.

The Fourth Lecture: What the University Must Be Primarily: Profession and Science

Ortega begins the fourth lecture by offering four propositions that follow from the principles discussed in previous lectures:

- Fundamentally, the university consists of the higher education that the ordinary student should receive.
- It is necessary to make this student a cultured person, living at the height of the times. The student should be taught physics (the physical scheme of the world), biology (the fundamental themes of organic life), sociology (the structure and function of social life), and philosophy (the plan of the universe).
- The student should receive expert training in a learned profession.
- The student should not and need not try to be a scientist.[37]

Ortega quickly adds that he knows that there will be a veritable volcanic eruption of objections from the faculty, but he insists on the importance of distinguishing between science, culture, and professional instruction. In this particular lecture, he considers the difference between science and the teaching of the professions. He insists that science is "one of the most sublime pursuits and achievements of mankind: more sublime than the university itself, conceived as an educational institution."[38] But, he continues, it is not the only one, and it is not for everyone. There is also professional instruction. Science involves investigation and inquiry—using the scientific method. It is critical for the world, but it is not necessary for the professional student. The ordinary student, a term Ortega uses to designate a typical undergraduate, needs only to receive the very best professional instruction. Here, Ortega makes a distinction between those who "do" science and those who "teach" science. He is all for students studying physics and biology, but only in a general sense—no labs, please. He worries that "the trend toward a university dominated by 'inquiry' has been disastrous"[39] and concludes that if his prescription were to be followed, the university could "teach the professions with greater efficiency and with greater depth, with less time and effort than at present."[40] Ortega favors the development of scientists and the training of professionals, but in his view, mixing the two is unhelpful—and perhaps dangerous.

Clearly, Ortega makes the distinction between scientific and professional instruction, but what about the relationship and tensions between science and general culture? This is the topic of his next lecture.

The Fifth Lecture: Culture and Science

In this short yet powerful lecture, Ortega makes the argument that science is important to the university but is not its central activity. The cardinal function of the university is the teaching of general culture so students can understand the system of vital ideas by which their age lives, and so they can grasp how to make meaning of life and embrace that meaning. Here, Ortega is pressing for students to learn about life in the biographical rather than biological sense. As he develops his argument, Ortega shows his existential leanings. Every human being must pick his or her way through life, and at times, "life is fired at us point blank."[41] We have to make sense of it and live in an enlightened way, at the height of the times. If not, the person lives beneath what would constitute a "right life" and is thereby swindled of his or her birthright—perhaps birth obligation would be a more accurate term. Thus, it is imperative that the university impart "the full culture of the time and [reveal] to mankind, with clarity and truthfulness, that gigantic world of today in which the life of the individual must be articulated, if it is to be authentic."[42] Too often, according to Ortega, science gets in the way. As he argued earlier, the student can only learn so much.

To ensure that enlightenment is maintained as the cardinal function, Ortega would make a faculty of culture the very centerpiece of the university. Those teaching in this faculty would be hired and promoted because of their genius for integration and their gift of teaching, pushing scientific inquiry to the periphery—still important but not central. In Ortega's view, creating such a faculty would shift the university's primary emphasis from research to the teaching of general culture and the training of professionals.

The Sixth Lecture: What the University Must Be "In Addition"

This is an intriguing question to us and for us. What *must* the university be in addition? It could be many things in addition, but what *must* it be? Ortega makes it clear that it must do two additional things. First, it must keep science close by. After making a strong case that science is not to be the dominant activity for the university and is not to be taught to all students, he turns right around and suggests that the university must have science encamped close by—their labs, research institutes, and centers—in constant interaction with the faculty of general culture and the professions. In fact, according to Ortega, science is the dignity and the soul of the university, without which the university slips back into scholasticism. So there is not only a place but also a crucial leavening role for science in the university after all. It isn't the German vision of the university, but a Spanish one—or at least Ortega's.

The second thing Ortega calls the university to do in addition is to remain an active part of public life, in contact with the present and "open to the whole reality of its time. It must be in the midst of life, and saturated by it."[43] If not, it will surely atrophy. The public needs the university to be a vital presence, too. According to Ortega, the church is lost in the past, and the state is too busy governing its own opinions rather than governing the people. Sadly, the public is left at the mercy of the only group or spiritual force still interested in current affairs—journalists. Even though Ortega jokingly admits that others refer to him sarcastically as a mere journalist, he sees the preeminent position of journalism in Spanish society as a danger. Journalists are not capable of nourishing and guiding the public soul. His hope is that the university will take on this leading role once again in Spanish society. Ortega ends the lecture series as he started—with more enthusiasm than faith. Still, he is a passionate orator to the end: "In the thick of life's urgencies and its passions, the university must assert itself as a major 'spiritual power,' higher than the press, standing for serenity in the midst of frenzy, for seriousness and the grasp of intellect in the face of frivolity and unashamed stupidity. Then the university, once again, will come to be what it was in its grand hour: an uplifting principle in the history of the western world."[44]

In the final portion of this chapter, we will summarize Ortega's primary arguments and ideas about the mission of the university, examine their implications and relevance for an institution that names Christ, and then pose some questions for further reflection and dialogue for all of us who try to live authentically before our students, helping them to make sense of both present and future. Certainly, we want our students to live in an enlightened way—at the height of the times. We know that life will be fired at them point-blank, so they will need the company of wise friends and mentors to make their way.

Mission Summary

Ortega summarizes the primary mission of the university in six points and cautions that it is important to see things as they are and not as we wish them to be—no utopian visions:

1. The university is to teach the ordinary student to be a cultured person and a good member of a profession.
2. The university will not tolerate false pretense, requiring of the student only what actually can be learned (not what the faculty would like them to learn).

3. It will not waste the time of the ordinary student by pretending that he is going to be a scientist. Therefore, scientific investigation will not be required.
4. The cultural disciplines and professional studies will be offered with the best pedagogy: systematic, synthetic, and complete.
5. The selection of professors will depend on their ability to synthesize and their gift of teaching rather than their ability as investigators.
6. After the students' requirements are reduced to the minimum, the university will be inflexible with the student.[45]

This is what, as Ortega puts it, the university must be primarily. In addition, he argues, the university must be associated with science to avoid scholasticism and must make its presence felt in society to prevent its own atrophy.

Key Ideas and Corollary Implications

Let's unpack this primary mission just a bit by looking at several ideas and their corollary implications.

The Ordinary Student

First, Ortega often refers to the "ordinary student." Ordinary students are simply undergraduates attending the university, but in many respects, they are not ordinary at all. Ortega believes deeply that a university education is for a select minority of persons. He holds no democratic inclinations when it comes to issues of university access. It is not and should not be for everyone. In this sense, Ortega is an elitist, distinguishing the classes (public leaders) from the masses (those who follow the leadership of the classes). While we must recognize the democratization of higher education that has taken place since the 1930s, particularly in the United States, we wonder if this trend has gone too far. Should everyone have access to higher education as students now have access to high school? Should everyone attend at least two years of college at a junior college as Robert Maynard Hutchins suggests?[46] If so, would the *higher learning* be reserved for professional training and graduate school for a select minority? Should it be? These are important and timely questions to ponder.

An Honest Education

Second, those who attend the university must be prepared to be leaders in whatever place they land. To help prepare for this reality, students must be active participants in their own education. Ortega is insistent that institutions do not *give* an education, they *offer* one, and students do not *receive* an education, they *acquire* one.[47] This is an important distinction for Ortega. The university must place honest demands on students, and it is up to them to rise to the occasion—or go home. We recognize that this sounds harsh, but we see much of value in the idea that a credible university program must demand something of substance from its students. No one deserves an "A" just because they paid tuition for the course and did their best.

General Culture

The third implication of Ortega's vision of the mission of the university is that a vital program of "general culture," to use his term, is essential if students are to be shaped and formed as public leaders and engaged professionals. Several corollaries follow from his view of general culture:

- The curriculum needs be student centered, not faculty centered, a theme that arises repeatedly among the thinkers we review in this book. Ortega is critical of university faculties that create programs and offerings based on what and when they want to teach rather than on what students actually need to learn.
- Faculty members need to have a genius for integration and synthesis and a gift for teaching rather than the desire and ability to do basic research. In such an institution, we suspect that the Boyer model of scholarship, particularly the scholarship of teaching, integration, and application, would not only be appropriate but would become the central priority.[48]
- The general education requirements will be trimmed to an essential minimum, and the best professors, employing the very best pedagogy possible, will teach them. Ortega does not give many details about the courses he envisions being offered, but it is fair to say that most of what we call the liberal arts would not be offered. This is a distinctly different vision of the university from that presented by

Newman or, we suspect, Sayers.[49] In some ways, Ortega's vision may be more in keeping with the pressing economic realities faced by institutions today.

- A faculty of culture is the very nucleus of university organization, because preparation for leadership is the fundamental reason the university exists. Without this faculty, the learned professions would send out students without a mission, unable to grasp a true purpose of life.[50]
- The university must reestablish itself as a major "spiritual power," a significant voice in the public square. No ivory towers. It gets its hands dirty; it gets up to its elbows in the formation of citizens, the renovation of institutions, and the recovery of meaning and purpose for the public good. This is, of course, a very grand and idealistic vision, but very much Ortega.[51]

QUESTIONS FOR REFLECTION AND DISCUSSION

Now that we have provided a summary of the mission(s) of the university and before we end this chapter on Ortega, we want to pose two significant questions for the Christian university (or college). We will use Ortega's two basic questions to frame the discussion and add a few others as a way to prime the pump:

What Must the Christian University or College Be Primarily?

- What would it mean to be truly student centered rather than faculty centered? Would the curriculum change, the times when courses are offered, or the mode by which they are delivered? What would it mean to have a faculty reward structure (including promotions and tenure) that encouraged and rewarded the genius of synthesis and integration (teaching) rather than one focused on original research and publications?
- Is a Christian university or college education for everyone? Would answering that it is not for everyone betray elitism, or might it be an expression of kindness?

- How would a faith-based institution operationally define what it means to be *in form*? What biblical and theological perspectives might we bring to answering the question of being *in form*? To what extent do compelling ideas give a sense of mission and task to our students? How could we do that? What are such ideas?
- What if professional preparation were acknowledged as central to the mission (since the middle ages) and not simply seen as a way for the administration to attract more students and make more money?
- What if we reenvisioned the dominant liberal arts idea of learning for learning's sake to mean preparing students to live at the height of the times? What if there were no departments divided into liberal arts disciplines, but rather a faculty of general culture? Would such organization bring energy and direction or mere chaos?
- What would living at the height of the times look like for a Christian in the twenty-first century? How can we help students live with a sense of the vital—in a Christian sense? What ideas would shape and form students in that manner? What about faculty?
- What would it mean to model for our students a tempered spirit of reform? How might that work out on our campuses, in our churches, and in our communities?

What Must the Christian College or University Be in Addition?

- What if basic research and the scholarship of discovery were moved to the periphery of the university instead of being the primary means of prestige and rewards for faculty? What if students were not expected to learn about scientific inquiry, but rather to learn the science that every civic and church leader would need to know? What if general culture and "enlightenment" trumped the laboratory experience? Would this be a gain or a loss? Is the university, especially the Christian university, stuck in modernity?
- What would it mean for a Christian institution to be *in form*? What about a faculty *in form*? Who would have to take the lead?
- Has the Christian university abdicated its role as a spiritual force in the public square? Has it lost its sense of vitality, its intellectual clarity, and its capacity to live life intensively?

We ask these questions, not as an indictment of our current ways of doing things, but in an honest effort to spur assessment and dialogue. Discourse, we believe, is the rare air of higher education. And we end this chapter with the same emotion with which Ortega began his lecture series in 1930—with enthusiasm. May we all have the courage to face the realities of our institutions with a tempered spirit of reform, with passion tempered by cool logic, courage, and a deep faith in the one who sustains our work. "We have arrived," Ortega once told an audience, "at a moment in which we have no other solution than to invent, and to invent in every order of life. I could not propose a more delightful task. One must invent. . . . Go to it!"[52] That, it seems to us, is living at the height of the times. Let's go to it!

FOR FURTHER STUDY

Ortega wrote widely and thoughtfully about philosophy, art, political action, university life, and modern culture. Unfortunately, to date his collected works are available only in Spanish. Fortunately, a good deal of his work has been translated into English. We do wish to highlight the following works and commend them to you.

IN ORTEGA'S OWN WORDS

Ortega y Gasset, José. *The Dehumanization of Art and Other Essays on Art, Culture, and Literature.* Princeton Paperbacks, 128. Princeton, NJ: Princeton University Press, 1972.
———. *An Interpretation of Universal History.* New York: Norton, 1973.
———. *Invertebrate Spain.* Translated by Mildred Adams. New York: W. W. Norton, 1937.
———. *Man and People.* London: Allen & Unwin, 1957.
———. *Mission of the University.* Princeton: Princeton University Press, 1944.
———. *The Revolt of the Masses: Authorized Translation from the Spanish.* New York: W. W. Norton & Co., 1932.
———. *Velazquez, Goya and the Dehumanization of Art.* New York: W. W. Norton, 1972.

BIOGRAPHIES

Gray, Rockwell. *The Imperative of Modernity: An Intellectual Biography of José Ortega y Gasset*. Berkeley: University of California Press, 1989.
Marías, Julián. *José Ortega y Gasset, Circumstance and Vocation*. Norman, OK: University of Oklahoma Press, 1970.
Niedermayer, Franz. *José Ortega y Gasset*. Berlin: Colloquium Verlag, 1959.
Ouimette, Victor. *José Ortega y Gasset*. Boston: Twayne Publishers, 1982.

OTHER SELECTED WORKS ABOUT ORTEGA

Bara, Francisco Esteban. "Wilhelm Von Humboldt, Cardinal John Henry Newman, and José Ortega y Gasset: Some Thoughts on Character Education for Today's University." *Journal of Character Education* 11, no. 1 (2015): 1.
Boyers, Robert. "Culture and the Intellectual at the Height of the Time. (José Ortega y Gasset)." *TriQuarterly* 80 (1991): 160.
Cate-Arries, Francie. "Poetics and Philosophy: José Ortega y Gasset and the Generation of 1927." *Hispania* 71, no. 3 (1988): 503–511.
Ceplecha, Christian. *The Historical Thought of José Ortega y Gasset*. Washington, DC: Catholic University Press, 1958.
Conway, James I. "Ortega y Gasset's 'Vital Reason.'" *Thought XXII* (1957): 594–602.
Corrigan, Robert. "José Ortega y Gasset: Master Teacher." *Kentucky Foreign Language Quarterly* 10, no. 3 (1963): 129–132.
DePuy, Ida Blanche. *The Basic Ideology of José Ortega y Gasset: The Conflict of Mission and Vocation*. Palo Alto, CA: Stanford University Press, 1961.
Díaz, Janet. *The Major Themes of Existentialism in the Work of José Ortega y Gasset*. North Carolina Studies in the Romance Languages and Literatures. No. 94. Chapel Hill, NC: University of North Carolina Press, 1970.
Dobson, Andrew. *An Introduction to the Politics and Philosophy of José Ortega y Gasset*. Cambridge Iberian and Latin American Studies. New York: Cambridge University Press, 1989.
Gonzalez, Pedro Blas. "Biographical Life and Ratio-vitalism in the Thought of Ortega y Gasset." *Philosophy Today* 46, no. 4 (2002): 406–418.
Homes, Oliver W. *Human Reality and the Social World: Ortega's Philosophy of History*. Amherst, MA: University of Massachusetts Press, 1975.
Jordan, Dylan. *Reason and History in the Philosophy of José Ortega y Gasset*. Portland, OR: Reed College, 2012.

Kerr, Clark. "Ortega y Gasset for the 21st Century." *Society* 28, no. 6 (1991): 79–83.

Marino, Joseph Francis. *José Ortega y Gasset: Perspectives on the Forms of Human Temporality.* New York: University of New York, 1980.

McClintock, Robert. *Man and His Circumstances: Ortega as Educator.* New York: Teachers College Press, 1971.

Neuhaus, Richard. "Ortega y Gasset Revisited." *Commentary* 82 no. 1 (1986): 53.

Pellicani, Luciano. "Ortega's Theory of Social Action." *Telos* 70 (1986): 115.

Raley, Harold C. *José Ortega y Gasset: Philosopher of European Unity.* Tuscaloosa, AL: University of Alabama Press, 1971.

Reid, Kenneth S. *Early Work of José Ortega y Gasset.* PhD diss., King's College, Newcastle-upon-Tyne, 1956.

Sánchez Villaseñor, José, and Joseph Small. *Ortega y Gasset, Existentialist: A Critical Study of His Thought and Its Sources.* Humanist Library 12. Chicago: H. Regnery, 1949.

NOTES

¹See "José Ortega y Gasset." *Contemporary Authors Online* (Gale Cengage Learning, Detroit: 2016), accessed on August 31 2016.

²The Spanish Students' Union Federation was a very active and powerful group, following the tradition of major student engagement and voice first established at the medieval university in Bologna and still observable in institutions in Latin America and Spain today. This is very different from the model of faculty control established in most northern European universities (stemming primarily from the University of Paris) and followed in most English-speaking universities. There are many excellent sources regarding faculty versus student power in the medieval university. For example, see Hastings Rashdall, *The Universities of Europe in the Middle Ages*, 3 vols. (Oxford: Oxford University Press, 1895); Alan Cobban, *The Medieval Universities* (London: Harper & Row, 1975); Helen Wieruszowski, *The Medieval University: Masters, Students, and Learning* (Princeton, NJ: Van Nostrand, 1966); and Ian P. Wei, *Intellectual Culture in Medieval Paris: Theologians and the University, 1100–1330* (Cambridge: Cambridge University Press, 2012).

³Christian Ceplecha, *The Historical Thought of José Ortega y Gasset* (Washington, DC: The Catholic University of America Press, 1958), 2.

⁴Ibid., 2.

⁵Ceplecha, 3; Andrew Dobson, *An Introduction to the Politics and Philosophy of José Ortega y Gasset* (Cambridge: Cambridge University Press, 1989), 17.

⁶Dobson, 18.

⁷Ibid., xii.

⁸Ibid., 11.

⁹Diego Sevilla, "José Ortega y Gasset," in *Fifty Major Thinkers on Education* ed. Joy A. Palmer (London: Routledge, 2001), 244.

¹⁰Sevilla, 244.

¹¹Ceplecha, 1.

¹²Robert McClintock, *Man and His Circumstances: Ortega as Educator* (New York: Teachers College Press, Columbia University, 1971), 211.

¹³John Wyatt, *Commitment to Higher Education* (Buckingham, UK: Open University Press, 1990), 41.

¹⁴Dobson, 132.

¹⁵Sevilla, 244.

¹⁶Ibid., 245.

¹⁷Ceplecha, 31.

¹⁸McClintock, 132–133.

¹⁹We recognize that McClintock did not use inclusive language (writing in 1971). Nonetheless, we quoted verbatim to be faithful to the text. With our readers, we recognize the inappropriateness of exclusive language.

²⁰McClintock, 176.

²¹A quotation from Ortega biographer Rockwell Gray, cited in John Wyatt, *Commitment to Higher Education* (Buckingham, England: Open University Press, 1990), 42.

²²Ouimette, 9.

²³Ibid., 151.

[24] Ibid., 3.
[25] Sevilla, 245.
[26] José Ortega y Gasset, *The Mission of the University* (New Brunswick, NJ: Transaction Publishers, 1992), 7.
[27] Ibid., 10.
[28] Ibid., 8–9.
[29] Ibid., 13.
[30] Ibid., 21.
[31] Ibid., 27.
[32] Ibid., 28.
[33] Ibid., 21.
[34] José Ortega y Gasset, *The Revolt of the Masses* (Notre Dame, IN: Notre Dame Press, 1985), 94.
[35] Ortega, *Mission*, 30.
[36] Ibid., 43.
[37] Ibid., 49.
[38] Ibid., 51.
[39] Ibid., 54.
[40] Ibid., 55.
[41] Ibid., 63.
[42] Ibid., 65.
[43] Ibid., 79.
[44] Ibid., 81.
[45] Ortega, *Mission*, 75.
[46] See Chapter Ten in this book, also Robert Maynard Hutchins, *The Higher Learning in America*.
[47] McClintock, 14.
[48] See Patrick Allen and Kenneth Badley, *Faith and Learning: A Guide for Faculty* (Abilene, TX: Abilene Christian University Press, 2014), particularly chapters 4–8, and 10.
[49] See John Henry Newman and Dorothy Sayers, Chapters Two and Six in this book, for details of their conceptions of the university.
[50] Whitehead might agree with Ortega on creating something like a faculty of culture.
[51] Ortega, *Mission*, xv–xvi.
[52] Quoted in McClintock, 485.

Robert Maynard Hutchins

The Higher Learning in America (1936)

ROBERT MAYNARD HUTCHINS WAS IN MANY RESPECTS THE LAST GREAT American university presidential personality, the most vocal, influential, and controversial leader in higher education for much of the first half of the twentieth century. His public persona was larger than life, only matched, some would say, by his ego. Del Weber, professor of education at Arizona State University, puts it this way: "Although Hutchins has been accused of many things—he has been called 'the most dangerous man in education,' a man whose ideas were so bad that even the Nazis threw them out—he has seldom been accused of lacking purpose, direction, or of failure to demonstrate leadership."[1] He didn't mince words, and he was once characterized by the eminent historian Frederick Rudolph as a "trenchant critic," sarcastic, bitter and sometimes funny, "a kind of strange and wonderful throwback to Jeremiah Day and the Yale Report of 1828."[2] Once, while scoffing at the incessant desire for credentials on the part of the American public, Hutchins quipped that every American should be granted the BA degree at birth. Then, colleges and universities would be free to educate only those students who were genuinely interested in learning.[3] Given the controversial context of his leadership, he may well be a throwback to the prophet Jeremiah, too.

Education and Professional Life

Maynard Robert Hutchins was born in Brooklyn, New York, on January 17, 1899, the same birthday of another from Brooklyn who would become a major figure in Chicago history—Al Capone. Yes, it was supposed to be Maynard Robert Hutchins, but at the christening ceremony, the minister became confused and presented the baby as Robert Maynard Hutchins. Being good Calvinists, his parents saw providence at work and did not attempt to correct his name. Both his grandfather and father were Presbyterian ministers, serving congregations for some time just blocks apart in Brooklyn. While his grandfather was a strict fundamentalist, his father was certainly more liberal, not believing in original sin, imputed guilt, or the historical accuracy of the Bible.[4] Still, he was a good preacher and pious enough to be offered a professorship in homiletics at Oberlin College, his alma mater. Robert and his brother, Will, wondered if they were to be exiled to Indian territory. As it turns out, they found themselves on a Puritan island instead.

Oberlin College

Hutchins attended both the academy and the college, and he loved every minute of it. He was a star student, but not a model one. It was a pious and conservative place with a great number of rules to follow—perhaps a few too many, as it turned out. He wrote and circulated this poem to express his views:

> In Oberlin, I must not smoke.
> I don't.
> Nor listen to a naughty joke.
> I don't.
> To flirt, to dance, is very wrong.
> Wild youths choose women, wine and song.
> I don't.
> In Oberlin I must not wink at pretty girls
> Or even think about intoxicating drink.
> I don't.
> I kiss no girls, not even one.

Why, I don't know how it is done.
You wouldn't think I'd have much fun.
I don't.[5]

One rule he didn't heed was "thou shall not steal." Thomas Henderson, a prominent member of the Oberlin community and a regular attendee at evening prayers, loved to park his new car right in front of the church—with the keys in the ignition. It was his pride and joy. Hutchins and his school friends would regularly take the car for a spin and return it before the service was over. That is, until one evening when the car ran out of gas. Discovering the "theft," Henderson immediately offered a $150 reward for its return and the apprehension of the criminals. Realizing that someone on campus would surely turn them in (since almost every student knew about the weekly escapades), they decided to return the car themselves and ask for mercy. Henderson read them the riot act, but decided that it was better to have the boys pray for forgiveness than to spend time in jail. So Hutchins and friends knelt down and vigorously prayed for forgiveness. Just to be sure it took, Henderson made the boys pray twice. On the way out, Hutchins, showing his audacious inclination to fund-raise at any opportunity, turned to Henderson and asked that since they returned the car and saved him the $150 reward, would he be inclined to share his savings with them? He was not so inclined. Many feel that Hutchins carried this youthful arrogance into his professional life and that it did not serve him well.[6]

Hutchins loved his time at Oberlin. Although he left after his sophomore year to serve as an ambulance driver during World War I before finishing his studies at Yale, he never forgot the combination of high academic standards, the classical curriculum, and an emphasis on piety and social engagement. It was a formative time. According to Hutchins scholar Mary Ann Dzuback, "The Oberlin of the early twentieth century exemplified for Hutchins the ideal intellectual community. It was a community he would spend his entire life trying to re-create."[7] Sadly, he never did.

Yale College

Hutchins's time at Yale can only be described as a meteoric rise, still almost unbelievable. After finishing his required undergraduate courses in the middle of his junior year, he turned his attention to the study of law. After graduating with a BA, he explored the idea of going into the ministry like his father but decided instead to teach English and history at the Lake Placid School.[8] After one semester, however, he received an offer from Yale College to return and serve as the secretary of the Yale Corporation. His duties included public relations and fund-raising, requiring frequent speaking engagements at alumni meetings, class dinners, and community events, and he was also responsible for planning and overseeing all of the university's public ceremonies. In addition, he supervised fifty staff members who produced all Yale publications, sat in on meetings of the corporation and its committees, and had access to all academic departments as the principal administrative assistant to President James Rowland Angell.[9] One could not ask for a better internship in university administration.

Hutchins thrived on the grueling schedule, gaining wide notoriety as a sharp and witty speaker. And on the side, he finished his law degree. With degree in hand, he took a position in the law school, appointed first as a professor and soon thereafter as dean. His leadership was sweeping, energetic, and at times controversial. However, it is difficult to tell how good a dean he would have become at Yale because in less than two years, he was named president of the University of Chicago. At his inauguration, he was thirty years old.

The University of Chicago

It is not possible to cover Hutchins's twenty-two years of leadership at Chicago in any depth in this short section.[10] Rather, our intent is to give a bit of context for his book, *The Higher Learning in America*. In Chicago, Hutchins hit the ground running. In many regards, it is surprising that he was offered the job at all, particularly given the poor recommendation he received from his former boss at Yale. President James Angell characterized Hutchins as young, inexperienced, temperamental, impatient, and intolerant—ready for a presidency in perhaps five or ten years, but not now. The board ignored Angell's negative review and extended the offer.[11]

In his inaugural speech, Hutchins announced that major changes in university structure, curriculum, and priorities were forthcoming. As you might expect, it made the faculty nervous. From the beginning, Hutchins worried about the nature of the pursuit of truth, fearing that the inductive methods used in the research university focused on the wrong end of the process, on producing small bits of facts and figures.[12] Instead, he wanted a deductive approach to scholarly work that would draw upon first principles for direction. In Hutchins's university, metaphysics would be the central and guiding force for the entire enterprise. This made the faculty very nervous (except the philosophy department).

Hutchins compounded this growing adversarial relationship by hiring key faculty and administrative staff without going through established university protocols. He would explain his actions, but he would neither apologize nor compromise. And he did much the same with academic reorganization. There was always some controversy brewing during his long and stormy presidency. Yet in the midst of this swirling storm, Hutchins boldly pressed his agenda not only for Chicago but for all of American higher education as well.

The Higher Learning in America

Twenty-five years after its first publication, a paperbound edition of *The Higher Learning* was released, and Hutchins wrote the preface. As the elder Hutchins looked back on the work of the younger Hutchins, he saw no need for any substantive changes—other than the necessity of second language study. In 1936 he had argued against it.

That is not to say that he was a kinder, gentler Hutchins. For example, pulling no punches, he notes that universities have demonstrated that they will do almost anything for money, and what is now called the higher learning has disintegrated because American educational standards have collapsed, taken over by specialization, vocationalism, and triviality. In fact, he wonders if these trends are even reversible, and perhaps it may be time to solemnly ask if it would be better to simply forget about most existing colleges and universities and plan new institutions to take on the important work that has been given up.[13] A solemn question indeed. Will the old wineskins hold new wine? Hutchins is doubtful.

In 1961, the elder Hutchins ended his preface in this way: "Let us hope that we can muster the imagination and courage to get education for our country before it is too late."[14] Hutchins, as we shall see in *The Higher*

Learning in America, never lacked in imagination, courage, or a sense of urgency.

Chapter 1: External Conditions

For Hutchins, the most striking feature of education is confusion. The university is confused with the high school, the junior college, and the liberal arts college. Sadly, the high school does not know whether to prepare students for work or for life. The junior college is simply an extension of the high school, and the liberal arts college has no direction at all. The university, which is commonly distinguished by professional schools and graduate degrees, really does not know what to do or why it should be done. In such a state of confusion, what is clear is that the magic is gone and danger lies ahead if the higher learning cannot clearly articulate its own mission. Hutchins observes, "Our people, as the last few years have shown, will strike out blindly under economic pressure; they will destroy the best and preserve the worst unless we make the distinction between the two somewhat clearer to them."[15]

Hutchins identifies three causes for this confusion. The first is the vulgar love of money.[16] It leads an institution to emphasize generating more and more revenue, a strategy that Hutchins calls both futile and fatal: "It is sad but true that when an institution determines to do something in order to get money it must lose its soul, and frequently does not get the money."[17] Many restricted gifts, he observes, cause more problems than they are worth, driving educational policy rather than the other way around. And the focus on student fees turns the university into a service station, offering something for everyone. This strategy, according to Hutchins, brings too many freshmen and sophomores to campus. Most could be educated better elsewhere. Universities that try to accommodate large numbers of underclass students by offering anything other than a strong general education program are simply headed for trouble. For Hutchins, the solution is to extend high school for another two years, K–14, joining the junior college with the high school in providing a good general education. Then, only those who truly desire the higher learning should attend the university.

In addition to the love of money, Hutchins identifies the confused notion of democracy as a second contributing factor, affecting the length, the content, and the control of education. According to this notion, students can study for as long as they like, in whatever fields they like, and seek any degrees they like. For Hutchins, this is nonsense. In actuality, the length of free public education is determined by the prevailing economic conditions. He suggests that it is time to extend free public education through grade fourteen: "This means that the public junior college will become the characteristic educational institution in the United States, just as the public high school has been up to now."[18] It is interesting to note that "up to now" was 1936. Today, with the growing number of calls to make the first two years of college free for all American students, it seems to us that Hutchins was spot on—and perhaps eighty years ahead of his time.

Along with the love of money and a flawed notion of democracy, Hutchins attacks a third confusing element for the mission of higher education—the erroneous notion of progress. He is most disappointed with the current emphasis on empiricism and the willingness to jettison the wisdom gained by past generations. The result, according to Hutchins, is an anti-intellectual university, justified by three rather odd (and wrongheaded) theories: the great-man theory, the character-building theory, and the hard-work theory. According to the great-man theory, you pay no attention to curricular details; the key is to have faculty stars. Their mere presence will inspire, stimulate, and exalt. Hutchins sees this as an excuse or alibi, "a vacuous reply to the charge that we have no intelligent program for the higher learning."[19]

The character-building theory aims to develop strong citizens by bringing together good people, good food, fellowship, and exercise in well-maintained buildings. In response, Hutchins sarcastically points out: "Undoubtedly, fine associations, fine buildings, green grass, good food, and exercise are excellent things for anybody. You will note that they are exactly what is advertised by every resort hotel. The only reason why they are also advertised by every college and university is that we have no coherent educational program to announce."[20]

As for the "teach students to work hard" approach, this is much better done through apprenticeship and trade schools. Hutchins bemoans the lack of content in higher education and scoffs at the focus on utility and superficiality of these approaches. In the end, the actions of the university and the sentiments of the public work together to degrade and render the work of higher learning into an enfeebled version of vocational education.

Hutchins ends this first chapter with a call to action. We must "stand firm and show people what the higher learning is. As education, it is the single-minded pursuit of the intellectual virtues. As scholarship it is the single-minded devotion to the advancement of knowledge."[21] If we can do this, he concludes, there might be some hope for the higher learning in America. The next three chapters are his attempt to work out the details.

Chapter 2: The Dilemmas of the Higher Learning

Hutchins begins by detailing his worries about the rapid addition and growth of professional schools in the university, noting that they consume a larger and larger portion of the time, energy, and resources of students, faculty, and administration. He also complains about the growth of preprofessional study programs in the undergraduate college: prelaw, prebusiness, predentistry, preengineering, and premedical, to name just a few of the more legitimate ones. For Hutchins, this kind of growth represents a creeping form of vocationalism.

Even inside such liberal arts departments as art, literature, and science, he sees an atmosphere that is highly professionalized. The result is that more and more faculty members are hired for their professional experience, and many possess little interest in scholarly research and even less sympathy for the intellectual mission of the university. Interdisciplinary conversations and connections cease, and the university becomes a series of silos.[22] When this happens, departments and schools work in isolation, and academic work becomes sterile and trivial—and the pursuit of knowledge for its own sake simply fades away.

This is particularly worrying for Hutchins because he sees no discernable public enthusiasm for the true mission of the university. He writes, "I do not need to tell you how hard it is in these times and in this country to keep this characteristic activity of a university alive. . . . Think where research in any meaning of the word would be if it had not been for the Rockefeller, Carnegie, and Harkness fortunes."[23] Wave after wave of vocationalism not only overwhelms the true mission of the university but also degrades the professional schools, too, turning them into trade schools. In the end, the professions suffer because young men and women entering the field lack intellectual preparation. They know how to follow a script, but they do not know how to think.

Sadly, the public does not seem to understand or care. This, Hutchins points out, is because the world is largely not only unintellectual but anti-intellectual as well, and he sees this epidemic operating much closer to home: "Even the universities are anti-intellectual. The college, we say, is for social adaptation; the university is for vocational adjustment. Nowhere does insistence on intellectual problems as the only problems worthy of a university's consideration meet such opposition as in the universities themselves. We try to help adjust students to life by giving them information about it, though we know the information will be archaic when they graduate. We try to adjust students to their life work by telling them how a professional man operates; we seldom bother to tell them why. The result is a course of study which is anti-intellectual from beginning to end."[24]

Thus, for Hutchins, the forces of professionalism have overrun the intellectual mission of the university, resulting in departmental isolation, vocational emphasis, and curricular triviality. All of this leads to an anti-intellectualism within the university that is fed by the public's incessant demand for credentials and jobs. Indeed, this is a troubling critique of American higher education, but Hutchins believes these dilemmas can be resolved. To do so, the professional schools and courses must be limited to those that have intellectual content in their own right, and the focus of study must be on the profession's great intellectual heritage that is studied for its own sake. In doing so, faculty in the professions will join the community of scholars, and advanced study in all professions will once again ultimately rest on a common body of knowledge, a general education. Of course, this is much easier said than done.

Before unpacking his prescription for an ideal general education in chapter 3, Hutchins ends this chapter with some hopeful words, knowing full well the daunting dilemmas faced by the higher learning: "The justification for the privileges of universities is not to be found in their capacity to take the sons of the rich and render them harmless to society or to take the sons of the poor and teach them how to make money. It is to be found in the enduring value of having constantly before our eyes institutions that represent an abiding faith in the highest powers of mankind. The whole world needs this symbol now as never before. It is the symbol that I hope the American universities may become."[25]

Enduring value. Abiding faith. Hope. These are powerful words. We agree that a vital higher education is needed now more than ever. For Hutchins, the highest powers of mankind are strictly intellectual. Our abiding faith in Christian higher education is in the life of the mind, too, but firmly rooted and sustained by the enduring, abiding, hopeful grace and character of God.

Chapter 3: General Education

To be clear, general education is not a part of the higher learning, but it is the essential foundation for it. Professors and students must have what Hutchins calls a common stock of fundamental ideas. Without it, "a university must remain a series of disparate schools and departments, united by nothing but the fact that they have the same president and board of trustees. Professors cannot talk to one another, not at least about anything important. They cannot hope to understand each other."[26] Without it, the higher learning is impossible.

In addition, general education will cultivate the intellectual virtues: intuitive knowledge (the habit of induction), scientific knowledge (the habit of demonstration), philosophical wisdom (scientific knowledge combined with intuitive reason regarding first principles and first causes), practical intellect (the capacity for a true course of reasoning), and prudence (right reason with respect to action). Such an education, Hutchins argues, is actually the most useful education imaginable—whether or not the student is destined for a life of the mind or a life of action. Hutchins agrees with John Henry Newman that such an education is a blessing, a gift, or a treasure; first for the owner, then through the student, for the world.[27]

Next, Hutchins takes on the caustic criticisms of John Dewey and other progressives of the day that such a conception of general education is a simplistic, one-size-fits-all solution that looks to the past rather than preparing students for future political, social, and economic changes. Hutchins dismisses the criticisms as shortsighted. He grants that there may be differences in organization, in administration, and in local habits and customs, but these, he insists, are simply details. At the heart of the matter, "education implies teaching. Teaching implies knowledge. Knowledge is truth. The truth is everywhere the same. Hence education should be everywhere the same."[28] This, in essence, is Hutchins's rationale for a general education for all. Truth is everywhere the same, and all knowledge is connected. We not only stand on the shoulders of those who came before us; we all stand on the self-same shoulders.

But what about all the practical things a student should know that will no longer be taught in the university? Hutchins suggests that students can learn these things better elsewhere. In fact, his principle of educational administration is that a college or university should do nothing that another agency or school can do as well. In order to address individual differences in learning and capacity, all requirements and course grades should be abolished except for general exams, which students take whenever they feel ready.

Even though Hutchins is ready to move general education out of the university, he is quite willing to dictate its content to the high school or junior college. What shall the curriculum be? Clearly, it will not be about social graces, the tricks of the trade, bodybuilding, or character development. Rather, it will be the study of the classics, the great books of the Western world. Why? First, he points out that they are simply the best books we have; and second, we cannot understand any subject or comprehend the world without them.[29] In order to be able to read and join the great conversation contained in the great books, Hutchins also prescribes the medieval university trivium—the study of grammar, rhetoric, and logic, to be taught along with the study of mathematics. In essence, students need these critical thinking skills if they are to profit from their engagement with the classic texts.

Although he acknowledges that students may find this curriculum uninteresting and difficult, Hutchins simply responds that good teaching will overcome the difficulties. What is needed, he presses, is the establishment of a new college or the conversion of some older ones to the true conception of general education. Displaying the urgency and impatience for which he was known throughout his career, Hutchins concludes his argument, "Unless some such demonstration or some such evangelistic movement can take place, we shall have neither general education nor universities; and we shall continue to disappoint the hopes of our people."[30]

It is not entirely clear to us what Hutchins means by *the hopes of the people,* but we know the Christian communities that sustain our institutions have hopes, too. We share a sense of urgency for the renewal and refocus of the Christian university as well.

Chapter 4: The Higher Learning

In this final chapter, Hutchins turns his attention to the nature of the higher learning and his vision for the renewal of the university. He starts by describing the ideal outcome of general education by the end of the sophomore year. (Remember that this is to be done in junior college or as an extension of high school.) Students would have a solid understanding of the foundations of the intellectual disciplines, the ability to distinguish and discuss subject matters, the facility of language and reason, and the understanding of humanity and its common connections. In short, the student "would have acquired some degree of wisdom."[31] It is at this point that the higher learning would commence.

Unfortunately, Hutchins laments that such a student today, ready for the higher learning, would find only disorder and confusion in the university, a jumbled mess of courses, departments, and schools offering a choice of anything and everything—but mostly nothing at all. Who can blame the student, Hutchins asks, who after gazing across the threshold of the higher learning and seeing nothing but chaos, would decide to leave the university and go into business?[32] The problem, as Hutchins sees it, is that the university lacks an ordering and proportioning discipline—it lacks unity. For the medieval university and for Newman, theology was that discipline, but regrettably, as Hutchins observes, "these are other times; and we are trying to discover a rational and practical order for the higher learning of today. . . . If we cannot appeal to theology, we must turn to metaphysics. Without theology or metaphysics a unified university cannot exist."[33]

For Hutchins, the ultimate aim of the university is wisdom, and because it deals with first principles and causes, metaphysics is the highest wisdom. This wisdom can bring perspective and order to all other disciplines since it is "impossible to keep metaphysics completely out of any consideration of any subject."[34] Thus, the metaphysics faculty will be the primary faculty of the university. Two other faculties are needed—a faculty of social sciences and a faculty of natural sciences. Although they are to stand on their own, they are always in conversation with and ultimately subordinate to the faculty of metaphysics. Interestingly, Hutchins has no particular metaphysical system in mind.[35] He writes: "I am not here arguing for any specific theological or metaphysical system. I am insisting that consciously or unconsciously we are always trying to get one. I suggest that we shall get a better one if we recognize explicitly the need for one and try to get the most rational one we can."[36]

According to Hutchins's plan, the student beginning in the junior year would study metaphysics, the science of first principles; the social sciences, the practical sciences dealing with human to human; and the natural sciences, dealing with humanity and nature. All three would be studied, with an emphasis on one—and without any vocational aim. Rather, the aim would be to think about fundamental ideas and problems in each field. This course of study would take about three years. All professional degrees and practical training would wait until after university study.

What about university organization? Hutchins allows for research and technical institutes to be affiliated with the university to provide necessary professional training in a particular field such as law or theology, but students would not be permitted to study in them until after they have completed their general and higher education. Only those teachers who are dealing with first principles would be considered as part of the university faculty. Academic departments and professional schools as presently known would disappear—simply fade away. The focus would be on interdisciplinary study, organized around the three new faculties. This massive reorganization would break what Hutchins refers to as the vicious circle, "a circle in which the products of a bad system grow up to be the operators and perpetuators of it,"[37] referring no doubt to the disciplinary departments and professional schools at the University of Chicago, and their resistance to change he experienced there.[38]

Hutchins notes that such changes, while admittedly sweeping and dramatic, are necessary to remove vocationalism and empiricism as the dominant elements in today's university. His hope is that if truth can be rationally pursued for its own sake, the true vision of the university can be restored. It is the only kind of university worth having. In addition, the three dilemmas described in chapter 2—professionalism, isolation, and anti-intellectualism—will be much easier to deal with. Just why this is so, he does not say.

With the optimism and passion of a fund-raising president, Hutchins, in typical fashion, concludes with these stirring words:

> If we can secure a real university in this country and a real program of general education upon which its work can rest, it may be that the character of our civilization may slowly change. It may be that we can outgrow our love of money.... Upon education our country must pin its hopes for true progress, which involves scientific and technological advance, but under the direction of reason; of true prosperity, which included external goods but does not overlook those of the soul; and of true liberty, which can exist only in a society, and in a society rationally ordered.[39]

Advance with reason, prosperity for body and soul, and a rationally ordered liberty for all. This is Hutchins's hope for the future.

Key Arguments and Corollary Implications

Hutchins, more than any other thinker we have explored in Part Two of our book, sees the university in danger of becoming irrelevant, proposes the most sweeping changes to its organization, curriculum, and educational sequence, and yet offers the most optimistic vision for the future of the university and society—provided, of course, that his plan of action is operationalized. It is interesting to us that someone who for all practical purposes was a professional academic administrator, trained as a lawyer, would be so opposed to the presence of professional schools in the university. He was not trained as a philosopher, yet he saw metaphysics as the ordering discipline. He was not a scholar, yet he argued passionately for scholarship and research focused on first principles. And while he was one of the best fund-raisers of his time, he chided universities for chasing after money. Indeed, Hutchins was a living paradox—full of ideas, passion, and hope, but constantly embroiled in criticism, controversy, and disquiet. In this section, we want to discuss five of Hutchins's ideas that have promise for those of us who are interested in the future of faith-based institutions. We will try to do so with as little hullabaloo and alarm as possible.

Vision

It is true that where there is no vision, the people perish.[40] The same does not hold true, however, for universities. Quality just goes down—and many hopes and dreams are lost and people hurt. Our institutions, we fear, are plagued by the love of money, too, ready to do just about anything for a buck or two. The criteria for approval for a new program or project are far too often determined by whether or not it will contribute to margin rather than whether it will further the institutional mission, and we have seen more than one restricted gift come back to haunt an institution. Examples can be found on almost every campus; buildings that are not needed, programs that have no mission purpose, and pet projects that are just silly. Somewhere along the line, the insight and courage to say "no" went AWOL. Without vision, any road will do, and universities end up racing down the nearest cul-de-sac.

However, having no vision was certainly not Hutchins's problem. He had a vision, not just for the University of Chicago but for all of American higher education. It was a dramatic, sweeping vision, but one with very little chance of succeeding. Of course, he thought he was right, and maybe he was, but those who propose such far-reaching changes without building understanding and buy-in are destined to partial success and persistent controversy at best.[41] We have heard more than one university president proudly declare that their institution was to become the Harvard of the West (or the state, or this side of the river).[42] It is far better, we believe, for leaders to dwell in the land of the doable.

Regardless of the goodness of the vision, it is rarely fully achieved. There are few, if any, complete successes in this line of work. For all of us in Christian higher education, it is important to remember that we are not called to be perfect, but to be faithful. Moving a project or an institution down the road is kingdom work, too, even if the final destination remains somewhat far off or necessarily left for another to complete. Keeping a clear, compelling, and doable vision before the university is a crucial leadership responsibility.

Partnerships
University presidents and provosts will tell you that hundreds and hundreds of good ideas besiege them each year. Clearly, they cannot undertake them all, and even some of those that they do undertake end up causing more difficulties than they are worth. The introduction of too many programs and projects, all possessing their own individual merits, adds to the complexity of the university, the very last thing most institutions need. Pound for pound, Christian institutions are among the most complexly organized universities on earth. We know of institutions that have more faculty committees than faculty members. It simply isn't healthy. In the end, the overabundance of programs saps the energy and kills the spirit of even the most dedicated people on campus.

One of Hutchins's principles of academic administration was that a college or university should do nothing that another agency or school can do as well. We find this notion quite interesting. What if this criterion came into play when deciding whether or not to undertake a new program? Are there others who can do this, or is this the province of our university? Far too often, we see universities getting bogged down trying to do things that other partners could and should do. For example, we see university students (with university sponsorship) start ministries to serve the poor, the hungry, the imprisoned, and the disenfranchised. We see the needs and applaud the initiative and biblical compassion of individual students, but we wonder if instead such efforts should be sponsored by a local church. Students could and should be involved as volunteers and leaders but as part of a worshiping congregation. The church and the university are closely related, but they do have different missions. The university is not a church. It is important to be clear about why students come to the university in the first place and what the university's obligation is to them for their having come. The Christian university needs partnerships.

Vocationalism

Hutchins does not like the emphasis on vocationalism in the university and wants no part of it. For him, it is outside the mission of the university. That is to say, it has nothing to do with the pursuit of truth. It only causes problems. First, it introduces an influx of professional programs and schools to the university and even taints the atmosphere of liberal arts departments with the pressures of professionalism. Hutchins deplores the insistence that the purpose of the university is to help someone get a job. For him, this vision demeans the mission of the university.[43] We recently heard of a presentation by a staff member of a Christian university to the board of trustees who said: "Our students don't need to learn any more about Plato, they need a job!"[44] Sadly, the trustees nodded in approval. We wonder how Hutchins would have responded if he were presiding over that particular board meeting.

Second, according to Hutchins, many professional faculty members lack interest in scholarship and research. While this may be a bit of an overstatement, there is much truth here. Our own experience is that many professors in professional disciplines struggle mightily with mastering the art of teaching after they are hired, and they are often left scratching their collective heads regarding the development of a scholarly agenda. Honestly, we do not fault these good colleagues. They are hired for their excellent field experience, but then they are evaluated for promotion and tenure on the basis of their peer-reviewed scholarship. They are hired for A but rewarded for B. This misalignment, it seems to us, is unfair, unproductive, and disingenuous. Christian universities that launch professional programs must think carefully about the alignment of their strategies and reward structures, and provide support and nurture for all those whom they invite to join the work.

Professional school faculty members are usually as bright, hardworking, experienced, and as committed to the institution as anyone. However, there is a "two-cultures" problem.[45] Professional and liberal arts faculty, not to mention the members of the arts and the sciences faculties themselves, speak very different languages. They often have different interests. If Christian universities are not to pursue the solution advocated by Hutchins (get rid of all professional programs), then we are left with a real difficulty—our faculties do not naturally talk with each other. They speak different languages, and the result is a university full of silos. Perhaps the starting point is to begin a conversation about the commonalities of our collective work—our common life in Christ, our shared mission, our commitment to bringing Christian perspectives to bear on scholarship and teaching (what so many call the integration of faith and learning), our focus on the whole person, our intention to teach, shape, and send our students, and the wisdom community that sustains our work. If we are called to this work, surely we can find ways to work productively and collectively for the good of the kingdom. Surely we are called to more than just our own self-promotion.

Interdisciplinarity

Hutchins is a big fan of interdisciplinarity, desiring to get rid of all discipline-based departments. Three general faculties would replace them: metaphysics, social sciences, and natural sciences. We are aware that similar attempts to develop a more divisional structure have been made, and they have met resistance similar to what Hutchins experienced. We suspect that the reaction might be even worse today, especially given the move toward more and more specialization. However, we wonder if Hutchins isn't on to something here. If we believe (which we do) that the rare air of higher education is academic discourse, and if we believe (which we do) that academic discourse is promoted by diverse voices, then we wonder if organizing differently might promote discourse. Could the Christian university come up with a different office arrangement for its faculty?[46] We wonder. Small colleges do this naturally because they have so few faculty members. Perhaps the university has something to learn from the small college here. Perhaps E. F. Schumacher is right—small is beautiful.[47]

We are aware that some attempts are being made to introduce students to an interdisciplinary approach to learning, particularly in general education. We applaud these efforts. Some of the most effective programs are organized as honors programs.[48] We worry, though, about the exclusivity of such programs. If Hutchins is right, and we think he is, this type of general education should be open to every student—at least through grade fourteen.

What would happen if the Christian university developed its entire general education program around this approach and infused the virtues and values of its own wisdom community? We think the results could be stunning.

The Higher Learning

Hutchins foresaw the need to extend a high school education for another two years; either have the high school provide the first two years of college (general education), or have a junior college take on the task. Today, we note that many students are graduating with a high school diploma and an AA degree at the same time. Some politicians are pushing for two years of college for all students at no cost. Of course, this is not exactly what Hutchins had in mind, but it is likely that free public education will be extended to grade fourteen in the near future. In that, Hutchins was prophetic. In many ways, we imagine that Hutchins would welcome this trend (saying it only took politicians eighty years to make it happen) and would push universities to focus on the higher learning. What would happen if the Christian university decided to focus on the higher learning—the last two years of traditional university study and graduate study? What if Christian higher education embraced the challenge to come up with a program of study that was fresh, challenging, and transformative? We believe such efforts are not only timely, but they would also pay huge dividends. Over the years, the Christian university has proven to be a nimble and adaptive institution. We believe the conditions are ripe to do so again. The question is this: are we going to tend the flame or guard the ashes?

The mission of the university is the pursuit of truth (this ideal is stated by all six U.S. regional accrediting bodies and by similar bodies in many other countries), and the Christian university is about the transformational tasks of teaching, shaping, and sending. We are challenged to provide a clear and rigorous program of instruction, spiritual formation, and vocational preparation. In short, we are asked to do it all. The Christian university is not a research institution (R1), but rather a transforming one (T1). For those who look to the future of the Christian university, this is indeed the higher learning—shaped in a community of faithful scholars in the pursuit of wisdom.

QUESTIONS FOR REFLECTION AND DISCUSSION

Robert Maynard Hutchins was brash, outspoken, and confident that his views were right. Surely, his musings invite many questions. A few of them are offered below for your deliberation.

Hutchins the Elder

Twenty-five years after publication of *The Higher Learning in America* in 1936, a paperback edition was released. Hutchins wrote the preface. He made several interesting comments as he looked back to 1936.

- According to Hutchins, three activities not closely related now occupy the attention of the university—research, vocational certification, and social accommodation. Do you agree that they occupy the attention of the Christian university, too? If so, can they coexist?
- Hutchins changed his mind about the importance of language study. Is study of another language important for all students?
- Hutchins wrote with a sense of urgency in 1961—we must change before it is too late. Does any corresponding sense of urgency exist today? Is your institution sleepwalking? What should it be concerned about?

External Conditions

- In 1936, Hutchins said the university is being confused with a high school and junior college. In what respects would this characterization be true of your institution?
- To what extent is the love of money evident at your institution? Is it driven primarily by concerns for the bottom line? Does your university operate like a service station? How so?
- Hutchins argues that the length of a university degree is determined primarily by economic conditions, and it could easily be completed in three years. What do you think about shortening the baccalaureate degree to three years?

Vocationalism

- Does the press for credentials and jobs at your university influence curricular decisions and recruiting? If so, do you see this as a healthy development?

- Do professional schools necessarily lead to isolation and anti-intellectualism in the university as Hutchins argues?
- Are professional-program faculty frustrated or confused about the expectations for promotion and tenure at your institution? If so, what can be done about it?

General Education
- How would you explain the purpose of general education to a trustee?
- Hutchins argues that all truth is connected and everywhere the same. Is this thinking spot-on or outdated?
- What would be the advantages and disadvantages of clustering faculty in interdisciplinary groups? Are there good conversations on your campus?

The Higher Learning
- If your institution asked you to develop a plan for the higher learning (merge upper-division study with graduate study), what would it look like at your institution, and how would you go about making it a reality?
- For Hutchins, the aim of higher education is wisdom. Do you agree? Is wisdom an explicit outcome of your educational programs? If so, how is it measured or expressed?
- Hutchins worries that higher education is disappointing the hopes of the people. What are the hopes of your constituents? Should their hopes and dreams determine the content of your curriculum? If not, what should?

FOR FURTHER STUDY

Robert Maynard Hutchins was a high-profile personality in higher education during his time as president of the University of Chicago and, as we have shared in this chapter, a controversial figure both on and off campus, too. For a sitting university president, he was indeed prolific. The list of his own works is daunting, but in recent years, scholarly interest in his work and works has waned. We wonder why. Certainly, though his interests and opinions were wide-ranging, most of his published works focused on some aspect of "the higher learning" as he understood the meaning of the term. Since Hutchins spoke more about the institutional aspects of university life than about specific academic disciplines, perhaps the interest in and production of scholarship has lessened over time because it lacks direct application. Perhaps the ideas have less traction today, understood to be too idealistic for the realities that higher education now faces. Or perhaps his enormous flow of ideas, while contributing to his notoriety and public persona, contained more heat than light, contributing little to the ongoing conversation about university life. Honestly, we do not know, but the lack of scholarly interested in Hutchins compared to other figures in the volume (Newman, Flexner, and Veblen, for example) is obvious from even a cursory search of a library's scholarly databases.

That is not to say, however, that there is nothing to gain from reading Hutchins or works about him. We know that he would urge all of us to join in the great conversation, and to that end, we suggest the following:

IN HUTCHINS'S OWN WORDS

Hutchins, Robert Maynard. *A Conversation on Education; Robert M. Hutchins Answers Questions from the Floor.* Santa Barbara, CA: Center for the Study of Democratic Institutions, 1963.

———. *The Democratic Dilemma.* The Gottesman Lectures, Uppsala University, 4. Uppsala, Sweden: Almqvist & Wiksells Boktr, 1952.

———. *The Education We Need.* Human Events Pamphlets No. 22. Washington, DC: Regnery, 1947.

———. *The Great Conversation: The Substance of a Liberal Education.* Great Books of the Western World, vol. 1. Chicago: Encyclopedia Britannica, 1952.

———. *The Higher Learning in America.* New Haven, CT: Yale University Press, 1936.

———. *Inaugural Address of Robert Maynard Hutchins, Fifth President of the University of Chicago.* Chicago: University Press, 1930.

———. *The Learning Society.* A Mentor Book, MY926. New York: New American Library, 1969.

———. *The New College Plan.* Chicago: University of Chicago Press, 1931.

———. *Some Observations on American Education*. Cambridge: Cambridge University Press, 2008.

———. *The University of Utopia*. Charles R. Walgreen Foundation Lectures. Chicago: University of Chicago Press, 1953.

Hutchins, Robert Maynard, and Mortimer Jerome Adler. *Contemporary Ideas in Historical Perspective*. Great Ideas Anthologies. New York: Arno Press, 1977.

BIOGRAPHIES

Ashmore, Harry S. *Unseasonable Truths: The Life of Robert Maynard Hutchins*. Boston: Little, Brown and Company, 1989.

Dzuback, Mary Ann. *Robert M. Hutchins: Portrait of an Educator*. Chicago: University of Chicago Press, 1991.

Mayer, Milton Sanford, and John H. Hicks. *Robert Maynard Hutchins: A Memoir*. Berkeley: University of California Press, 1993.

OTHER SELECTED WORKS ABOUT HUTCHINS

Ashmore, Harry S. "Robert Maynard Hutchins: The Higher Learning in America." *Society* 33, no. 5 (1996): 69–75.

Botstein, Leon. "Wisdom Reconsidered: Robert Maynard Hutchins' The Higher Learning in America Revisited," in *Philosophy for Education*, edited by Seymour Fox, 17–38. Jerusalem: The Van Leer Jerusalem Foundation, 1983.

Brownell, Herbert. "Robert Maynard Hutchins, 1899–1977." *The Yale Law Journal* 86, no. 8 (1977): 1547–1551.

Campbell, James. "Hutchins, Robert Maynard, and Mortimer Adler: A Great Idea at the Time: The Rise, Fall, and Curious Afterlife of the Great Books." *Biography* 32, no. 1 (2009): 230.

Cohen, Arthur A. "Robert Maynard Hutchins: The Educator as Moralist," in *Humanistic Education in Western Civilization*, edited by Arthur Cohen, 3–17. New York: Holt, Rinehart and Winston, 1964.

Epstein, Joseph. "The Sad Story of the Boy Wonder (Robert Maynard Hutchins)." *Commentary* 89, no. 3 (1990): 44.

Gideonse, Harry D. *The Higher Learning in a Democracy: A Reply to President Hutchins' Critique of the American University*. New York: Farrar & Rinehart, 1937.

Kelly, Frank K. *Court of Reason: Robert Hutchins and the Fund for the Republic*. New York: Collier Macmillan Publishers, 1981.

Leach, Royal B. *The General Philosophical Position Underlying Robert M. Hutchins' Educational Proposals*. Tacoma, WA: College of Puget Sound, 1953.

Martin, Oliver. *Two Educators: Hutchins and Conant*. Hinsdale, IL: Henry Regnery Company, 1948.

McNeill, William H. *Hutchins' University: A Memoir of the University of Chicago, 1929–1950*. Chicago: University of Chicago Press, 2010.

Shils, Edward. "Robert Maynard Hutchins." *American Scholar* 59, no. 2 (1990): 211–235.

Weber, Delbert D. *Hutchins [and] Conant: A Contrast in Educational Views*. Tempe, AZ: Arizona State University Bureau of Educational Research and Services, 1965.

NOTES

¹Del Weber, *Hutchins and Conant: A Contrast in Educational Views* (Tempe, AZ: Bureau of Educational Research and Services, Bulletin no. 17, Arizona State University, 1965), 43.

²Frederick Rudolph, *The American College and University* (New York: Alfred A. Knopf, 1968), 479.

³Christopher J. Lucas, *American Higher Education: A History* (New York: St. Martin's Griffin, 1994), 217.

⁴Mary Ann Dzuback, *Robert M. Hutchins: Portrait of an Educator* (Chicago: University of Chicago Press, 1991), 6.

⁵Ibid., 13.

⁶Harry S. Ashmore, *Unseasonable Truths: The Life of Robert Maynard Hutchins* (Boston: Little, Brown and Company, 1989), 12.

⁷Ibid., 2. (We recommend Dzuback's work for an insightful exploration of the influence of evangelical culture on Hutchins's thought.)

⁸Ashmore, *Unseasonable Truths*, 37–38. He wrote to several church officials inquiring about taking a church, but his letters bore no fruit.

⁹Ibid., 38–39.

¹⁰For in-depth coverage of Hutchins's leadership at the University of Chicago, we recommend the scholarly work of Dzuback and Ashmore.

¹¹Ashmore, *Unseasonable Truths*, 60.

¹²Context-free facts and figures remained an abiding concern for several of our selected thinkers, including Whitehead, Sayers, and Jaspers.

¹³Robert Maynard Hutchins, *The Higher Learning in America* (New Haven, CT: Yale University Press, 1970), xi–xiii. (All page numbers cited in this chapter correspond to the 1970 edition unless otherwise indicated.)

¹⁴Ibid., xix.

¹⁵Hutchins, 3–4.

¹⁶Our job is not to speculate on the genesis of Hutchins's concern about the love of money, but we cannot avoid noting that he was not the first to identify it as the source of all kinds of problems.

¹⁷Ibid., 4.

¹⁸Ibid., 16.

¹⁹Ibid., 28.

²⁰Ibid., 29.

²¹Ibid., 32.

²²On this point, he agrees with Whitehead completely; students get isolated bits of knowledge with no integrating framework within which to make it cohere.

²³Hutchins, 43.

²⁴Ibid., 52–53.

²⁵Ibid., 58.

²⁶Ibid., 59.

²⁷Ibid., 64. Note that Hutchins holds Cardinal Newman's ideas about the university in high esteem. See Chapter Six.

²⁸Ibid., 66.

[29] Ibid., 78–79. We are fully aware that the value of teaching the Western canon is much less clear today than when Hutchins articulated his vision. At this point in our chapter, we see our job as reporting.

[30] Ibid., 87.

[31] Ibid., 91.

[32] Hutchins may have been ahead of his time at this point, or perhaps he has simply identified a perennial problem. Recall from Chapter Two, on Dorothy Sayers, that some recent assessments of the decline of liberal arts enrollments point to the hollowing out of the liberal arts so that, for some professors, suspicion is now the only appropriate posture toward the titles Hutchins thought constituted the great conversation.

[33] Hutchins, 97.

[34] Ibid., 103.

[35] Like our readers, we see some naïveté in this view, as if university life has no politics. Not to specify which— or, should we say, *whose*—metaphysics would simply not work in today's university.

[36] Hutchins, 105.

[37] Ibid., 117.

[38] During his tenure as the president of the University of Chicago, Hutchins, along with his dean, Mortimer Adler, tried to institute the organizational changes he envisioned. Faculty resistance was stiff and the results mixed. While an interdisciplinary undergraduate college was established as part of Hutchins Chicago Plan, most of the academic departments and professional schools did not simply fade away as Hutchins had hoped. In fact, today the University of Chicago is most known for the strength of its research programs and professional schools. Clearly, this is not the university Hutchins envisioned.

[39] Hutchings, *The Higher Learning*, 118–119.

[40] Proverbs 29:18.

[41] We note here the emerging field known as implementation science, the study of how ideas are implemented in policy and practice. Although implementation science originated in health and mental health fields, it is now finding applications in many fields. The National Research Implementation Network now serves researchers and policy makers in several fields. See http://nirn.fpg.unc.edu/

[42] And we suspect that the vision casters of Harvard often state that their goal is to become the McGill of the United States or the Chicago of the Northeast.

[43] We remind our readers of our discussion of whether a university education should lead to a job in Chapter Two's treatment of Dorothy Sayers and her rationale for the liberal arts.

[44] We purposely do not name the employee or the institution, but we can say that the remarks fell very close to home.

[45] See C. P. Snow, *The Two Cultures and the Scientific Revolution* (Cambridge: Cambridge University Press, 1959). Snow observed that science and literary faculty do not talk to each other, that they speak different languages.

[46] We remind readers of the intellectual bounty that came forth from MIT's Building 20. See Jerome Lehrer's very interesting *New Yorker* article, "Groupthink: The Brainstorming Myth" (January 30, 2012, online at http://www.newyorker.com/magazine/2012/01/30/groupthink) or see the Wikipedia article on "Building 20." Building 20 was erected quickly during World War II as a temporary research structure. It survived for

four decades after the war, and various departments colonized it because the university gave it little oversight. Lehrer even credits the inconvenience of getting to the washroom with some of the interdisciplinary work scholars did there; people had to walk through departments other than their own to get where they were going. Interdisciplinary conversation inevitably happened.

[47] See E. F. Schumacher, *Small is Beautiful* (New York: Harper and Row, 1973).

[48] We recommend the honors programs at Baylor University, Biola University, and George Fox University as good examples of interdisciplinary programs. Many universities have begun politics/philosophy/economics interdisciplinary majors. Others have launched first-year, interdisciplinary programs with names such as "Arts One" or "Science One." The Association of Interdisciplinary Studies (formerly Association of Integrative Studies) supports the development of such programs and offers related resources: http://wwwp.oakland.edu/ais/.

Karl Jaspers

The Idea of the University (1946)

ONE MIGHT WONDER WHAT AN EXISTENTIAL THINKER WOULD HAVE TO say about the university as an institution, but as you will see, Karl Jaspers has much to say to all of us about the idea of the university, the institution that is the university, and the individuals who work and study there. We can think of no better person to conclude our survey of voices from the past. As has been our custom, we will provide a brief biography, a synopsis of his classic work, a discussion of applicable ideas for Christian higher education, and some questions for reflection and discussion.

Childhood and Major Career Events

Karl Jaspers was born on February 23, 1883, in Oldenburg, an independent city in the state of Lower Saxony, Germany. His mother grew up in a local farming family, and his father, although having studied law, worked primarily as the financial manager of the local bank and served as a local and regional politician. From childhood, Karl was melancholy and sickly, two difficulties that would trouble him throughout his life, and he had an independent streak, too. At high school graduation, he refused to give the formal "leaving speech" in Latin, noting that it was beneath him and beyond his classmates' comprehension. In response, his schoolmaster retorted:

"Nothing can become of you anyway, because your illness is an organic fact of life."[1]

In fact, his illnesses did change the course of his professional life in a way. On his way to study law at the University of Freiburg in 1901, Jaspers became so ill that he had to take a leave of absence to recuperate. The time spent in medical clinics must have made a deep impression on him because after several dismal semesters studying law, he decided to study medicine instead. Over the next ten years, and with financial support from his father, he completed his studies in medicine, passed the state medical examination, married Gertrud Mayer, worked as an unpaid medical volunteer in the Heidelberg Clinic of Psychiatry, finished his doctoral dissertation on "Homesickness and Crime," and published his first book, *General Psychopathology*. In 1913, he was accepted as an unpaid lecturer for psychology (part of the philosophy faculty at Heidelberg), and in 1916 won an assistant professorship (with salary) in psychology. During this time, his attention shifted to philosophy. Finally, in 1921, he was appointed full professor of philosophy, a crowning professional achievement in the German university.

In 1923, Jasper's concerns about the decline in the intellectual quality of university life and the increased politicization of German universities provoked him to write and publish an essay, *The Idea of the University*. It was a forceful argument about the necessity of academic freedom in the life of the university. As it turned out, the courage of his convictions and his personal commitment to academic freedom would be tested the very next year.

That testing started when an unpaid lecturer in statistics, Emil Julius Gumbel, made a provocative comment at a local political rally. In essence, he said that the German war dead from World War I were not national heroes. Rather, they died a horrific and unnecessary death. After the local newspaper reported his remarks, he was summoned to the rector's office where he quickly retracted his remarks and later offered a public apology. However, many faculty members were not satisfied, wanting to suspend his teaching privileges. Jaspers was appointed to a three-person review committee to investigate Gumbel. The committee voted two to one to discipline him, with Jaspers disagreeing because he believed that such an action was a clear violation of academic freedom. He argued that the university's roots were medieval—not national—and that it was unhealthy, even dangerous, for the university to become embroiled in contemporary national politics. The university senate adopted the majority report and suspended Gumbel's teaching rights. There was only one dissenting vote in the university senate—Karl Jaspers. Gumbel was ultimately vindicated when the Ministry of Education in Karlsruhe did not uphold the university's action, but Jaspers no doubt paid a personal price for his stand. And it would not be the last time his convictions would be tested.

Jaspers did not follow the lead of his friend, Martin Heidegger, who joined the Nazi Party when they came to power in 1933. He could not. He did not agree with their politics or tactics, and his wife, Gertrude, was Jewish. Because they had no children, they were classified as a privileged "mixed marriage," one that offered no immediate threat to the Nazi regime. However, as Nazi power and oppression increased, that privilege faded away. Jaspers lost his professorship in 1937 (he was simply notified via post that he was now retired), and in 1938 he was forbidden to publish his works. He attempted several times to emigrate but did not succeed, either because the academic arrangements could not be worked out or because the German government would not let his wife leave the country. After 1938, living in semi-seclusion and in constant fear, the couple made a suicide pact in the event that they received a notice of deportation, keeping the suicide capsules in their bathroom medicine chest. When the Allies entered Heidelberg in April 1, 1945, they discovered that month's deportation manifesto. Included on the list were the names of Karl and Gertrude Jaspers.

Jaspers professorship was ultimately restored, and he joined the task of rebuilding the university and the country. For the next twenty years, he remained an active and productive philosopher and scholar, eventually accepting a professorship in 1948 at Basel University in Switzerland. He died in Basel on February 26, 1969, on his wife's ninetieth birthday. Gertrude lived in Basel for another five years.

Jaspers's notes that the 1923 and 1946 versions of *The Idea of the University* are essentially the same, with only some minor reorganization (published in English in 1959). Having lived through two world wars and dealt with their aftermaths, Jaspers is quite clear about his passionate conviction that the university must pursue truth at all costs. We will explore this abiding mission as we make a synopsis of his classic work in the following section.

The Idea of the University

This small but dense and powerful book cannot be read in a cursory fashion, due in part to its being translated from German in such a way that the English version reflects Jaspers's deliberate meter and his careful and particular style. Moreover, Jaspers is one of the most penetrating thinkers we know. This book is packed with insights, observations, arguments, and ideas; no words are wasted.[2] The result is a "slow read," one of the most perceptive books ever written about the idea of the university. Jaspers is always mindful of the human condition of those who find work and life in that institution, and he is consistently careful to keep their prospects in view while stressing his own hopes for the wholeness and healing of the human spirit.[3]

In the introduction, Jaspers outlines his case: "The university is a community of scholars and students engaged in the task of seeking truth," and in order to do so, they must have academic freedom. This freedom is both a privilege and an obligation "to teach truth, in defiance of anyone outside or inside the university who wishes to curtail it. . . . For it is a human right that man must be allowed somewhere to pursue truth unconditionally and for its own sake."[4] For Jaspers, that somewhere is the university, the corporate realization of the basic human desire to know.[5] As such, its foremost concerns are research, teaching, and formation of the whole person. For Jaspers, science and scholarship are meaningful only insofar as they are part of a comprehensive intellectual life, the very lifeblood of the university. It is this sustaining intellectual life that Jaspers examines in chapters 1–3 of this work.

Chapter 1: The Nature of Science and Scholarship

Science and scholarship produce a kind of knowledge that is methodical, cogent, and universally valid.[6] That is, it implies a precise and careful method that results in purely rational evidence that can be verified by anyone, the fundamentals of the scientific method. Jaspers reminds us that it is essential for science not to overstep its bounds and attempt to represent the entire universe of knowing. This is always a temptation, but science must recognize its own limits and assumptions. For example, "thinking which illumines by flashes of insight is not part of science but has its own independent roots."[7]

What, then, are the limits of science? According to Jaspers, science is conclusively limited because it studies clearly designated objects rather than being itself, a dimension about which science is philosophically ignorant. In addition, scientific knowledge cannot provide direction for life. And science cannot even explain itself. Its existence is "due to motives whose truth and cogency are themselves beyond scientific demonstration."[8] For Jaspers, this is as it should be. He notes that the notion that science is limited is a source of bitter disappointment for people who expect more from science than it is able to provide.[9] Science is not God.

What are the basic assumptions of science? Jaspers makes it clear that without assumptions, there is no such thing as science, and science is obligated to recognize and clarify these assumptions in a self-critical spirit. Science presupposes that the rules of logic are valid, that scientific knowledge is desirable, that we choose from an infinite number of possibilities to study, and that we permit ourselves to be guided by ideas. Jaspers makes it clear what we need not assume "that the world is entirely knowable, or that knowledge deals with Being itself; or that knowledge is somehow absolute. . . . The converse is true the moment we reflect on the limits of knowledge."[10]

Jaspers also recognizes that science has a sense of direction, a journey that starts from within, from an unqualified will to know. "It is the road," he writes, "along which I travel so that I may grow aware of the transcendence guiding my will to know."[11] However, if we lose our sense of direction, getting caught up in busywork, Jaspers notes how our conscience turns as "we give in to mere 'industry' to drown our sense of hopelessness. Such 'industry' cannot disguise the deadly inertia of meaningless work."[12]

Science, Jaspers insists, can dispense half-truths that we don't want to face, keeping us from deceiving ourselves because it springs from and produces honesty. But to do so, it must follow proper methods and always distinguish what is cogently known and what is not. In the pursuit of truth, the scientific attitude must always be willing to accept criticism, for "criticism is the necessary condition of life. . . . He who avoids criticism essentially does not want to know."[13]

Jaspers closes the discussion on the nature of science and scholarship by discussing the interdependence of science and philosophy. For Jaspers, science keeps philosophy from promulgating unfounded statements and imaginary proofs, from moving into the land of make-believe. Philosophy helps provide a sense of vision and grounding for scientific work. They are better together than apart.

Chapter 2: Spirit, Human Existence, Reason

In this very short and concise chapter, Jaspers continues his analysis of science by appraising what makes science work. For Jaspers, spirit, self-actualization, and responsive reason make up the all-inclusive context of our lives. They form the underlying context for science, too, giving meaning and vitality to scientific work. Without spirit, science remains stale, lacking creative intuition and imagination. Without a commitment to wholeness, science is hedonistic, irresponsible, and empty. Without reason, science is arbitrary, haphazard, and self-centered. In essence, these three qualities constitute the foundation of the scientific outlook, even though they are rarely recognized as such. They bring humility and humanity to scientific work by giving credit where credit is due, by causing us to recognize what we do not know, and by amplifying the instinct for craftsmanship and thorough effort. "Without them," Jaspers concludes, "science has no meaning for us."[14]

Chapter 3: Culture

According to Jaspers, culture is an integrated system of associations, gestures, values, and ways of putting things that is shaped by a given historic ideal. For the university, the historic ideal is scholarly and scientific discipline, the ability to suspend one's own values for the sake of objective knowledge, and to set aside bias in order to conduct an impartial analysis of data. But this outlook encompasses far more than simply producing facts and figures. The goal is for our whole person to be transformed in accordance with reason. One can never simply think as one pleases and forget everything else.

However, foreshadowing the observations of C. P. Snow,[15] Jaspers notes that natural science and humanism have two distinct cultural ideals—two cultures, but ideally they would be joined to one another for their mutual benefit. He notes with sadness that "their mutual enlightenment has not been realized so far."[16]

The chapter ends with a spirited call for scientists to be guided by something more than a myopic focus on facts and figures that results in "an essentially dead and meaningless knowledge."[17] That something more is an authentic commitment of the whole person to the discipline of science. Jaspers admits that this is an ideal, rarely fully achieved, but it can be a life-giving journey nonetheless.

Chapter 4: Research, Education, and Instruction

Students come to the university full of hope for something more than instruction in labs, lectures, and seminars. They are on an intellectual (dare we say existential) quest for a sense of wholeness and search for the unity of truth. They are searching for the life of the mind. Sadly, their expectations are seldom fulfilled. They slowly give in to the massive influx of facts and figures that perverts true effort to the point where they seek "an edifying frame of mind, rather than scholarship," and mistake "the classroom for the pulpit."[18] They simply end up doing what they are told to do, and ultimately they have to make their own way without the benefit of an adequate inner compass. For Jaspers, this is a serious problem. Students need a compass.

In order to avoid producing intellectual automatons, the university requires three things: research, instruction (in professional training), and the education of the whole person. For Jaspers, these three must be united as part of a living whole, the very spirit of the university. Research, of course, is central, but it is often lonely, hard work. Jaspers warns that research can become an endless drudgery unless one also has a chance to play with ideas and contemplate the ultimate unseen connection of all of life. This is best achieved when the researcher remains in dialogue with other intellectually productive people and groups. Discourse, then, is the rare air of higher learning, and it is the obligation of the university to preserve it at all costs.

Unlike other thinkers we have discussed in this volume, Jaspers argues for the inclusion of professional training in the university and the merger of research and teaching. In fact, he insists that only people who are engaged in research as a vital part of their own intellectual search for the unity of knowledge should teach. Thus, it is the obligation of the university to provide professional training with a twin foundation: "a growing lifelong commitment to the scientific outlook as well as to the search for the unity of knowledge."[19] Jaspers calls this a philosophical point of view. Professional training without a scientific outlook and a philosophical point of view is simply "unthinking and inhuman." Unlike deficiencies in professional routine that can be eliminated with practice, "basic deficiencies in scholarly and scientific training are irremediable."[20]

Before discussing pedagogy, Jaspers pauses to reflect for a moment on education as formation. He distinguishes three basic forms of education: scholastic instruction, apprenticeship, and Socratic education. In all three forms of education, respect, humility, and excellence set the tone, but Jaspers clearly favors the Socratic approach because it fosters personal responsibility and independence for students. And because the professor is a learner, too, no hero worship is permitted. "The teacher knows that he is only human, and demands that his students differentiate between human and divine."[21] Above all, a Socratic education demands a ruthless will to know, giving the student both clarity of purpose and great humility about all that remains unknown.

Before concluding the chapter, Jaspers offers several intriguing observations about the mechanics of instruction, particularly lectures and discussions. Regarding lectures, he wonders what would happen if senior professors welcomed lectures as a genuine part of their professional work, the "high point of one's professional responsibility and achievement."[22] What a remarkable approach, one that might revolutionize undergraduate experience on many Christian campuses, so long as professors do not conceive of the lecture only as a set of PowerPoint slides.[23]

On the topic of discussions, one the most intimate forms of teaching, Jaspers offers a startling perspective. These provide for a serious and lively give and take—but not every student is capable of participating intelligently. In fact, Jaspers argues that while high schools have an obligation to teach all their students, universities do not. The university should focus on a small number of select people who have intellectual zeal and the mental wherewithal to do the work. In the classroom or lab, the professor should never aim at the middle of the student talent pool, but rather Jaspers suggests, at a minority who are capable of growth and initiative. Interestingly, Jaspers sees no need to focus on the few geniuses in the class. They will do just fine on their own. It is the next tier down, the talented minority who, on his account, should receive the lion's share of the instructor's time. The rest of the students will either rise to the occasion or leave the university.

Chapter 5: Communication

For Jaspers, maintaining the community of scholars is just as important as recognizing the unity of all knowledge, and discourse is the key—again, it is the rare air of higher learning. He admits that the intellectual life at a university is truly fragile and the search for truth can be a tough business at times, especially when the mode of discourse turns from discussion to debate. In a debate, power comes into play as each party tries to win. However, in Jaspers's view of a discussion, conclusions are merely stepping-stones and therefore nobody needs to win. In a healthy discussion, it is not necessary to have the last word; Jaspers would call us to be content to have our say and then listen.

Jaspers also recognizes the power of ideas and the responsibility to be careful with words. He characterizes Nietzsche as one "who threw into the world every idea in its most radical and destructive form. He was intoxicated, yet horrified, by the magic of extremes; he shouted without communicating into the hollowness of his time."[24] Sadly, those who fail to filter their words not only hurt the community of scholars but their own careers, too.

Jaspers concludes by sharing some reflections on the university as a necessary meeting place of different disciplines and world outlooks. He argues that it is important to remain in community with those who disagree with one's basic worldview, as long as all retain respect for the disciplined, scholarly pursuit of truth. He suggests:

> The university does this because it wants to thrive in freedom only and would perish rather than carefully shelter itself from unfamiliar ideas and withdraw from intellectual conflict where

fundamentals are involved. All the university must require of its members is this: professional and intellectual standing, mastery of their tools, and integrity.[25]

These words from Jaspers ring with importance at a time such as our own, when financial pressures bear so heavily on our choices about what is worth sheltering, what is worth defending, and for that matter, what is the value of integrity. Jaspers does not need Newman's help, but we believe that in these remarks he is addressing the question of the well-being of the university, and he therefore deserves our full attention.

Chapter 6: The University as an Institution

The idea of the university is never fully realized. Jaspers sees perennial tension between the ideal and the corporate reality. Why? To start, although in theory academic departments are free to choose the very best faculty candidate, they often do not. Rather than the excellent ones, second-tier candidates win many appointments.[26] Weaker departments often lack the capacity to run a good search and the courage to bring in stronger colleagues. The "safest" candidate (theologically) rather than the most qualified wins the day, and the implications for quality are devastating.[27] As Howard Lowry, former president at the College of Wooster, was fond of saying, "Any college lives and dies by its appointments."[28]

A second failing is that departments often give preferential treatment to their own graduates, and other departments rarely speak up because they intend to do the same thing. Mutual "respect" turns out to mean "that everybody approves everyone else's candidates for academic appointment simply in order to have freedom in this matter oneself."[29] Basic criticism, even constructive criticism, is avoided. Thus, personal sympathy and familiarity take precedence over ability. Again, quality suffers.

Sounding much like Flannery O'Connor, Jaspers notes that jealousy, envy, and the lust for power lead to destructive criticism, something that drives discourse underground and saps the intellectual spirit.[30] He offers this bit of wisdom: "It is one of the maxims of the sensible university teacher never to acknowledge purely negative criticism or the intrigues which grow out of it, to deal with it as if it were nonexistent, or at least to blunt its impact so that fruitful, cooperative work may continue to flourish in the interests of the university as a whole."[31] Wise advice, indeed, but we note that it is much easier said than done. Remaining silent in the face of unfair and undeserved criticism takes the rawest kind of courage.[32]

University leadership can also be less than ideal. According to Jaspers, the leader should be a productive person with a talent for leadership. Incompetent leaders try to make up for their poor self-image and lack of intelligence by using power as a tool of self-promotion. On the other hand, strong leaders, aware of their own limitations, give their subordinates freedom to accomplish far more than they themselves could possibly achieve.

Jaspers acknowledges that despite all its shortcomings, we do need the institution of the university, and in fact, it is an honor and privilege to be part of it—one of the best places to work in the world. Academic work is a lifetime pursuit, letting the idea of the university shape and form us as we work to teach, shape, and send our students. It is certainly a picture worth pondering, indeed a high calling.

Chapter 7: The Cosmos of Knowledge

Although the actual existence of the university stands for that oneness and wholeness of all knowledge, Jaspers worries that the universe of knowledge is growing at great speed while the university is changing at a snail's pace. The result is an aggregation of isolated and unrelated professional training schools, an intellectual department store promising something for everyone. For him, this is not a compliment.

Of course, he acknowledges that there is no way for the university to represent and organize all fields of knowledge,[33] and academic departments do not necessarily reflect a rational division of knowledge. They are a local political settlement, and as anyone who has thought about academic reorganization at a university can tell you, there are no universal governing principles for disciplinary organization. All faculties view their discipline as the center of the curriculum. Thus, the course catalog is really a result of historical accumulation and necessary compromise. Yet, as the university expands, and it certainly will, it will be important to keep sight of the unity of knowledge and the daily work to revalidate it. Mere factual and technical instruction cannot reign supreme. According to Jaspers, this daily work is a task faced not only by the university, but also by the entire modern world—and its very survival may be at stake. (Remember that Jaspers wrote this portion of the book right after World War II.)

Technology poses an ominous problem for the university—perhaps the ultimate problem for modernity, too. On the one hand, it is impossible to exclude technology's pervasive influence from the university curriculum.[34] On the other hand, Jaspers worries that technology, like many other disciplines, may lose sight of its own ideals and corrupt the university. His solution is to embrace technology, but at arm's length. That is to say, the university could set up a loose affiliation with technology schools, but not allow them to actually become a part of the university until they mature and demonstrate their commitment to the life of the mind and scientific process. Just how this is to be done, he does not say.[35] He ends by asking a question that he does not answer: "Does the university embody the aspirations of *all* men and is it therefore called upon ultimately to accept all applicants and to elevate to a higher level each and every branch of human knowledge and technique? Or does it contain an esoteric element, forever intelligible only to a minority?"[36]

In the final two chapters of his book, Jaspers turns his attention to the people who come together at the university, and the power of state and society whose will and needs sustain it. In doing so, he does provide, at least in part, answers to the questions we have just posed.

Chapter 8: The Human Factor

For Jaspers, "all of university life depends upon the nature of the people participating in it. The character of a given university is determined by the professors appointed to it . . . (*but even*) the best professors flounder helplessly at a school where the student body is unfit."[37] However, the problem is that the best students can rarely be determined beforehand. The place to begin the admissions process is to look for a variety of aptitudes—concentration, speed, resistance to fatigue, ability to take instruction, and the ability to distinguish differences, to name just a few. In addition, intelligence proper, spirituality, the ethos of intellectual excellence, and creativity should be considered. In the end, however, "what matters most is informed firmness of purpose and self-discipline. . . . A person with strong intellectual motivation may be hampered by his imperfect initial equipment, but if he has genuine enthusiasm and willingness to sacrifice he must be allowed to follow his calling."[38] If we can ignore the exclusive language in these passages, then we can easily imagine ourselves in a faculty discussion of admissions, despite being six or seven decades removed from Jaspers.

But how do we identify strong intellectual motivation and gauge to some degree a student's initial equipment? Jaspers suggests that examinations, personal interviews, and elections by majority vote are appropriate (these methods were in use at Heidelberg), but he admits that they have their shortcomings, too. Ultimately, the best we can do is screen out those who are clearly unfit by ability or motive, and then admit a large enough cohort to account for those who will fall out along the way. Crassly put, the cream will rise to the top, and the university will make butter with it. Other organizations will have to deliver the milk. For Jaspers, this is an honest recognition of what the university must be, how scholarly preparation works, and the personal responsibility carried by the student. There are no guarantees of success.

Chapter 9: State and Society

Given that Jaspers was "retired" without his consent by the Nazi government, banned from lecturing, prohibited from publishing his work, internally exiled, and made to live in fear for his life, we might be excused for wondering if Jaspers changed his views about the relationship of the university to state and society. He makes his case with dispassionate grace. He concedes that there will inevitably be politics both inside and outside the university. The university exists only as the state wills, and any state afraid of the search for truth and the limitation of its power will have to close the university down. And from personal experience, he notes that radical regimes and ruthless dictatorships will do so with outright violence.[39]

Jaspers is quick to point out, however, that politics are a reality inside the university as well.[40] Academic life is "ever prone to its own set of corruptions, which threaten to muddy the pure atmosphere of intellectual activity. Suspension of value judgments may degenerate into mere naturalist indifference; suspension of practical action, into laziness; intellectual caution, into neurotic fear of any challenge to enfeebled energies."[41] Jaspers remains hopeful that despite the tensions within and without, there can be true cooperation between state and university in the protection of academic freedom.

For this cooperation to occur, the university needs a strong leader who will care for the academic life as a gardener tends a precious plant, who "without vanity derives satisfaction from knowing that he has contributed to the flowering of a world not of his own making, but under his care and dependent on that care."[42] Sadly, we have witnessed presidents who run the university as their own, or even more troubling, think that they are the university, without any challenge from those who are to hold the institution in trust—as long as the enrollment and financial numbers add up (as Veblen noted).[43] The long-term impact of poor leadership can be as debilitating to the university as the actions of an intrusive and oppressive government, perhaps more so.

Jaspers concludes by conceding that the pursuit of truth is a difficult but necessary task, and it will "live or perish with our ability to realize the ideal of the university in its ever-changing forms."[44] Yes, the pursuit of truth is a difficult but necessary task for all of us who serve in faith-based institutions, too. We know that our institutions do not always live up to their ideals or our highest hopes, but in all honesty, the same could be said about us as individuals, too. We all fall short. So in light of today's realities and the uncertain times ahead, what does Jaspers have to say to us about the future of Christian higher education? In the following section, we will address several of the compelling ideas and arguments that he believed universities had to consider in the mid-twentieth century, and that we believe are still worth considering today.

Key Arguments and Corollary Implications

When we began to list key arguments and ideas worthy of discussion in this section, we stopped counting at fifty. As we acknowledged in the introduction to the chapter, Jaspers left us a short but powerful book. For this section, we will focus our remarks on four ideas: the mission is everything, the formative scholarly virtues, the university is not a high school, and the ideal and the reality of institutions.

The Mission Is Everything

For Jaspers, it is a human right (and obligation) to pursue truth *unconditionally*, and each society must create its own place to do so. In our culture, the university is such a place, a place where intellectual life is prized and academic freedom is protected. When the intellectual life of an institution is alive and well, the first fruits will be rich and genuine discourse. Students who are introduced to such rare air are lucky indeed. It is formative beyond imagination.

The primary protection for academic freedom in most universities is tenure, a lifetime contract given to a faculty member that can be revoked for only a few specific reasons.[45] The key idea is that tenure will protect a faculty member's academic freedom, and the tenured members of a faculty will protect the freedom of their nontenured colleagues by their willingness to speak to power when necessary. As Jaspers notes, it takes vigilance and a readiness to sacrifice. At least, that is the ideal.

The reality, however, on many Christian college campuses is much different. That is to say, the mission is different. For starters, the pursuit of truth is *conditional*. Truth can only be pursued within the bounds of a guiding theological framework. Those who hold positions outside this framework are simply not welcomed as part of the faculty, and those who migrate to such positions while serving as faculty members are simply not welcome to share their movement. When they do, they put their jobs on the line. In spite of the arguments for the necessity for a diversity of voices on a campus to promote discourse,[46] Christian colleges can easily become intellectual or theological shelters where criticism is unwanted, driven by the desire for safety, certainty, and purity. Much of this, it seems to us, stems unnecessarily from fear. While the American Association of University Professors (AAUP) stipulates that religious institutions can make infringements on academic freedom based on their own religious tradition as long as that right is clearly stated at the time of hiring, we wonder if this practice is used far too often and for the wrong reasons. We challenge institutions to face their fears and to move away from the isolation and insulation they maintain in the name of faith and purity. If an institution claims to be a "university," then it is a matter of integrity to act like one.

We recognize that all institutions are pressed in one way or another to hold the line, stay pure, and keep that faith.[47] But, we insist, if conversations about any subject are disallowed on a Christian college campus, then where on earth are they to be carefully and constructively held? If the mission of the Christian college is not to pursue truth unconditionally, then what is it? The starting point needs to be abundantly clear. As Jaspers points out, mission is everything. Far too often, the mission of the church (or the sponsoring denomination) and the mission of the university are confounded. Certainly they are related, but they are not the same. This invites the question: what is the mission of the Christian college—your college?

Can tenured faculty speak about that mission? Can those with tenure speak up for their non-tenured colleagues? We recognize that tenure is not granted at some Christian colleges, and at many others, tenure is being granted to fewer and fewer faculty members or no longer granted at all.[48] On many Christian college campuses, the percentage of faculty members with tenure is in decline. Thus, faculty voice continues to fade. If the mission is to pursue truth freely, then this trend is indeed disturbing.

Perhaps even more disturbing are instances when longstanding faculty members are dismissed or forced out, with the reasons either unexplained or obviously false or insincere, and no one speaks up on their behalf—no one. As Jaspers astutely observes, it takes a readiness to sacrifice. Sadly, we see such readiness in short supply.[49]

Something is clearly wrong or misaligned. If all truth is God's truth, why do we fear other points of view or hide behind half-truths? We do our students a grave injustice when we isolate or drive away those who ask tough questions about the party line. Again we ask, if not on a Christian college campus, where else on earth will these conversations fruitfully happen? As Christian higher education looks to the future, mission is still everything. What exactly will our universities protect?

The Formative Scholarly Virtues

Of course, all virtues and vices are formative, but here we focus on three scholarly virtues that are key to the formation of a scholar, whether professor or student. The first is humility. For all of us, learning is a journey in humility. There is the humility that stems from the recognition that no one knows it all and never will. Students need to see that modeled for them. There is the humility that stems from the knowledge that you could be wrong. Students need to hear that, too. And finally, there is the humility that stems from the confession that we are not God, even if at times our students think we are. Hero worship can be heady, but it is a professional obligation to be sure your students know the difference. Simply put, we are all learners. Practicing these three aspects of humility will keep your scholarly feet solidly on the ground, and they will ground your students in humility, too.

When scholars approach their work with humility, a genuine respect for other scholars' work will also come into play. After all, are not all true scholars actually fellow and sister pilgrims, motivated by the innate will to know and dedicated to the pursuit of truth? The work of other scholars, even when we disagree with their conclusions, should be treated with utmost respect and care. It is the golden rule of scholarship. Running roughshod over another's work to make a point makes the wrong point, and students will notice.

The third scholarly virtue is hospitality, a genuine openness and appreciation for other points of view. It stems from a welcome embrace rather than a fearful withdrawal. As we practice and students see these virtues, honest conversations and confessions will emerge. Students also need to see those conversations and confessions.

The University Is Not a High School

Jaspers makes it clear that a university is not a high school. Unmistakably, he is an intellectual elitist. Of course, we recognize that the democratization of education in North America since the Second World War has changed the dynamics of higher education in ways that Jaspers would find unimaginable, yet his questions remain relevant for us today: who should attend the university, and how will success be measured?

When faith-based institutions struggle to maintain enrollments, they may be tempted to pay less attention to the question of who should and who should not attend their institutions. Yet we raise this issue on behalf of two student groups that we see engaged in a perennial struggle on our campuses—the ill prepared and the misguided.

Jaspers would argue that students who are not prepared for an educational program should not be admitted to it. This seems obvious, but every year students whose educational records indicate they will not be successful in university work are admitted as "probationary students," and every year, while a few do succeed, most do not. It is one year and done. Far too often, these students lack fundamental academic proficiency in reading, math, writing, and critical thinking, and the college lacks the infrastructure to assist them effectively. It is a prescription for failure. We ask simply: if a Christian college knows full well that the vast majority of a particular student group will fail, should it admit those students? Jaspers would let the process run its course on behalf of the few who will succeed. We do not agree. The misery levels and failure rates are simply too high, and the diversity of talent in the classroom imposes an almost impossible instructional task on the professor. University work is not for everyone.

We also question the wisdom of admitting students who have absolutely no desire to attend and who lack the motivation for serious academic study. These students see it as a trial year, or their parents see it as a good experience—for at least a year. Jaspers observes that the best indicator of success is a determination to know. We observe simply that a college is not a teen camp, and those students who treat it as such pay an extraordinary price for that experience.

We realize that we are walking on thin ice here, pushing back against the idea that everyone should go to college and somehow God will make a way. One of the rarely acknowledged facts about Christian colleges and universities is that the four-year graduation rate for many institutions is about 50 percent, sometimes less. It is a systemic failure of massive proportions, yet no one notices (or wants to notice). Nothing is said about the large numbers who come in as freshmen and never finish. As we look to the future, it is time to say that Christian higher education is not a one-size-fits-all proposition.

The Ideal and the Reality of Institutions
Jaspers makes it clear that institutions rarely live up to the ideal—theirs or his—and he points out that people are usually the major part of the frustration. Of course, he is right, but he remains optimistic. In fact, he sees

university work as perhaps the best thing people can do with their lives if they are so called. We agree.

We remain optimistic about the future of Christian higher education, too. Without doubt, our institutions fail to live up to their ideals, and people can be frustrating, but we also believe that working on a Christian college campus can be the best job in the world. We can think of no better way to craft a simple, sincere, and serene life. Of course, it will demand the discipline to live within one's means (as we note at other points in this book, in this work we trade money for time), but doing so will provide a lifestyle like none other. It can be like working in the Magic Kingdom, only the relationships are deeper, the discourse richer, and the returns eternal. It is pure joy to serve in a place when our values are congruent with the values of the institution.

We close with a word about administrators. Jaspers notes that we need them, and it is much better when they are good at what they do. He is correct, of course, and we add that it is best when they work from a clear sense of calling and a deep commitment to the institution's mission. It is hard but honorable work, particularly when approached with a servant's heart. As Jaspers puts it, they tend a garden that is not their own. In the end, the ideal of the university will not be achieved without dedicated faculty and administrators—who love their work, love their students, and love each other.

QUESTIONS FOR REFLECTION AND DISCUSSION

Reading Jaspers brings many questions to mind. A few are listed below for your consideration.

The Pursuit of Truth
- In Jaspers's ideal university, truth is pursued unconditionally. How would you characterize the pursuit of truth at your institution?
- We have noted that discourse, rich and free, is the rare air of higher education. How would you rate the air quality at your institution?

- To what extent are other voices, especially the voices of critics, welcomed at your institution? Should they be?
- Academic tenure is both an honor and an obligation. How seriously does your institution take that obligation?
- Jaspers places his trust in the unity of all knowledge. Given what we know today about ways of knowing and the role of perspective in epistemology, how do you think Jaspers would respond? How do you respond?

Acting Like a University, Not a High School
- Is a college education for everyone? Who should attend?
- Jaspers argues that the best indicator of success for a prospective student is informed firmness of purpose and self-discipline. Do you agree?
- Should the teacher aim at the middle of the class, the upper middle of the class, or at the very top of the class? Can a teacher aim at several places at the same time?
- For Jaspers, a 50 percent failure rate would be acceptable. Would you agree? How do you define failure and success at your institution?

Academic Work
- Are humility, respect, and hospitality practiced at your institution? In your work?
- Jaspers argues forcefully that only someone engaged in research (scholarly work) can be an effective teacher at the college level. Do you agree? Explain.
- Who gives the general lectures at your institution? Are senior faculty involved?
- What do you think would happen if your faculty considered the lecture the high point in one's professional responsibility and achievement?

Mission and Vocation
- How do you understand the mission of the university in relation to the mission of the church?

FOR FURTHER STUDY

We were not able to give Jaspers's thought or biography as much attention as they deserve. What a challenging and fascinating life—both before, during, and after the Nazi reign of terror. We recommend the following for those who wish to read more of his own works, learn more about his life, or join the ongoing conversation about his philosophy, commitments, and religious faith.

IN JASPERS'S OWN WORDS

Karl Jaspers. *The Future of Germany*. Chicago: University of Chicago Press, 1967.
———. *The Future of Mankind*. Chicago: University of Chicago Press, 1961.
———. *The Great Philosophers*. New York: Harcourt, Brace & World, 1962.
———. *The Idea of the University*. London: Owen, 1960.
———. *Man in the Modern Age*. New York: H. Holt, 1933.
———. *Nietzsche and Christianity*. Chicago: H. Regnery Gateway, 1961.
———. *Origin and Goal of History*. New Haven, CT: Yale University Press, 1959.
———. *The Perennial Scope of Philosophy*. New York: Philosophical Library, 1949.
———. *Philosophical Faith and Revelation*. Religious Perspectives, vol. 18. New York: Harper & Row, 1967.
———. *Philosophy and the World: Selected Essays and Lectures*. Washington, DC: Regnery Gateway, 1989.
———. *The Question of German Guilt*. Perspectives in Continental Philosophy, no. 16. New York: Fordham University Press, 2000.
———. *Reason and Anti-Reason in Our Time*. London: SCM Press, 1952.
———. *Tragedy Is Not Enough*. London: V. Gollancz, 1953.
———. *Way to Wisdom: An Introduction to Philosophy*. Yale Paperbound; Y-27. New Haven, CT: Yale University Press, 1960.
Jaspers, Karl, and Michael Bullock. *The Origin and Goal of History*. New Haven, CT: Yale University Press, 1953.
Jaspers, Karl, and Rudolf Bultmann. *Myth and Christianity: An Inquiry into the Possibility of Religion without Myth*. New York: Noonday Press, 1958.

BIOGRAPHIES

Gottschalk, Herbert. *Karl Jaspers*. Köpfe Des XX. Jahrhunderts; Bd. 43. Berlin: Colloquium Verlag, 1966.

Kirkbright, Suzanne. *Karl Jaspers: A Biography: Navigations in Truth.* New Haven, CT: Yale University Press, 2004.
Salamun, Kurt. *Karl Jaspers.* Beck'sche Schwarze Reihe; Bd. 508. Munich: Beck, 1985.
Schilpp, Paul Arthur. *Karl Jaspers.* Philosophen Des; 20. Jahrhunderts. Stuttgart: Kohlhammer, 1957.
Wallraff, Charles Frederic. *Karl Jaspers.* Princeton Legacy Library. Princeton, NJ: Princeton University Press, 2015.

OTHER SELECTED WORKS ABOUT JASPERS

Amin, Sonal K. *Karl Jaspers and Existentialism.* New Delhi: Anmol Publications, 1992.
Andrén, Mats. "Nihilism and Responsibility in the Writings of Karl Jaspers." *European Review* 22, no. 2 (2014): 209–216.
Arendt, Hannah, Karl Jaspers, Lotte Köhler, and Hans Saner. *Hannah Arendt/Karl Jaspers Correspondence, 1926–1969.* 1st Harvest ed. San Diego: Harcourt Brace, 1993.
Carr, Godfrey. *Karl Jaspers as an Intellectual Critic.* Frankfurt, Germany: Peter Lang, 1983.
Clark, Mark W. "A Prophet without Honour: Karl Jaspers in Germany, 1945-48." *Journal of Contemporary History* 37, no. 2 (2002): 197.
Durfee, Harold A. "Karl Jaspers' Christology." *The Journal of Religion* 44, no. 2 (1964): 133–148.
Ehrlich, Leonard H. *Karl Jaspers: Philosophy as Faith.* Amherst, MA: University of Massachusetts Press, 1975.
Heidegger, Martin, Karl Jaspers, Walter Biemel, and Hans Saner. *The Heidegger-Jaspers Correspondence, 1920–1963.* Contemporary Studies in Philosophy and the Human Sciences. Amherst, NY: Humanity Books, 2003.
Howey, Richard Lowell. *Heidegger and Jaspers on Nietzsche: A Critical Examination of Heidegger's and Jaspers' Interpretations of Nietzsche.* The Hague: Nijhoff, 1973.
Miron, Ronny. *Karl Jaspers: From Selfhood to Being.* Value Inquiry Book Series. Amsterdam: Editions Rodopi, 2012.
Nixon, Jon. "Hannah Arendt and Karl Jaspers: The Time of Friendship." *Journal of Educational Administration and History* 48, no. 2 (2016): 160–172.
Rabinbach, A. "The German as Pariah—Karl Jaspers and the Question of German Guilt." *Radical Philosophy* 75 (1996): 15–25.

Salamun, Kurt. "Moral Implications of Karl Jaspers' Existentialism." *Philosophy and Phenomenological Research* 49, no. 2 (1988): 317–323.

Schilpp, Paul Arthur. *The Philosophy of Karl Jaspers.* Library of Living Philosophers. La Salle, IL: Open Court Pub., 1981.

Trivers, Howard. "Reminiscences of Karl Jaspers." *Man and World* 16, no. 2 (1983): 139–144.

Wallraff, Charles Frederic. *Karl Jaspers.* Princeton Legacy Library. Princeton, NJ: Princeton University Press, 2015.

Walters, Gregory J. *The Tasks of Truth: Essays on Karl Jaspers's Idea of the University.* New York: P. Lang, 1996.

Wyatt, J. F. "Karl Jaspers' The Idea of the University: An Existentialist Argument for an Institution Concerned with Freedom." *Studies in Higher Education* 7, no. 1 (1982): 21–34.

Young-Bruehl, Elisabeth. *Freedom and Karl Jaspers's Philosophy.* New Haven, CT: Yale University Press, 1981.

NOTES

¹ Suzanne Kirkbright, *Karl Jaspers: A Biography* (New Haven, CT: Yale University Press, 2004), 11.

² See Godfrey Carr, *Karl Jaspers as an Intellectual Critic* (Frankfurt, Germany: Peter Lang, 1983), 15. He describes Jaspers's prose style as one that both invites and frustrates rapid reading, "using short sentences and a syntax so simple that it promises easy assimilation of meaning. However, the formulations in the sentences are complex, betraying a challenging tautness and nervosity of thought." We agree.

³ For an excellent analysis of Jaspers's existential argument for freedom in the university, see John Wyatt, "Karl Jaspers's The Idea of the University: An Existential Argument for an Institution Concerned with Freedom," in *Studies in Higher Education* 7, No. 1 (2006): 21–34, accessed September 3, 2015, doi:10.1080/03075078212331379281.

⁴ Karl Jaspers, *The Idea of the University* (Boston: Beacon Press, 1959), 1–3.

⁵ Here Jaspers echoes Thorstein Veblen's idea that the desire to know is a basic human instinct, resulting in the disinterested pursuit of esoteric knowledge; see Chapter Eight.

⁶ Remember here that *wissenschaft* (translated as science or scientific) refers to both science and the humanities. Thus, there is a narrow and broad understanding of science used in this book. We will try to clarify the meaning throughout the synopsis.

⁷ Jaspers, *The Idea of the University*, 12.

⁸ Ibid., 13.

⁹ Clearly, Jaspers saw both the importance of scientific knowledge and its limits, noting other ways of knowing must enter into the discussion of ultimate things. This is one of the reasons why he felt it was important for scientific research to be a part of a broader community of scholars.

¹⁰ Jaspers, *The Idea of the University*, 19.

¹¹ Ibid., 22.

¹² Ibid., 23.

¹³ Ibid., 24.

¹⁴ Ibid., 28.

¹⁵ See Charles Percy Snow, *The Two Cultures* (London: Cambridge University Press, 1959). He observes that science and literature professors speak entirely different languages, literally two different cultures—and this is true on both sides of the Atlantic.

¹⁶ Jaspers, *The Idea of the University*, 33.

¹⁷ Ibid., 35. Note at this point how much Jaspers sounds like both Whitehead with his complaint about inert knowledge and Sayers with her concern that education seems to produce people who know things but cannot make the connections between them.

¹⁸ Ibid., 40.

¹⁹ Ibid., 45–46.

²⁰ Ibid., 47.

²¹ Ibid., 50.

²² Ibid., 58.

²³ In the hands of some professors, the truth comes home with a vengeance that power corrupts but PowerPoint corrupts absolutely.

²⁴ Ibid., 63.

²⁵ Ibid., 68.

[26] As we noted in Chapter Four, Flannery O'Connor's stock in trade is human frailty. To our knowledge, she never addressed the ways search committees worked, but she certainly knew about pride, and she understood how egos get in the way of both clear thought and moral decision-making.

[27] For a discussion of this phenomenon, see Patrick Allen and Kenneth Badley, *Faith and Learning* (Abilene, TX: Abilene Christian University Press, 2014), 225–226.

[28] Elton Trueblood, *The Idea of a College* (New York: Harper & Brothers, 1959), 63.

[29] Jaspers, *The Idea of the University*, 74.

[30] We do not know if he knew Flannery O'Connor's work, although he certainly could have done so. As we noted in Chapter Three, he knew Arendt well, and similarities between these remarks and her own assessment of power and its working are likely not incidental.

[31] Ibid., 73.

[32] As Arendt taught us, *not* keeping silent when others face unfair criticism takes the same kind of courage.

[33] The encyclopedist movement in eighteenth-century France began with the ambition of organizing all knowledge; with the passage of time, it adjusted its ambitions.

[34] Our readers will know that hundreds of observers since Jaspers have warned about the same thing. These concerns appeared as early as Plato, who, in *The Phaedrus*, registered his concerns about what the invention of writing would do to memory.

[35] For a thoughtful discussion of Jaspers and modernity, see George Pepper, "Jaspers's Response to Modernity," in *The Task of Truth: Essays on Karl Jaspers's Idea of the University*, ed. Gregory Walters (Frankfurt, Germany: Peter Lang, 1996), 55–68.

[36] Jaspers, *The Idea of the University*, 97. We raised the same question in our discussion of access to the liberal arts in Chapter Two.

[37] Ibid., 101.

[38] Ibid., 110–111.

[39] The preferred method today in some jurisdictions is to impose year-by-year reductions in state funding for research that a particular government does not want to see done, for example, on climate change. This approach is less violent and therefore garners less attention in the press and among the public.

[40] We deal with these realities in more depth in Chapters Three and Four, on Arendt and O'Connor.

[41] Ibid., 122.

[42] Ibid., 126,

[43] See Chapter Nine.

[44] Jaspers, *The Idea of the University*, 136.

[45] In most instances, tenure can only be rescinded for financial exigency, gross incompetence, moral turpitude (professional misconduct), or sustained contempt for the institution's mission.

[46] See Elton Trueblood, *The Idea of a College*, 27.

[47] We call for this while recognizing that many universities operating without any connection to Christian faith have nevertheless seen their freedoms carved away by various ideologies, whether corporate and neoliberal on the one side or by any number of *-isms* on the other. Thus, in a sense, many universities operate within the constraints of a de facto statement of faith. We make this sad observation not to be clever, only to point out that openly faith-based schools are not alone in being based on faith.

[48] We also note that the percentage of full-time, tenure-track faculty at many institutions is in serious decline. The heavy use of adjunct, part-time, and one-year appointments has further degraded the faculty's voice.

[49] We can point to an instance or two where faculty have banded together and pushed back, but these are the exception rather than the rule. We do wonder if the use of social media will invite a much broader outcry and sense of support for faculties who find themselves in opposition to the powers that be.

Conclusion

Part One: The Classroom and the Student

IN PART ONE WE INTRODUCED SOME COMPELLING IDEAS AND SEMINAL thinking from some interesting and, in a few cases, unlikely candidates for serious discussion of teaching and learning in higher education: Alfred North Whitehead, Dorothy L. Sayers, Hannah Arendt, Flannery O'Connor, and Maria Montessori. We saw several common themes emerge, and some disagreements.

We started with Alfred North Whitehead and his deep concern that students see the curriculum as a whole, a passion he shared with Dorothy Leigh Sayers. A century and a half-century ago, respectively, they called for integration and connection. They raise a question for us: In our concern that students attend classes taught by experts, have we parceled out too much undergraduate education? Have we given students only the parts but unwittingly denied them the whole? The Christian university sits in a unique position to address the problem of curricular atomization. If we are willing to believe that Christ holds all things together and to apply that claim to the curriculum and the student's experience, we may be sitting on a curricular model that would address Whitehead's and Sayers's complaints. And not at all coincidentally, four of the writers in Part One—Whitehead,

Sayers, O'Connor, and Montessori—would all say *amen* to a model founded in Christian theology and faith.[1]

Whitehead also called for an end to standardized, external examinations. Recall that he did so because he believed the teachers in actual day-to-day contact with students were best positioned to know what students understood and therefore would be the best judges of students' performance. Here, Whitehead sounds like Maria Montessori, who also envisioned a classroom where teachers knew their students and therefore knew where to begin instruction and how to structure it. To us, these ideas make complete sense. That they are not far-fetched leaves us wondering why we do not implement them more widely in Christian higher education. What are the difficulties, or why is there resistance? What would it take to learn our students' names compared, say, to getting the technology in every classroom to work properly every instructional day? Not much: assembling and printing a photo directory, producing a few name cards, enduring a few moments of mild embarrassment early in the term. What would it give? From experience, we can both say it helps build a learning space in which students want to produce their best work. It increases year-to-year retention. We may respond that we do not need Whitehead and Montessori schooling us in these basics, but apparently someone needs to because it's been a century since they wrote and thousands of students still report that not one professor has learned their name.[2]

Whitehead and Sayers drew our attention to the curriculum. On this matter, they did not agree with each other, but both forced us to think. Like Newman, Hutchins, and Ortega (all of whom we treat in Part Two), Sayers views the liberal arts as necessary for the life well lived. Whitehead did not address the liberal arts directly. But in different ways, both called for depth. Link those calls for depth with their shared concern for integration, and you get a picture of a curriculum that, with the right professors in place, students would embrace; they would line up to sign up.

We included Flannery O'Connor and Hannah Arendt here because they address the ways we view and treat our students. To be quite blunt, O'Connor and Arendt make us (the authors, not the royal us) uncomfortable; could we not produce an upbeat book about Christian higher education without having to talk about sin and evil? Yes, we certainly could. In fact, we talked about doing just that. But we believe these two women bring something essential to the conversation about how we function in the academy.

In Chapter Three, we noted Gouldner's account of how academics like words and ideas. As Christian academics, we sometimes go at problems in our classrooms, departments, and institutions as members of the new class first and Christians second, if at all. By this, we mean that academics, including Christian academics, tend to assume a given problem has arisen out of a shortage of information, or out of miscommunication, or from a lack of understanding. Through further reflection or with the right explanation, we can agree and move ahead in harmony, a quite rationalistic, modern approach to problem solving. Sometimes, these factors do figure in the problems we encounter in class or in the department. But imagine for a moment what Hannah Arendt or Flannery O'Connor might say if they knew what was troubling us at that moment. "Have you considered whether this person's action is rooted in narcissism or plain old ambition?" Or perhaps, "Why don't you just admit that you have a mean-spirited colleague?" We need not repeat here what we called in Chapter Four the catalog of bad types that populate O'Connor's fiction. Our point is, yes, of course we would have preferred to say more uplifting things in our book, but we believe that as Christian higher educators, we might be a bit more serene within our work contexts if we accepted the fact that sin is at work. After all, this concept is part of our lexical stock, so to speak.

Arendt also spoke about authority and where its roots lie. We included her for her reminder about this important matter. We see many professors who think that their expertise, their experience, their contract, and their possession of the classroom remote control give them all the authority they need to teach their classes. Arendt reminds us that groups confer authority (what she called power) as they engage in dialogue and come to agreements. We included Gouldner's new class theory in that context, as well as some ways that the Internet has changed students' epistemology, all with the aim of persuading our readers that we work in a new landscape, one where we might be the only ones in a given classroom who assume that we have the right simply to stand and start teaching.

Taken together, the thinkers we included in Part One have some important ideas for us to consider or reconsider. For a century, higher educators have read Whitehead's views of education. To our knowledge, few have asked whether Montessori had application to higher education. O'Connor wrote dozens of letters to educators, especially to professors who wanted her explanation of the "meanings" of various stories. But she did not address education or higher education in a general way. Neither did Arendt. Sayers did, but her primary interests lay elsewhere. We recognize the risks involved in including writers who did not address education directly, trusting that their ideas and concerns will not be summarily dismissed as irrelevant or misguided. But we remain convinced—deeply so—that if Christian higher educators took these five thinkers' and writers' ideas seriously and put them into action in some of the ways we have suggested, we and our students would gain huge educational benefits.

Part Two: The Faculty and the Administration

IN PART TWO WE REINTRODUCED SIX LARGELY FORGOTTEN FIGURES IN higher education, all of whom contributed a major work to the classical literature of higher education: John Henry Newman, Abraham Flexner, Thorstein Veblen, José Ortega y Gasset, Robert Maynard Hutchins, and Karl Jaspers. Interestingly, two wrote from the perspective of a president or rector (Newman and Hutchins), three were professors for the majority of their academic careers (Veblen, Ortega, and Jaspers), and one (Flexner) never held an appointment in any university of any kind, serving instead in supporting or ancillary organizations. They all suffered major disappointments and troubles during their careers, lending an earned wisdom and seasoned perspective to their writings. They all recognized the fragility of an institution's mission, knowing full well that a university can lose its way from pressures within and without. And from time to time, they angered and frustrated friend and foe alike. However, they all carried a deep faith in the enduring idea of the university, a commitment to scholarly habits of mind, and a shared belief in the necessity of an institution to pursue truth in an organized way—and at all costs.

They did not agree, though, on how this pursuit of truth was to be organized and conducted. For example, they disagreed about who should go to college, when they should go to college, what they should be taught, how they should be taught, how long they should study, and who should pay for the education. They also disagreed about who should teach, how faculties should be organized, the role of the professional studies, graduate instruction, research, and the proper governance role of trustees, presidents, and faculties. And even though they all agreed on the necessity of the pursuit of truth, they disagreed on the fundamental nature of truth and how it was to be pursued. Some thought truth must be pursued inductively (through the scientific method), and others argued for a deductive approach (proceeding from first principles). Some believed in the unity of all truth, that all things are ultimately connected; others, not so much.

Given these fundamental disagreements, is there a unifying message to all of us who serve in faith-based institutions and wonder about the future? We believe there is. First, while there is no one right way to organize or operate, they all agree that a common mission and sense of place is vital. Ultimately, the mission is a locally negotiated reality, but it can easily be hijacked by egos, money, metrics, misunderstanding, or mismanagement. Mission care reduces mission drift.

Second, the core of the institution, the academic program, must be honored and protected. It is the pearl of great price. Institutions easily lose their way when external and peripheral activities take center stage. And, sadly, the mission of the institution can be clouded when leaders act as though the institution is there for their own pleasure. Even more sadly, institutions can easily go off the rails when leaders cannot distinguish between themselves and the institutions they are supposed to serve.

Third, whatever the mission of the curriculum, there is no place or substitute for quality and hard work. No one is well served by disinterested or distracted teaching. Whatever is to be done, it is to be done with passion, dedication, excellence, and care. The same goes for students. The university is not a teen camp. The focus must be on learning, not on country club activities.

Finally, all the writers we reviewed in Part Two agreed that the university serves an important social function, the pursuit of truth, and this pursuit requires a degree of independence. Academic decisions are best made by academics. We could write an entire book on the unintended consequences of outside interventions. This is not to say, however, that the university can exist in isolation, ignoring social concerns, interested only in its own business. If it does so, it will soon become stagnant at best and irrelevant at worst. A university must always be a vital part of the society or group that sustains it, and this mutual relationship must be cultivated and nurtured.

Closing Comments

In closing, we would like to offer a few comments about glitz, glue, and hope.

Glitz

We have been in more than one faculty discussion making light of the marketing and branding efforts of an institution. Faculty derive a kind of perverse joy and a false sense of superiority from second-guessing and mocking serious efforts by the administration to promote the university. If radio advertisements are used, we would prefer television. If television advertising, we prefer Internet advertising. If Internet advertising, we prefer that the website have these buttons on the home page, not those. If billboards are used, they are in the wrong place or promote the wrong program or are just too expensive. We wonder if funds dedicated to marketing efforts would not be better spent on our own department's wants and needs. And when the president starts using business jargon and marketing lingo, faculty check out and head for the doors in droves. Honestly, it seems like a strange and foreign language, and in some respects, it is.

However, we recognize the fiercely competitive environment our institutions face as they attempt to recruit students and convince donors to invest in us, and we see nothing to indicate that it will get any better anytime soon. In fact, it will probably get even more competitive, particularly given the growing interest in providing the first two years of college at no cost to all students and the constant entry of new competitors in the higher education marketplace. Whether faculty like it or not, institutions without a bit of glitz will be at a serious disadvantage. Therefore, Christian higher educators must give careful attention and a portion of the budget to marketing, branding, recruiting, and building. Students will not simply show up on their own because we have solid academic programs. Like moths, they are attracted to the bright lights of branding, image, buildings, and social media. Like it or not, we have to have some bright lights, too.

So glitz is now a requirement. Most administrators know this, but there seems to be a distrustful atmosphere on the part of faculty that university leaders are somehow misguided, if not downright crass, when they make these efforts. This, it seems to us, is a serious mistake. If Christian colleges and universities are to have a future, their administrators will need partners, not critics. Shared governance must come to mean a respectful, collaborative relationship dedicated to the well-being of the institution rather than a defensive, protective stance. The old adversarial, dual-organization model—a philosophical and administrative Berlin Wall running across campus with the administration on one side and the faculty on the other—is a prescription for disaster. Recruitment, branding, and image have become everyone's business.

Glue

At the same time, the thinkers examined in this book, in one way or another, have made it clear that glitz alone is not enough; a vibrant central academic core is needed to provide the glue. To paraphrase John Henry Newman, glitz is sufficient for *being*—for looking like—a university, but it is not sufficient for its *well-being*. Glue is needed, too, if the institution is to hold together and to have integrity.

Now we turn the tables. It seems to us that faculty understand this intuitively, and they work very hard to create and protect the *genius loci*, the character of the place. In fact, in many respects, they carry the ethos of an institution. They focus their best efforts on teaching, scholarship, and character formation. They love their students and want the best for each of them. They know each one by name. Administrators, however, who pay so much attention to marketing, media, metrics, and margins, can project a lack of care about these faculty values, and sadly, we know of more than a few who actually do not care, even who view faculty as an obstacle to the university's flourishing. The future will require a new approach for administrators, too. The deeply embedded values of the faculty are not obstacles to be eliminated, but rather the glue of the place to be valued and promoted.

The misaligned interests of the administration (margins) and the faculty (personal promotion) must both give way. The idea of the Christian university and its primary reason for existence is neither to make money nor to support individual faculty research interests. There are other institutions dedicated to these ends. The genius of the Christian university is to create a wisdom community where the primary functions are to teach, to shape, and to send. Christian universities must develop and prize their own spirit of place, their own distinctive character. At its heart, the Christian university is what we call a transformational (T1) institution, not a research (R1) institution, or a poor imitation of it. Our ultimate mission is the transformation of students, and the future of the Christian university will require the cooperative efforts of faculty and administrators dedicated to that end.

Of course, resources will always be needed, and faculty research can play an important role in the transformation of students, but the future will require a new understanding and cooperative spirit on campus. Absent that cooperation, other institutions better organized and aligned to produce revenue on the one hand or to produce new knowledge on the other will do the job that we have done until now. We predict a bright and hopeful future for those Christian universities willing to embrace and enhance their T1 mission. Why? They, among the many types of universities, are best equipped for this mission. In our view, this mission is our competitive advantage in the twenty-first century.

Hope

There is good reason to be hopeful about the future of Christian higher education. In *Theology of Hope*, Moltmann distinguishes between optimism and hope.[3] Optimism, according to Moltmann, is looking at past events and projecting them into the future with some degree of certainty. For example, if it snows every August in Anchorage, Alaska, and has done so for the past thirty years, one can project with optimism that it will snow again next August. Hope, on the other hand, stems from our confidence in the character of God, who continues to make all things new. Think of the incarnation. Such a wonder could not have been predicted from the events of the previous ten decades. At just the right time, however, something totally unexpected came into this world, and it changed the way we go about our lives and think about the future.

It is our hope that the Christian university will become a new thing, too, something heretofore unimagined. At the very time that higher education seems to be spinning out of control and dividing into mean-spirited interest groups, the Christian university can, with confidence and integrity, embrace its future as a transforming institution for the sake of students, church, and society; that is, for the sake of the kingdom.

In Chapter Ten, we quoted Ortega, and we do so again in closing: "We have arrived at a moment in which we have no other solution than to invent, and to invent in every order of life. I could not propose a more delightful task."[4] Nor could we. Onward and upward!

NOTES

[1] And we recognize that they would do so using quite different language.

[2] One national magazine has now begun to include this question in the annual polls it uses to produce its university rankings: do your professors know your name? If Christian universities are to take our transformational task seriously, we must recognize the power of this simple intentional act. See http://www.macleans.ca/education/where-professors-know-your-name/.

[3] See Jürgen Moltmann, *Theology of Hope* (New York: Harper & Row, 1967).

[4] Robert McClintock, *Man and His Circumstances: Ortega as Educator* (New York: Teachers College Press, Columbia University, 1971), 485.